Fundamentals of
Insurance

second edition

TENA B. CREWS

SOUTH-WESTERN
CENGAGE Learning

Australia • Brazil • Japan • Korea • Mexico • Singapore • Spain • United Kingdom • United States

SOUTH-WESTERN
CENGAGE Learning™

Fundamentals of Insurance, 2nd Edition

Tena B. Crews

Vice President of Editorial, Business: Jack W. Calhoun

Vice President/Editor-in-Chief: Karen Schmohe

Vice President/Marketing: Bill Hendee

Executive Editor: Eve Lewis

Senior Developmental Editor: Enid Nagel

Editorial Assistant: Virginia Wilson

Assistant Marketing Manager: Linda Kuper

Content Project Management: Pre-Press PMG

Technology Project Manager: Mike Jackson

Senior Manufacturing Buyer: Kevin Kluck

Production Service: Pre-Press PMG

Senior Art Director: Tippy McIntosh

Cover and Internal Design: Kim Torbeck, Imbue Design

Cover Images: ©Getty Images/Michael Blann, Arthur S. Aurbry; ©iStock

Photography Manager: Amanda Groszko

For product information and technology assistance, contact us at
Cengage Learning Customer & Sales Support, 1-800-354-9706

For permission to use material from this text or product,
submit all requests online at **www.cengage.com/permissions**
Further permissions questions can be emailed to
permissionrequest@cengage.com

Library of Congress Control Number: 2009921218

Student Edition ISBN 13: 978-0-538-45015-7
Student Edition ISBN 10: 0-538-45015-0
Instructor's Edition ISBN 13: 978-0-538-45016-4
Instructor's Edition ISBN 10: 0-538-45016-9

South-Western Cengage Learning
5191 Natorp Boulevard
Mason, OH 45040
USA

Cengage Learning products are represented in Canada by Nelson Education, Ltd.

For your course and learning solutions, visit **school.cengage.com**

Printed in China
2 3 4 5 6 7 8 9   15 14 13 12

Chris T. Autrey
Teacher, Business Education
Dacula High School
Dacula, Georgia

Steve Avila
Professor, Risk Management and
  Insurance
Ball State University
Muncie, Indiana

Lou Ellen Blackmon
Teacher, Career and Technology
  Department
Socastee High School
Myrtle Beach, South Carolina

Janice Bosman
Teacher, Business Department
Hanna-Westside Extension Campus
Anderson, South Carolina

Norma Brown
Teacher, Marketing Education
Dutch Fork High School
Irmo, South Carolina

Cindy Gleason
Career and College Research Development
  Coordinator
Academy of Business Team Leader
Blake High School
Silver Spring, Maryland

Christine A. Haff
Assistant Director, South Carolina Virtual
  Enterprise Network
Roebuck, South Carolina

Gregg Koeller
Faculty, Business Department
Glenbard East High School
Lombard, Illinois

Tammi Riddle Metz
Instructor
Mississippi State University
Starkville, Mississippi

Karen Murri
Teacher, Business Education Dept.
Havre High School
Havre, Montana

Marsha M. Owczarski
Teacher, Business/Computer Science Dept.
Southwick-Tolland Regional High School
Southwick, Massachusetts

Eva W. Rutiri
Teacher, Career and Technology Education
Charlestowne Academy
N. Charleston, South Carolina

Terri Vick-Phillips
Teacher, Business Education
White Knoll High School
Lexington, South Carolina

ABOUT THE AUTHOR

Tena B. Crews has taught traditional and online business education and technology courses at the secondary, technical, and university levels for over twenty years. She has served as the Director of Business Education at the University of West Georgia and the University of South Carolina.

She currently serves as the Director of Online Learning and Development for the College of Hospitality, Retail and Sport Management and Associate Director of Technology Teaching Excellence at the Center for Teaching Excellence at the University of South Carolina.

iii

Contents

INSIDE THE STUDENT EDITION

climbing the ladder

From Insurance Claims Clerk to Auditor

DaSheena has worked for the North Star Insurance Company as a claims clerk for three years. She has a degree in art history but became interested in insurance due to issues she had at her last job.

She was previously employed as a tour guide at the Glandour Museum of Art and was injured on the job. She had disability insurance through that position, but not a substantial amount and not an amount large enough to provide for her family while she was out of work. She had to work closely with the company's human resources representative and the insurance claims clerk to settle her claim.

Through this experience, her interest in insurance grew, and she obtained a position at a local insurance company. She now works as an insurance claims clerk. Her duties include reviewing insurance claim forms, contacting the insured to obtain missing information, calculating the amount of the claim, and transmitting claims for payment or further investigation. DaSheena particularly enjoys any type of work that is investigative and more broad-based than working with a single client.

Therefore, she is looking into the possibility of becoming an insurance auditor. Auditors examine and analyze business records to determine financial status and prepare reports noting strengths and deficient areas. Through this type of position, DeSheena would consult with company officials about particular regulations and financial matters.

She would be able to utilize her communication and critical thinking skills and would be required to use problem-solving skills. She realizes, however, she will probably need additional education. She would need to enhance her bachelor's degree in art history by taking more accounting and finance courses. However, her experience in the insurance industry will serve her well.

DaSheena is willing to take more classes and even earn a master's degree to get a job as an auditor. One coworker suggested DaSheena talk to several auditors and ask the following questions about their jobs.

- What type of degree do you have?
- What skills are the most important in performing your job successfully?
- How much time do you spend sitting at a desk?
- What is a typical day like in your position?
- How often do you work with groups?
- How often do you work alone?

The answers to these questions should help DaSheena determine if being an auditor is the right job for her. DaSheena wants to be sure she is headed in the right direction.

Upper Rungs to Consider

DaSheena enjoys many aspects of her current position as an insurance claim clerk, but she wants to progress in the field of insurance and move on to other jobs. She is ready for a change. She will continue to analyze the work environment for auditors, educational opportunities, and job openings in the area.

Preparing for the Climb

Different careers have different requirements. What career are you thinking about? What questions would you like to ask about the career? Who could you ask?

Insurance

8.1 Disability Insurance

goals

+ Explain the principles of disability insurance.
+ Describe ways to reduce the risk and cost of disability insurance.

terms

+ disability insurance
+ elimination period

Insurance Scene

Ron Hall is an apprentice electrician. He works for a company specializing in outdoor, high-voltage power systems; therefore, he spends a lot of time on ladders, on scaffolds, and in bucket trucks. He had one potentially serious incident stepping off a scaffold, and once he forgot to stabilize the truck before starting up in the bucket. So far he has not been injured. Ron jokes about his absent-mindedness. He says his union insurance plan includes 90 days of full disability benefits and that's long enough for a broken leg to heal. He's young and strong, has no dependents, and has siblings and cousins who could nurse him through a disabling injury. What does Ron not understand about potential disability? What would you say to him about reducing risk? What would you advise him to do about financial risk?

SPECIAL FEATURES ENHANCE LEARNING

flat world...

Driving in Canada and Mexico

The U.S. Department of State posts information on its website about driving in foreign countries (http://travel.state.gov). Although most U.S. auto insurance policies do not cover driving overseas, some policies cover driving in Mexico and Canada. Even if your policy is valid in one of those countries, it may not meet that country's minimum requirements. For example, in most parts of Canada, you must have at least $200,000 in liability insurance. If you have an accident in Mexico and your car is not covered by theft, third-party liability, and comprehensive insurance, you will need to post a bond that could be as high as 50 percent of the value of the vehicle.

Think Critically What do you think are your options for complying with Canadian law? Do you think those options apply to Mexico? Where would you find the information you need?

> **FLAT WORLD** provides international banking connections relevant to today's current events.

tech talk

> **TECH TALK** provides information about new technology that is being used in insurance.

Green Car

Researchers continue to work on the development of a green, environmentally friendly vehicle. Technology plays a big role in the creation of such a vehicle. Hybrid technology (the combination of an electric motor and a gasoline-powered motor) and emission control technology (the elimination of auto pollutants) are essential to improving the environment. Technology also plays a role in the development of an alternative fuel for vehicles.

Think Critically Why would insurance companies be interested in the development of a green car? How can you research the advantages and disadvantages of an environmentally friendly vehicle? What automotive technology other than that mentioned above is essential to improving the environment?

Ethics in Action

A visitor backs into the fiberglass fender of Ethan's deteriorated 1972 VW Beetle parked at the museum where he works. The fender splits, and a security guard who sees the incident stops the visitor from driving away. The claims adjuster from the visitor's insurer sends Ethan to a body shop where he receives an estimate of $162.73 to fix the fender. After providing an estimate, the body shop owner advises Ethan that he'd be better off mending the fender with duct tape and using the money for something he cares about more than the car. Ethan takes the advice.

Think Critically

Did the body shop owner act ethically? Did Ethan act ethically? Explain your answers.

> **ETHICS IN ACTION** provides a real-world situation where students decide an ethical action.

SPECIAL FEATURES ENHANCE LEARNING

NET Bookmark

NET BOOKMARK
incorporates Internet activities into every chapter.

If you were purchasing your first home or condominium, or renting your first apartment, how would you ensure that your home/apartment and personal belongings are covered in case of loss? How could you find out everything you need to know? What is standard in an insurance policy? What are the different types of homeowner's insurance policies? Access www.cengage.com/school/pfinance/insurance and click on the link for Chapter 6. Choose four questions about homeowner's or renter's insurance addressed on the website. Find answers to your questions and write a one-page report. Share your report with the class.

www.cengage.com/school/pfinance/insurance

Insurance Math *Connection*

Alfredo and Tonya pay $536 a year for their home insurance. Their deductible is $250. They could raise their deductible to $500 and decrease their premium by 12 percent each year. One day Tonya realizes they have lived in their home for ten years and have never filed a claim. How much money could they have saved over the past ten years by raising their deductible to $500?

Solution

Percent decrease $\times$ Annual premium = Annual savings
0.12 $\times$ $536 = $64.32
Annual savings $\times$ Number of years = Total savings
$64.32 $\times$ 10 = $643.20

INSURANCE MATH CONNECTION worked examples that reinforce and review math concepts.

interesting *facts*

In 2008 there were approximately 75 million dogs in the United States. Emergency rooms see approximately 1,000 Americans per day due to dog bites. Homeowner's insurance pays over $300 million per year for dog bite claims. Owning a dog may make getting renter's or homeowner's insurance more difficult or costly.

INTERESTING FACTS provides an interesting fact about the topic.

COMMUNICATE provides activities to reinforce, review, and practice communication skills

"communicate"

You are one of several witnesses to a serious accident. You are contacted by an attorney who asks you to write a short statement about what you saw. Write a description of what details to include in your report.

ONGOING ASSESSMENT

✔ checkpoint

Why is it important to purchase renter's or homeowner's insurance?

CHECKPOINT Short questions within lesson to assist with reading and to ensure students are grasping concepts.

THINK CRITICALLY Provides opportunities to apply concepts.

MAKE ACADEMIC CONNECTIONS Provides connections to other disciplines.

TEAMWORK provides you with opportunities to work with classmates on cooperative learning projects.

CHAPTER ASSESSMENT Contains Chapter Summary, Vocabulary Builder, Review Concepts, Apply What You Learned, and Make Connections

chapter 2 assessment

Chapter Summary

2.1 Automobiles and Risk
A. Having automobile insurance does not keep you from having accidents, but it helps protect you from financial loss.
B. Insurance premiums vary according to individual risk factors, including age, gender, type of vehicle, geographic location, and driving history.

2.2 Personal Auto Policies
A. Most people are insured with a Personal Auto Policy (PAP) including four basic types of coverage: liability, medical expenses, physical damage, and uninsured/underinsured motorist.
B. Read and understand your insurance policy. The declarations page is a summary of coverages purchased, while the policy itself details the coverages and exclusions, conditions, definitions, and general provisions of the policy.

2.3 Reporting Accidents
A. The most important things to do in an accident are to help the injured, contact the police, and prevent further accidents. Gather insurance information from other drivers, obtain names and addresses of witnesses, and cooperate with the police.
B. When filing a claim with the insurer, make sure you provide details such as name, address, policy number, car year and make, date, time, location, and injury information. If you are liable for the losses from an accident and they exceed your liability coverage, there is a possibility you may be sued by the injured party.

Vocabulary Builder

Choose the term that best fits the definition. Write the letter of the answer in the space provided. Some terms may not be used.

a. accident zones
b. aggressive driving
c. bodily injury liability
d. collision coverage
e. comprehensive coverage
f. declarations
g. depreciation
h. endorsement
i. exclusions
j. medical expenses coverage
k. Personal Auto Policy
l. Personal Injury Protection
m. points
n. property damage liability

_____ 1. Important personal policy information
_____ 2. Policy for personal use of a private passenger vehicle
_____ 3. Losses not covered by the policy
_____ 4. Covers injuries caused by the insured
_____ 5. An amendment to your insurance policy
_____ 6. A license that has specific requirements attached to it
_____ 7. Covers treatment for injuries to driver/passenger of insured vehicle
_____ 8. Coverage for damage to insured's vehicle in case of collision
_____ 9. Covers damage to vehicles and property of another
_____10. Coverage for damage to insured's vehicle other than by collision
_____11. The reduction in the value of a car as it gets older

---

assessment 2.3

Think Critically

1. Why should you try to preserve the scene of an accident?
2. Why should you get the names and addresses of witnesses of an accident?
3. Why should you carry sufficient liability coverage?
4. What happens when losses exceed coverage?

Make Academic Connections

5. **RESEARCH** Using the Internet, find information about traffic accidents. Write a report explaining how experts reconstruct accidents from skid marks, debris placement, window shatter patterns, and so on.
6. **CONSUMERISM** Review your family auto and homeowner's/renter's insurance policies. Compare the two. Are the liability coverages for similar amounts? Look at the uninsured/underinsured motorist coverage. Does it match your liability coverage? Does anyone in your family remember how these amounts were chosen? From what you've learned about insurance so far, would you revise these policies? Make a presentation to your family.
7. **INSURANCE LAW** Some states have "comparative negligence" or "shared negligence" laws that distribute the liability for some accidents between drivers instead of assigning all the liability to one. Does your state have such a law? Find out and summarize it.

 Teamwork

In a small group, discuss additional ways in which you can be prepared for an accident. Make a list and present your suggestions to the class.

Review Concepts

13. List ways to reduce risk when you drive.

Apply What You Learned

24. In addition to protecting your own interests, why is it important to buy liability insurance?

25. Do you feel you have an ethical as well as a legal responsibility to obey traffic laws?

Make Academic Connections

28. **SOCIOLOGY** Describe your life 10 years from now. Answer these questions: How old will you be? Where will you be employed? What is your job title? What type of vehicle do you drive? Where do you live? Are you married? Do you have children? How many vehicles do you own? After answering these questions, describe your automobile insurance needs. Check with an automobile insurance agent or go online to get a quote on an insurance premium based on your answers to these questions.
29. **RESEARCH** Log on to an insurance company website and research the crash protection ratings of your dream car. Would you purchase this vehicle after reviewing the ratings? Explain why or why not.

30. **CONSUMERISM** Open the *Yellow Pages* and look at the ads for at-

CHAPTER

Insurance Basics

PHOTODISC/GETTY IMAGES

climbing the ladder

From Claims Adjuster to Certified Insurance Service Representative

Katrina had been working for the Garmen Insurance Company as a claims adjuster for three years. As a claims adjuster, she settled claims between her company and those filing claims. In her position, she had to determine the extent of the insurance company's liability and the insurance coverage, interview the insured, and develop a reasonable settlement.

By working in a variety of areas of insurance, Katrina learned a tremendous amount about the insurance industry. She also demonstrated her people skills and improved her time management and organizational skills. By effectively processing claims applications and coordinating with the insured, she proved to be a valuable employee to the company.

The aspect Katrina enjoyed most about her job was serving as a coordinator between the Garmen Insurance Company and customers. She enjoyed building relationships. When Katrina decided she was ready for another challenge in her career, she began investigating the opportunity of becoming a service representative. In this type of position, she would be the coordinating person between insurance companies and insurance agents. Katrina knew she was up for the challenge and applied for the position at another company. During the interview process, she was able to discuss her communication and relationship skills. Due to her work experience, her dedication to her employer, and excellent references provided by her employer, the company recognized her potential. The company talked to her about becoming a Certified Insurance Service Representative (CISR).

The company would provide her with the opportunity to take courses and an examination to become a CISR. This certification is recognized throughout the United States and designates the person as one who has a comprehensive understanding of risks and insurance.

Katrina accepted the job and, soon after, started taking the CISR courses. After completing the courses, she passed the certification exam. She now completes professional continuing education courses each year to keep her certification current.

As a CISR, Katrina enjoys traveling throughout the state, working with a variety of people, and building relationships. As she continues to learn about insurance and risk, she remains an eager, viable employee.

Upper Rungs to Consider

Katrina finds her current position as a CISR rewarding, yet demanding. She continues to improve her communication and time management skills and looks forward to other opportunities for growth in the insurance industry. She plans to continue her professional development and seek other possible insurance certifications in the future.

Preparing for the Climb

Many careers demand soft skills. Soft skills typically include personal traits such as listening, teamwork, and communication skills but may also include conflict resolution and leadership skills, especially when dealing with consumers. Are there things you can do now to improve your soft skills to help prepare for a future career?

PHOTODISC

1.1 Insurance and Risk

goals

+ Define risk.
+ Describe how insurance works.

terms

+ risk
+ insurance
+ insured
+ premiums
+ insurer
+ insurance policy
+ coverage
+ claim
+ uninsured
+ underinsured

Insurance Scene

The wedding was picture perfect, and they enjoyed their honeymoon, but Aaron and Susan came home to some bad news. They've both been dropped from their parents' health insurance coverage because of their new marital status. Their part-time jobs don't offer health insurance, and they have three more semesters before they graduate from college and begin working full-time. They are already paying for insurance on two cars and for renter's insurance, which Aaron's dad insisted they purchase. Aaron wants to cancel the renter's insurance and buy health insurance, but Susan thinks they don't need health insurance because they are young and in good health. Do you agree with Aaron or Susan? What are some other options they should consider?

LIFE CARRIES RISKS •

Risk is involved in any situation in which some kind of loss or misfortune is possible. When you are exposed to the chance of loss or damage, whether personal or material, risk is involved. Risk is a part of life. The loss might involve any one of or a combination of the following:

• Financial, such as a $15,000 hospital bill for an appendectomy

• Physical, such as injury or death

• Material, such as a wrecked car, burned home, or a stolen cell phone

Insurance is designed to protect against risk, because individuals who buy insurance are financially compensated in case of loss. Individuals who are concerned about potential risks pay insurance companies for protection against specific types of risk such as floods, medical costs, car accidents, and many others. Purchasing insurance does not remove risk. It merely provides compensation for the loss and spreads the cost of sharing the risk.

Because insurance is intangible—you cannot actually see or touch what you are getting—some individuals are not motivated to purchase insurance. Risks are intangible, too, and many times are not realized until you experience a loss or survive a close call.

PHOTODISC/GETTY IMAGES

Risks, like life, depend on the circumstances that surround you. Although many individuals face similar risks, no one faces exactly the same risks. For example, although cars are fitted with air bags and seat belts to protect you in a collision, someone who is six feet tall who weighs 200 pounds will suffer different injuries than someone five feet tall who weighs 100 pounds. Risk changes based on circumstances throughout your life. Your risks change as you become employed, change your marital status and number of dependents, and increase or decrease income and savings.

Dealing with Risk

There are several ways to deal with risk. For example, smoking is a risk-filled behavior. To deal with risks associated with smoking, you can choose to do one of the following:

- **Avoid risk,** by not smoking

- **Reduce risk,** by limiting the number of cigarettes you smoke

- **Ignore risk,** by smoking three packs a day

- **Transfer risk,** by buying health insurance to compensate you for medical treatment for conditions caused by smoking.

Dealing with risk by transferring it is the underlying principle of insurance. Insurance transfers risk.

 checkpoint

List and describe four ways to deal with risk.

_____

_____

_____

interesting *facts*

An *underwriter* is a person who reviews and evaluates the eligibility and risk factors of insurance applicants. This word dates back to times when groups of investors shared the costs—and the risks—of a sea voyage. They wrote their names and the amount of their investment *underneath* the description of the ship, its cargo, and the voyage. ▪

HOW INSURANCE WORKS •

Individuals who buy insurance are the **insured**. The insured agrees to transfer risk by paying periodic payments, **premiums**, to the insuring company, the **insurer**. These premiums create a pool of money that the insurer invests to earn more money, which is used to compensate the insured for losses.

Individuals who pay premiums to the insurer are protected against the risk of financial loss by transferring the risk to a large group of individuals who then share the financial loss. Depending on the type of insurance, premiums are paid as follows:

- monthly, once each month

- semiannually, every six months

- annually, once a year

It is important that you budget accordingly to be able to pay premiums when they are due. Some insurance companies offer the option of paying smaller premiums more often to make budgeting easier, but you will pay a fee, and thus a higher overall yearly premium, for this convenience.

An **insurance policy** is a written contract between the insurer and the insured. Each individual contract is designed to cover specific future losses such as theft, accident, fire, flood, illness, or death. Each kind of specific loss is identified as a type of **coverage** on an insurance policy. For example, you may have flood or fire coverage. Individuals agree to pay premiums on an insurance policy, and the insurer agrees to reimburse them for their loss on the specific coverage included in their policy.

When a loss occurs, the insured files a claim. A **claim** is a written request for reimbursement to cover loss or damage that occurred from a specific event.

PHOTODISC/GETTY IMAGES

flat world...

Natural Worldwide Disasters

You may only be aware of natural disasters that occur in the United States, but they happen everywhere. Listed below are world disasters that occurred within a two-month period (May and June) in 2008. Natural catastrophes have led insurance companies to increase premiums worldwide.

Philippines: Typhoon Fengshen
Suriname: Floods
India: Floods
Central America: Tropical Storms Alma and Arthur
Colombia: Earthquake
Chile: Floods
Philippines: Tropical Cyclone Halong
China: Earthquake
Chile: Volcano Chaitén
Myanmar: Tropical Cyclone Nargis

The question is not *if* a natural disaster will occur, but what will be the extent of damages incurred by individuals and insurance companies *when* the disaster does occur. In the China 7.9-magnitude earthquake, an estimated 70,000–85,000 people were killed, and approximately 5 million people were left homeless.

Think Critically

1. What does the number of insured losses tell you about the future cost of insurance premiums in other countries?
2. How do disasters in other countries affect insurance in the United States?
3. Do you think there will ever be a "worldwide" standard insurance premium for certain types of insurance, such as flood or earthquake coverage?

Who Provides Insurance?

Most insurance is provided by private, for-profit corporations. The U.S. government also provides some insurance, for example, to military employees. Additional insurance programs are provided jointly by federal and state governments. The main difference between private corporation and government-supplied insurance is the cost of the premiums. Most individuals who receive government insurance pay minimal or no premiums for coverage.

Increasing Costs

Over the past years, insurance premiums for most kinds of insurance have increased dramatically. Growth in premiums continues to proceed at a higher rate than growth in workers' earnings and growth in the economy. Consequently, the high cost of insurance causes many Americans to be **uninsured** (having no insurance at all) or **underinsured** (not having enough insurance). Some consumer advocates blame high premiums on the insurance industry, saying it is fleecing the public by charging too much for premiums. Others blame increasingly sophisticated medical technology and prescription costs for rising health insurance costs. Insurance industry defenders blame consumers and attorneys who bring malpractice claims

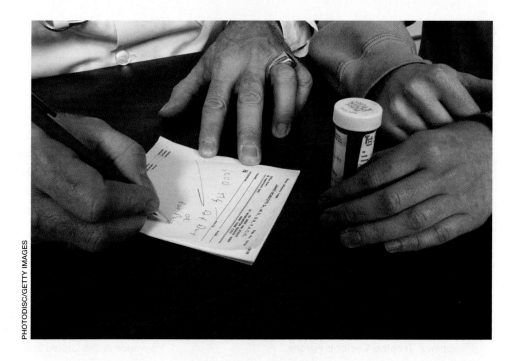
PHOTODISC/GETTY IMAGES

to court, thus raising costs for insurance companies. The debate continues about the rising costs of insurance.

One undeniable factor behind high premiums is the string of catastrophic earthquakes, hurricanes, floods, and wildfires that have occurred. Natural catastrophes doubled between the 1960s and 1990s. The year 2001 was later noted as having the highest estimated insurance losses in history. This was due to a hailstorm in St. Louis, Missouri, a tropical storm in Houston, Texas, and the terrorist attacks on September 11, 2001. But 2001 did not compare to the financial losses due to Hurricanes Katrina, Wilma, and Rita in 2005, making it the year with the highest insurances losses to date.

Insurance costs for so many widespread natural disasters caused insurance companies to raise premiums substantially or cancel policy coverage in specific areas. If individuals built homes in areas prone to wildfires or flooding, insurance companies would exclude wildfires or floods from those customers' coverage or charge much higher premiums.

 checkpoint

Do you think insurance companies or consumers have more responsibility for the rising cost of insurance? Why?

_____

_____

_____

assessment 1.1

Think Critically

1. Why do individuals need insurance?

_____

_____

2. Why is insurance intangible?

_____

_____

3. How can you transfer risk?

_____

_____

Make Academic Connections

4. **PROBLEM SOLVING**   Think about four different risks you face in your life and how you deal with each risk. Can you think of better ways to manage these four risks?

_____

_____

5. **CREATIVE WRITING**   Think of a circumstance in your life or a friend's/ family member's life in which insurance coverage was needed. Write a story describing the incident, insurance needs, and the outcome of events.

6. **PSYCHOLOGY**   Some individuals are uninsured or underinsured because they cannot afford to pay the premiums. Can you think of a reason why individuals who can afford to pay remain uninsured or underinsured?

_____

_____

_____

 **Teamwork**

Sometimes risk cannot be avoided, nor should it be avoided under certain circumstances. As a class, brainstorm about situations in which risk-taking behavior is useful, necessary, or even noble.

1.2

Basic Policy Types

goals

+ Describe basic property and casualty policies.

+ Describe basic life, health, and disability policies.

terms

+ liability

+ real property

+ personal property

Insurance Scene

LaShawne owns a house on a large lot in a neighborhood where there are many children. He often finds children playing in his yard, even though it is fenced. He has made his yard as safe as possible, putting locks on his outbuildings and keeping his dogs inside unless he is home. He wants to install an in-ground swimming pool. What safety and insurance issues will LaShawne have to consider?

PROPERTY AND CASUALTY INSURANCE • • • • • • • • • • • • • •

Property and casualty insurance includes insurance policies for homes, cars, and businesses. It protects the insured against losses to his or her property or losses caused by injury to other people or damage to others' property. Events such as fire, burglary, and other damage, as well as liability, are covered by such policies. **Liability** refers to a legal responsibility to provide compensation for certain types of injury or loss. For example, if a person falls down stairs in your home because they were holding onto a loose railing, you may be liable for paying any medical bills incurred. Therefore, property and casualty insurance protect you from a financial loss due to liability.

Both real property and personal property are covered by property and casualty insurance policies. **Real property** includes permanent structures and objects such as buildings, fences, and built-in appliances. **Personal property** includes anything not permanently attached, such as cars, RVs, furniture, clothing, and personal items.

Automobile Insurance

Because automobiles can be dangerous possessions, the most important automobile coverage is liability. Most states mandate a minimum amount of liability insurance individuals must carry to cover property damage and personal injury in case of an auto accident. Each state has specific regulations for types of automobile insurance policies including no-fault, uninsured, and underinsured motorist coverage.

- **No-fault insurance** coverage provides compensation in the case of an accident regardless of who was at fault.

- **Uninsured motorist** coverage provides compensation through an individual's insurer to recover damages caused by a driver who is not insured—uninsured.

- **Underinsured motorist** coverage provides compensation through an individual's insurer for amounts not covered by the insurance company of the driver at fault because he or she is underinsured.

Comprehensive Coverage   A comprehensive automobile insurance policy protects an individual against automobile theft, collision, vandalism, and damage from fire. The policy covers an individual's liability in an accident that is his or her fault, and it provides uninsured and underinsured motorist coverage. As the name implies, this type of policy is comprehensive in nature.

Due to the high cost, many individuals do not purchase comprehensive coverage insurance. Instead, they carry the minimum coverage required by state law. An individual may choose to carry additional coverage but should not pay for more collision insurance than the car is worth.

Homeowner's and Renter's Insurance

Homeowner's and renter's insurance vary on coverage. For example, homeowner's insurance covers more than the building itself. Such policies provide several basic coverages, including damage to or loss of the dwelling itself, other structures such as garages and sheds, and personal property on the insured premises. Coverage might also include loss of use of the property, personal liability, and medical payments in case of an accident on the property.

Renter's insurance provides coverage for those renting an apartment, condo, or home, but typically does not cover the dwelling itself. The owner of the apartment or home should have insurance to cover the structure. However, renter's insurance covers personal possessions and liability. If a loss occurs, typically the policy will compensate the insured for the replacement value of the possessions lost. Both renter's or homeowner's policies purchased and options selected depend on the circumstances of the insured.

✔ checkpoint

Describe the difference between real property and personal property.

_____

_____

_____

LIFE, HEALTH, AND DISABILITY INSURANCE • • • • • • • • • •

Life expectancy in the United States continues to increase. In 2008, the life expectancy was 78.1 years of age. Life expectancy varies among races and by gender. For example, white females typically live the longest with a life expectancy of 81, followed by black females, 76.9, followed by white males, 76, and black males, 70.

Modern medical technology enables individuals requiring assistance and skilled care to live longer. Elderly individuals live longer, even if they are frail. Because the probability is good that you will live longer, you may need a variety of life, health, and disability insurances, such as long-term care, and different kinds of social insurance, such as Social Security and workers' compensation.

Life Insurance

Life insurance pays a set amount of money to specified beneficiaries upon the insured's death. A *beneficiary* is a person or entity named in the insured's will who should receive the benefits upon the insured's death. Life insurance was an early form of insurance developed to protect families financially when their major wage earner died. The life insurance funds can be used to pay funeral expenses, debts, and fees incurred in settling the estate of the deceased. When purchasing life insurance, consider the standard of living you want for your beneficiaries based on your particular circumstances.

Life insurance is a viable and important tool for family protection, but it is also used for financial planning as well. Estate planning to reduce taxes, salary continuation after death, and deferred compensation are often considerations in purchasing life insurance. Loans can even be obtained against a life insurance policy during the life of the insured.

NET Bookmark

Learning about insurance may be new to you. It's important to learn basic insurance terms to continue to develop your understanding of insurance. Access www.cengage.com/school/pfinance/insurance and click on the link for Chapter 1. At the Insurance Information Institute website, browse the Glossary of Insurance Terms. Review the definitions for several terms discussed in this chapter, and write your own personal definition of three insurance terms.

www.cengage.com/school/pfinance/insurance

Don't Buy What You Don't Need   Not everyone needs to purchase life insurance. If you do not have *dependents* (a child or another person who relies on you for financial support), and your *assets* (the money and property you own) would cover your debts and funeral expenses, you could use the money you would pay for insurance premiums for more important purposes. You could invest the money, buy certificates of deposit (CDs), or enroll in a savings plan.

PHOTODISC/GETTY IMAGES

nmunicate"

Interview two adults—relatives, family friends, or neighbors—about the risks each faces in his or her job. Write a one- to two-page report on what you learn and how they could reduce their risk. Present your report to the class.

Health and Medical Insurance

Typically the terms *health insurance* and *medical insurance* are used interchangeably. Health/medical insurance plans provide compensation for medical care costs due to disease or injury. These plans range from managed care to more traditional fee-for-service plans and can be purchased by individuals or on a group basis through your employer. Managed care plans may cover preventive treatments for a nominal fee, while traditional fee-for-service plans require individuals to pay a larger percentage of all care received. Most plans offer options from which to choose.

Federal health and medical programs are provided by the government for those in need of health and medical care. They include the following:

- **Medicare** provides hospital, medical, and surgical benefits to individuals age 65 or older or those under 65 with certain disabilities.

- **Medicaid** is a government medical assistance program based on need. It provides medical benefits to low-income families with children and others in need who cannot afford medical insurance.

Long-Term Care Insurance

Due to the aging population in the United States, as well as better survival rates for individuals who are severely disabled, long-term care insurance has become important. Long-term care policies include compensation for nursing homes, home health care, institutional care, assisted living facilities, personal care, and other related services for the elderly and disabled. The cost of premiums for long-term care insurance is affected by existing health problems, lifestyle choices, age, and family history, as well as the desired level of care. Long-term care is for everyone in need of medical assistance for a long period of time. You may need long-term care if you are in a disabling accident or have a disabling disease.

PHOTODISC/GETTY IMAGES

Ethics in Action

Sean works for a bicycle courier service and was injured during a delivery. Through his employer's workers' compensation insurance program, Sean has been receiving a temporary income while unable to work. However, Sean is now physically able to return to work, but he is pretending he is still disabled so he can continue to collect workers' compensation benefits.

Think Critically

Why are Sean's actions unethical? How might his fraudulent behavior be uncovered? What do you think the penalty should be if he is caught? Do you think Sean's boss can do anything to prevent this from occurring again?

Social Insurance

Most U.S. citizens are protected by various forms of social insurance required by law and financed, completely or partially, by employers, employees, and/or the government. Social insurance is provided through government-sponsored programs that provide monthly benefits, benefits to dependents of deceased workers, and disability benefits. Social Security is the best known example of social insurance, which includes workers' and unemployment compensation as well.

Workers' Compensation and Unemployment Compensation   Federal and state legislation determine much of the employer costs for workers' and unemployment compensation.

• **Workers' compensation insurance** pays benefits to employees or an employee's family for work-related bodily injury, occupational diseases contracted at the worksite, or a work-related death. Benefits may be paid for medical expenses, lost income, and/or rehabilitation.

• **Unemployment insurance** provides temporary income to eligible unemployed individuals who meet certain criteria and are involuntarily unemployed or laid off.

checkpoint

Describe the importance of government social insurance programs.

_____

_____

_____

assessment 1.2

Think Critically

1. Why should you buy liability insurance?

_____

_____

2. Describe why individuals may need Medicare or Medicaid.

_____

_____

3. Discuss ways in which workers' compensation is similar to liability insurance.

_____

_____

Make Academic Connections

4. **CONSUMERISM** Do you think it is possible to waste money by buying too much insurance or the wrong kind of insurance? Visit at least two websites for insurance buyers and list 5 to 10 ways to protect you as a consumer.

_____

_____

5. **GOVERNMENT** Do you have or know someone who has been in a nursing home or needed extended care in a medical facility? Discuss how Medicare, Medicaid, workers' compensation, or unemployment insurance was or may have been beneficial to that individual.

_____

_____

6. **SOCIOLOGY** Individuals who suffer severe spinal and brain injuries may require lifelong assistance. If you were severely injured, what kind of impact would it make on your lifelong plans? Write a few paragraphs about how you might handle such an event and what type of insurance you would need.

 **Teamwork**

Working in groups, make a list of people in your families. Explain which types of insurance they should purchase depending on their individual circumstances.

Purchasing Considerations

goals

+ Discuss insurability and probability.
+ Explain product options, price, and company ratings.

terms

+ insurability
+ product options
+ deductible

Insurance Scene

Santino, age 19, is a college sophomore. When he was in high school, he was cited twice for speeding and also for three minor accidents. His parents carry him on their auto insurance policy, but they make a point of showing him how much extra they must pay to cover him. Santino decides to reform his driving habits so he can afford to buy insurance when he graduates and is living on his own. How can he demonstrate that he is a safe driver? Are there insurance discounts for safe drivers? If so, how do they work?

ARE YOU INSURABLE? •

There are some types of insurance coverage no one should go without. Unfortunately, not every person is eligible to obtain all types of insurance. For example, if you received a number of traffic citations for high-risk violations such as speeding or running red lights, you would be considered a less desirable customer because you are less insurable.

Insurability is the ability of an individual who has applied for insurance to be accepted by the insurer. The insurer determines whether you are insurable and meet the company's conditions to be insured. The insurer reviews factors such as health, occupation, lifestyle, and age. Insurance companies are for-profit businesses designed to make money. By analyzing insurability factors, they decide whether you are likely to file more claims than they would like to pay. If so, insurers will either refuse to sell you insurance or will charge high premiums.

Probability, Insurance, and You

Because life is uncertain and the future difficult to predict, insurance companies struggle with ways to determine who is insurable. To determine your insurability, the insurer draws heavily upon the laws of *probability*, the branch of mathematics that measures the likelihood of some event occurring.

Probability theories assist insurers in predicting the likelihood of claims payments for a variety of lifetime events. Life insurance in particular is based upon probability, using mortality tables (also called actuarial tables)

Insurance companies check information on your application for insurance very carefully. All states have some type of insurance fraud listed as a crime, and most states have developed Fraud Bureaus set up in the State Attorney General's office. Don't lie on an application for insurance! ◼

to determine death rates. If insurers were unable to accurately predict the likelihood of claims, more claims would be paid, and the insurers would be required to compensate more individuals than expected. Their costs would rise, and they would have to charge higher premiums, or go out of business.

Are You a Risk to the Insurer?

To reduce cost to the insurer and keep premiums as low as possible, a screening process is completed before an application for an insurance policy is approved. As your policy application is reviewed, the insurer considers your personal characteristics, such as age, gender, and family history. The company also looks closely at lifestyle choices, such as whether you smoke or whether you have points on your driving record, to determine the probability of your filing claims. This analysis determines whether you are eligible for the insurance, and it may also affect the cost of the premium if you are accepted.

Many health insurance companies will require evidence of insurability. You must supply personal medical information on the insurance application form to provide your evidence of insurability. Evidence of insurability may be requested before you initially enroll, increase coverage, or add dependents to the policy. Because evidence of insurability is based on facts, all questions must be answered honestly and in good faith. If asked, "Do you smoke?" and you do not answer truthfully, you may later be considered uninsurable because of your misrepresentation. Many insurance companies also check for pre-existing medical conditions or injuries that occurred prior to the purchase of the policy. For example, if you had cancer before applying for insurance, this would be considered a pre-existing condition. The insurance company can refuse to insure you, charge higher premiums, or restrict benefits.

©CORBIS

 **checkpoint**

What is the difference between insurability and evidence of insurability?

BEFORE YOU BUY •

Before you purchase any kind of insurance, it is important to analyze your specific needs. The four basic steps in making insurance decisions are as follows:

1. **Determine what risks you face.** For example, if you want to buy a house in the country as opposed to the city, what risks do you face?

2. **Determine the causes of the risks.** Fire insurance in rural areas, far from fire hydrants and professional fire departments, is more expensive because the risk of complete loss is higher.

3. **Identify ways to handle each risk.** You can *avoid* the risk by abandoning your country house plan. You can *transfer* risk by paying high insurance premiums. You can *reduce* risk by buying a house in town instead of the country, or by buying a brick rather than a frame house. Or you can *ignore* the risk by buying your country house and not insuring it as thoroughly as you should.

4. **Make a plan of action.** If your plan of action is to insure yourself against risk, you must do some research. Before you decide to buy any type of insurance, you must consider the options available for a particular policy, the price of the premiums, and the rating of the insurance company.

PHOTODISC/GETTY IMAGES

Insurance Math *Connection*

The Horizons Travel Agency wants to add employee dental insurance to its health coverage. The insurance company needs to determine how much to charge Horizons for this coverage. One factor in determining the premium for the dental coverage is employee age. Given all of the employees' ages below, determine the average employee age.

20	21	22	23	24	24	25
26	28	28	30	30	30	31
33	35	38	39	45	48	51

Solution

Add the ages of all the employees to find the total age. The employees have a total age of 651 years.

Divide the total age by the number of employees to find the average age.

Total age ÷ Number of employees = Average age
   651   ÷   21   =   31

The average age is 31.

Product Options

When you review an insurance policy, you should ask yourself two questions: "What is the basic policy coverage?" and "What are the available product options?" **Product options** are special features added to a basic policy. For example, options for an automobile insurance policy may include collision, car rental, and comprehensive coverages. These options provide for a variety of circumstances and give you flexibility, allowing you to customize an insurance policy to your specific needs. Product options typically increase the cost of the premiums. When considering options, ask yourself, "What is the worst thing that might happen if I don't have this coverage?" The answer to this question may help you make an effective decision on which options or coverage to buy or not buy.

Policy Pricing

Remember, insurance companies are profit-making, competitive organizations. Prices for the same coverage will vary among insurance companies so it is important to

comparison shop. Search the Internet. Ask friends about their policies. Contact different insurance companies and seek whatever discounts you can, such as the "B or above" student discount for auto insurance. Obtain at least three quotes from insurance companies before you buy.

While you are searching for the best policy price, remember the cheapest policy is not always the best policy. For only a slightly higher premium, one company may offer you a significantly better policy than another. Sometimes it is difficult to compare policies because coverages are grouped differently by each company. Sit down with a variety of policies and investigate each coverage, item by item, to get a better idea of what each policy offers.

Reducing Your Rate   Besides reducing risky behaviors, another thing to consider is raising the policy deductible. By raising the policy deductible, you can reduce the overall rates of the insurance policy.

A **deductible** is the amount of money you, the insured, agree to pay in the event of a loss, prior to the insurer paying the rest of the claim amount. As you know, the premium must be paid by the insured consistently. You don't pay the deductible unless you file a claim.

Company Ratings

Some insurance companies do go out of business, and their policyholders lose not only their coverage but also the amount of money they may have invested in the policy. When you purchase a policy from an insurer, you want to be sure the company is in stable financial health. You can obtain such financial information from a ratings service.

Standard & Poor's (S&P) and A.M. Best are two commonly used insurance rating services. They rate the financial strength and reputation of insurance companies worldwide. These rating services are necessary to analyze an insurance company's financial strength to make sure it can meet its policy contract obligations to everyone who buys a policy.

The ratings provided are important to the insurance companies and consumers. Insurance companies can use the ratings to build consumer

tech talk

Insurance Online

The number of individuals contacting insurance companies online is increasing. Prospective customers can obtain a premium quote online or compare premiums from several companies before making a decision. Current customers can submit a claim, change policy options, and change personal information online. The popularity of these services has increased the demand for insurance companies to produce more interactive websites to allow prospective customers access to company products.

Think Critically   Describe three advantages and three disadvantages of accessing an insurance company online.

confidence in the company's stability. Sample ratings of an insurance company by a variety of rating services are listed below.

A.M. Best	Financial Strength Rating: A++ Superior The outlook is stable.
Standard & Poor's	Financial Strength Rating: AAA
Moody's Investors Service	Holds AAA Rating
Fitch	Insurer Financial Strength: AAA Exceptionally Strong Highest Rating Possible

Ask Your State

Each state has an insurance department to regulate all insurance types. In addition to regulating insurance laws and practices, the state insurance department provides consumers with basic information and educational material. Your state's insurance department provides this information online.

Remember that no matter what kind of insurance you buy, rates for the premiums should be adequate, reasonable, and nondiscriminatory. If you have questions or wish to report insurance fraud, your state insurance office is the place to go.

PHOTODISC/GETTY IMAGES

 checkpoint

Explain four things you should do before you buy insurance.

assessment 1.3

Think Critically

1. Why do insurance companies assess prospective customers for insurability?

2. How can your lifestyle affect your insurability?

3. Why do product options increase the cost of insurance?

Make Academic Connections

4. **PROBLEM SOLVING**   Taking both your family history and lifestyle into account, make a list of your health risks. What health practices, including making changes to your lifestyle, can you undertake to reduce your risk of illness or premature death? Which practices would increase your insurability?

5. **CONSUMERISM**   Select a car and get quotes from at least three auto insurance companies online. Compare the companies' basic policies and options and determine the best buy. Defend your answer.

6. **RESEARCH**   Using two different ratings services, research the ratings of the companies whose quotes you investigated above. After reviewing the ratings, does the best buy still seem like the best buy? Defend your answer.

 **Teamwork**

Work in teams to investigate probability. Flip a coin 50 times and keep track of the results. What is the probability that heads will appear on any given flip? Does each group have the same results? How is probability applied to insurance?

chapter 1 assessment

Chapter Summary

1.1 Insurance and Risk

A. Risk is involved in any situation in which some kind of loss or misfortune is possible. You can choose to avoid, reduce, ignore or transfer risk by buying insurance.

B. Insurance premiums paid by the insured soften the impact of a loss by spreading the loss among a large group of individuals. Premiums are paid at regular intervals to create a pool from which claims on the insurance are paid.

1.2 Basic Policy Types

A. Property and casualty insurance include coverage for losses to homes, cars, and businesses. They protect against losses caused by injury to other people or damage to property.

B. Life, health, and disability insurance protect individuals and families in case of death, medical costs, or disabling injury. Social insurance, such as unemployment, workers' compensation, and Social Security, also protects individuals and families from financial consequences when they are unable to work or they involuntarily lose a job.

1.3 Purchasing Considerations

A. Insurers use probability to determine insurability. Probability helps the insurer determine whether it risks losing money if it covers a particular individual. For reasons ranging from pre-existing conditions to lifestyle choices, some individuals are considered uninsurable.

B. Because product options increase premiums, it is important to analyze insurance needs, compare pricing from several companies, consider reducing risks and increasing the deductible, and explore company ratings.

Vocabulary Builder

a. claim
b. coverage
c. deductible
d. insurability
e. insurance
f. insurance policy
g. insured
h. insurer
i. liability
j. personal property
k. premium
l. product options
m. real property
n. risk
o. underinsured
p. uninsured

Choose the term that best fits the definition. Write the letter of the answer in the space provided. Some terms may not be used.

_____ 1. Individual who agrees to transfer risk by paying certain sums of money to the insurer

_____ 2. Legal responsibility

_____ 3. Sum of money paid by the insured to the insurer to create a pool of money used for compensation

_____ 4. Amount paid by insured before insurer pays on a claim

_____ 5. Contract designed to cover specific future losses

_____ 6. Ability of an individual to be accepted by the insurer

_____ 7. Special features added to a basic policy that increase the cost of the premium

_____ 8. Protection taken against risk

_____ 9. Request for reimbursement to cover losses due to an event

_____10. An individual who has no insurance at all

_____11. Property such as a cell phone, clothes, and car

Review Concepts

12. Define and give examples of a loss.

13. How does the payment of premiums transfer the risk to a large group of individuals who share the financial loss?

14. What is the purpose of no-fault insurance?

15. Name the types of coverage options for homeowner's insurance.

16. Name the purposes of life insurance.

17. Describe workers' compensation in your own words.

18. Explain why you should comparison shop before buying insurance.

19. Describe what you can do to lower the cost of insurance.

20. Explain the difference between Medicare and Medicaid.

_____

_____

_____

_____

_____

Apply What You Learned

21. Why do you think government regulates the insurance industry?

_____

_____

_____

22. Why do you think auto liability insurance is mandatory?

_____

_____

_____

23. Do you think it is ethical for insurers to refuse to insure individuals with pre-existing medical conditions?

_____

_____

_____

24. You have been asked in this chapter to use the Internet to research insurance companies. Would you feel comfortable buying insurance online? Why or why not?

_____

_____

_____

Make Academic Connections

25. **PROBLEM SOLVING**   Most insurance is bought to protect the insured against the possibility of loss, except life insurance. People buy life insurance to prepare for death. Can you explain how life insurance works?

_____

_____

_____

_____

26. **CREATIVE WRITING**   Pretend you are 30 years old and have a spouse and two children. Create a story of your life, identify the types of insurance needed, and explain why.

_____

_____

_____

_____

27. **RESEARCH**   The easiest way to reduce risk of injury in an auto accident is to buckle your seat belt every time you get into the car. Find an auto safety website giving the statistics on seat belt use to learn what a dramatic difference this can make. Summarize the important points.

_____

_____

_____

_____

28. **COMMUNICATION**   Using the research you did on seat belts for question 27 above, assume a friend/family member does not use a seat belt. Write a letter to persuade this person to start buckling up.

_____

_____

_____

_____

29. **MARKETING**   Create an advertising campaign to promote a low-risk lifestyle for individuals your age. Describe what message you would like to send and where you would place ads. Mock up a print ad or script a radio or TV ad.

_____

_____

_____

30. **GOVERNMENT**   Visit your state's department of insurance online. Review the website and read the consumer information you find the most interesting. How can you apply this information to your own life right now? Do you think it is appropriate for government to take this sort of role? Why or why not? Write a few paragraphs explaining your thoughts.

_____

_____

_____

_____

2

Automobile Insurance

COMSTOCK IMAGES/JUPITER IMAGES

climbing the ladder

From Insurance Sales Agent to Insurance Underwriter

Kacey expressed an interest in business as a career in high school and took several business courses. After high school, she completed an associate degree in business from Cambridge Community College (CCC). She took accounting and economics courses at CCC and an insurance course as an elective. Kacey did so well in her insurance course her professor encouraged her to seek a career in the insurance industry. Kacey was open to the professor's suggestion because she found the insurance course to be interesting and challenging.

Kacey now works for Hartsmith Insurance Company as an insurance sales agent. She enjoys the opportunity to work with clients to review and explain the terms of policies. She is often the first contact with clients at Hartsmith, and she strives to help individuals, families, and businesses choose the best insurance policy to meet their diverse needs.

She sells several types of insurance, including life, health, disability, long-term care, and property and casualty. She also maintains sales records, writes reports, and finds and recruits new clients. She uses word processing and spreadsheet software to complete many of her duties. Her written and oral communication skills have improved because of her work as an insurance sales agent.

Kacey has also had the opportunity to work extensively on the insurance company's Web page to assist clients online. The combination of working with people and working with technology is an enjoyable part of her job.

While working for Hartsmith, Kacey was provided with an opportunity to continue her education. The company provided financial support as long as she maintained a 3.0 (B) average. She just completed her bachelor's degree. She majored in business, which included more insurance and accounting coursework. With a bachelor's degree, she realized she had more career opportunities with the company.

Her degree helped her qualify for and obtain an insurance underwriter position at her company. Insurance underwriters typically have a degree in business administration or finance with coursework in accounting.

Her key duties as an underwriter include identifying and calculating the risk of loss, deciding who will receive a policy, writing policies to cover the appropriate type of risk, and establishing the proper premium. Basically, Kacey uses computer software to analyze information prospective clients provide in their applications for insurance. Her computer skills continue to increase as she attends training sessions at the central office.

Upper Rungs to Consider

Kacey is pleased with her increased salary and new position. She is considering earning a master's degree in insurance and risk management to expand her opportunities in the insurance business.

Preparing for the Climb

Computer skills are important to Kacey's new insurance position. Many careers in business require computer and other technology skills. Are you currently developing computer and technology skills? What computer or technology skills are essential to obtaining your career goal?

PHOTO DISC

2.1 Automobiles and Risk

goals

+ Discuss ways to reduce risks when driving.

+ Discuss factors to consider when purchasing auto insurance.

terms

+ aggressive driving

+ restricted license

+ points

Insurance Scene

Jason Zachary is 18 years old and is buying his first car. He will be going away to college and won't be able to park close to the dorm. He will also be driving home and back to school (an approximate 100-mile trip) several weekends throughout the year. Before he buys a car, what should he consider? Before he buys car insurance, what should he consider?

DRIVER BEWARE

You may be a mild-mannered, careful person who wouldn't dream of doing anything dangerous like skydiving or bungee jumping, but the fact is, every time you get into a car, you're putting yourself at risk. If you drive, you are also putting the life, health, and property of others at risk. Cars are dangerous. They're heavy and they travel fast. Even under the best circumstances, they take time and varying distance to come to a complete stop.

Americans drive more than three trillion miles every year. Given so much time on the road, accidents are inevitable. And because most cars, trucks, and vans weigh at least a ton and can travel at high rates of speeds, some accidents are bound to be serious. In fact, approximately 45,000 Americans die in auto accidents every year. The Centers for Disease Control and Prevention (CDC) provides statistics to the public about motor vehicle crashes as well as many other injuries or deaths.

The leading cause of death for teens in the United States is motor vehicle crashes. Approximately 5,000 teens die each year in auto accidents and another 400,000 are injured and require medical attention. The economic cost of vehicle accidents involving teenagers is over $40 billion annually.

What Insurance Does

Automobile insurance won't keep you from having an accident, but it will protect you financially in case you are involved in an accident. A minor accident in which no one is injured can still result in thousands of dollars of damage to one or more vehicles. The other component to consider in an accident is medical coverage in case of injury. The amount of potential loss can skyrocket when medical bills are included. Serious injuries involving physical therapy, rehabilitation, and lost wages can easily run into six figures. If you are found to be at fault in a serious accident, you might also

DIGITAL VISION/GETTY IMAGES

be sued for pain and suffering or prosecuted for negligence or reckless driving. In either case, legal fees, as well as any compensatory costs, penalties, or fines you may be ordered to pay will add to your financial loss.

Because of the high costs of auto accidents, every state requires drivers to either carry automobile insurance or prove they have the financial resources to pay a claim. Automobile insurance is the easiest way to document such financial resources.

What You Can Do

Insurance merely transfers risk. You also have the power to reduce your risk of having an accident or at least reduce the damage if you are involved in an accident. Many people who become traffic fatalities tend to cluster risky behaviors—for example, they speed and don't use their seat belts. The best way to reduce risk is to be mindful of and follow safety rules and regulations.

TEEN CRASH STATISTICS

- Motor vehicle crashes are the leading cause of death for American teenagers ages 16–19.

- Over 5,000 teenagers (ages 16–19) die in motor vehicle crashes each year.

- Approximately 2 out of every 3 teenagers killed in vehicle crashes are male.

- Over 60 percent of teenage passenger deaths occur in vehicles driven by another teenager.

- Over 50 percent of vehicle crash deaths among teenagers occurred on Friday, Saturday, or Sunday.

Use Your Seat Belt   Using your seat belt is probably the single easiest way, statistically speaking, to increase your life expectancy. Insist your passengers use their seat belts as well.
Seat belts may prevent you or your passengers from being ejected in a crash, which is a common cause of fatality. Using a seat belt will often reduce injuries you might suffer, as noted by the National Highway Traffic Safety Administration (NHTSA). Safety belts prevent approximately 16,000 fatalities, 350,000 serious injuries, and over $65 billion in economic costs associated with traffic injuries and deaths every year.

PHOTODISC/GETTY IMAGES

Observe Speed Limits   Experts are not exaggerating when they tell you speed kills. The faster you drive, the harder it is to maneuver, the longer it takes to stop, and the farther you travel while reacting to the situation. The odds of death and serious injury double for every 10 miles per hour over 50 miles per hour. The protective capability of seat belts and air bags drops as speed increases. Speed is a factor in approximately one-third of traffic fatalities.

Concentrate on Driving   Give your full attention to driving. Don't talk on the phone or send text messages while driving. Some states have laws against it. Check your mirrors and blind spots before changing lanes and always use turn signals. Be aware of signs noting speed limits, curvy roads, or construction. A reduced speed is necessary in construction zones. Keep all distractions to a minimum and pay full attention to the road. Your life, and the lives of others, depends on it.

Be Patient   Aggressive driving, such as speeding, tailgating, running red lights, weaving in and out of traffic, or acting out—"road rage"—is on the rise as roads become more congested. You can reduce your need for rapid travel by allowing extra time to reach your destination or taking an alternate route if there is traffic congestion. Be a safe and courteous driver. Auto accidents are devastating—physically, emotionally, and financially. Reduce your risk of being in an accident by being patient.

Observe Motorcycle Safety   Motorcycle safety is also important. Helmet laws are not consistent from state to state, so as a motorcyclist, you must be aware of the state laws before driving across state lines. Helmet law regulations include 100 percent helmet free (4 states); full helmet laws for all motorcycle riders (20 states); helmet laws for those under 18 (19 states); and helmet laws for those under 21 or a specific regulation on age (7 states).

Head injury is the leading cause of death in motorcycle crashes. Helmeted motorcyclists are less likely to suffer fatal head injuries than those not helmeted. Helmets reduce the likelihood of a motorcycle crash fatality by approximately 40 percent. So be smart—wear a helmet if you are operating a motorcycle.

Don't Drink and Drive   Approximately 17,000 fatalities occur each year due to alcohol-related accidents. An alcohol-related fatality occurs every half hour, and an alcohol-related injury occurs every two minutes. These accidents cost about $51 billion. Male drivers are twice as likely as females to be involved, and the overall risk of being involved in alcohol-related accidents is greater for young people than for older people.

The organization Mothers Against Drunk Driving (MADD) reported in 2008 that 41 percent of the approximately 43,000 total traffic fatalities were caused by alcohol-related accidents. The organization also notes that 3 out of every 10 Americans will be involved in an alcohol-related accident in their lifetime.

✔ checkpoint

Why is it important to purchase automobile insurance?

_____

_____

VARYING RISKS, VARYING RATES • • • • • • • • • • • • • • • • • •

Automobile insurance is a huge component of the insurance industry. In order to be competitive in the market, insurance companies have studied all factors to determine which of their policyholders are at highest risk of loss and, therefore, tend to file the most claims. Insurance companies have also determined what kinds of claims a particular policyholder is likely to file. Some drivers, and some vehicles, carry more risk than others.

Policyholders falling into high-risk categories will be charged higher premiums for basic policies. Those falling into a low-risk category will be charged less. Pricing is individualized to some degree by driving record. If you're cited in an accident, your premium may rise. If you drive for several years without a traffic ticket, you may receive a discount. If you file many claims, your policy may either skyrocket in price or be canceled.

Age

It is statistically proven that the youngest and oldest drivers are at the highest risk for accidents of any age groups. They are also at the highest risk for fatal accidents.

PHOTODISC/GETTY IMAGES

Teens   While all teenagers are at high risk, 16-year-olds are clearly at the
highest risk. Young individuals between the ages of 15 and 20 have the
highest rate of fatal crashes. Young drivers are three times more likely to be
involved in a fatal crash than drivers age 65 to 69. This suggests that driver
inexperience is a major factor in accidents.

Teens tend to drive at a higher rate of speed than other age groups and
tend to leave less distance between their vehicle and the vehicle in front of
them. Teenagers are also more likely than other age groups to engage in
speeding and other risky, dangerous behaviors. The combination of inexperience and risky behavior is frequently lethal and explains why teenagers
are involved in significantly more fatal single-vehicle crashes than other age
groups. This is why many states have implemented rules and regulations
for young drivers.

For example, in some states a conditional license or beginner's permit
is the first type of license 15- or 16-year-olds may obtain. Then, a **restricted
license** that has specific requirements attached may be obtained. These requirements may include the right to drive alone only during daylight hours
unless accompanied by an adult age 21 or over. Another regulation prohib-
its young drivers to drive with other passengers under the age of 21 unless
accompanied by an adult 21 or over. Typically, a good driving record for
12 months with no points against your record and no accidents is required
to obtain an unrestricted license. **Points** accumulate on a person's driving
record because of traffic violations and accidents.

Over 65   Older drivers drive fewer miles than other age groups but suffer a higher proportion of fatal crashes than any other group, except young
drivers. Due to the frailty of older drivers, they are less likely to survive an
accident than younger individuals. Many seniors suffer from diminished
eyesight and slower reflexes. Because seniors' typical traffic offenses involve
running stop signs and traffic lights, turning improperly, and failing to
yield, they tend to be involved in multiple vehicle crashes at intersections.

The National Highway Traffic Safety Administration estimates that people age 65 and older will represent 25 percent of the driving population and 25 percent of fatal crashes by the year 2030. Over 6,000 individuals age 65 or older are killed in traffic accidents each year.

Gender

Males tend to drive more miles than females and also are more likely to engage in risky road behaviors, as well as drinking and driving. These factors explain why males of all ages are at a strikingly higher risk than females of dying in a traffic accident. Two-thirds of the teenagers killed in motor vehicle crashes are males. Males age 20 to 24 are two and a half times more likely than females to be a fatality. However, 16-year-old females are closing this gap because they are having more accidents. The gender gap narrows somewhat until it rises again at age 60. By age 85, three times more males than females die in traffic accidents.

Cell Phones

Cell phones have proved to be a major distraction while driving and have been the cause of many crashes. There has been a decline in using hand-held phones due to Bluetooth and other hands-free technology advances, but the use of cell phones while driving, in general, is high. Several states have cell phone laws about usage while driving. For example, more than 15 states have laws that prohibit young drivers from using cell phones while driving. Other states have banned the use of cell phones while driving for all drivers regardless of age. Many states also prohibit text messaging while driving.

Vehicle Type and Crashworthiness

The car you drive can make an enormous difference in risk and a substantial difference in your premium as well. Expensive, high-performance cars always cost more to insure. They are more likely to be involved in accidents and to be stolen, and they cost more to repair. Some insurers are contemplating raising premiums on sports utility vehicles (SUVs) because in collisions with cars, SUVs tend to cause a lot of damage.

Depending on size and design, some vehicles protect passengers better than others, thus reducing risk. Some models incur less damage in accidents than comparable models and may cost less to repair. In general, larger, heavier vehicles tend to protect you better than smaller, lighter ones. However, this is not always the case. Many newer, smaller cars with the latest design and safety features will fare better in an accident than heavier cars

NETBookmark

Over the past several years, car dealers have been offering hybrid vehicles for sale, and more and more of them are being seen on roads. Hybrid vehicles are being heavily promoted as a way to save gas as well as a way to help protect the environment. But do hybrids have an impact on insurance rates? Access www .cengage.com/school/pfinance/insurance and click on the link for Chapter 2. Read the article on insurance costs for hybrid vehicles and write a one-page report to answer the following questions: Are insurance rates higher or lower for hybrid vehicles? What factors help determine rates?

www.cengage.com/school/pfinance/insurance

lacking these features. Also, vehicle performance may vary dramatically in different kinds of accidents. The same SUV that is barely scratched in a collision with a car that is totaled may have a dangerous tendency to roll over if it hits a guardrail.

Safety Features Seat belts and air bags are now standard features, but you may be able to get a lower premium for a vehicle equipped with side air bags and an antilock brake system. Consumer reports are available on automobiles so you can check the reliability and safety of your vehicle. Be sure to check crash safety ratings before you buy any vehicle.

Theft A vehicle is stolen about every 25 seconds in the United States. While expensive cars are as attractive to thieves as to the people who buy them, many popular, moderately priced cars are also rated as top theft bait. Why? Because they are popular and easy to resell. Which vehicles are the most popular varies from city to city. For example, four-wheel drive vehicles may be stolen more often in areas with a higher snowfall ratio than those areas that typically do not get snow. Because some manufacturers have streamlined production by using interchangeable components, cars are often stolen and immediately disassembled in "chop shops" to be sold in less easily identifiable pieces. Before you buy, be sure to check a vehicle's theft rating.

Driving Record

Because statistics show that people follow patterns of established behavior, if you are cited for an accident or receive multiple traffic tickets for moving

flat world...

Driving in Canada and Mexico

The U.S. Department of State posts information on its website about driving in foreign countries (http://travel.state.gov). Although most U.S. auto insurance policies do not cover driving overseas, some policies cover driving in Mexico and Canada. Even if your policy is valid in one of those countries, it may not meet that country's minimum requirements. For example, in most parts of Canada, you must have at least $200,000 in liability insurance. If you have an accident in Mexico and your car is not covered by theft, third-party liability, and comprehensive insurance, you will need to post a bond that could be as high as 50 percent of the value of the vehicle.

Think Critically What do you think are your options for complying with Canadian law? Do you think those options apply to Mexico? Where would you find the information you need?

violations, your premiums will rise because you are at an increased risk of an accident. On the other hand, if you reform your driving habits, after a period of time (usually three to five years) with no moving violations or accidents, your premium may be reduced. Some insurers will give you credit for completing a driver safety course, and some will give you a refund if you have a consistent safe driving record.

Geographic Location

If you live in an area where the cost of living is high, insurance premiums are higher too. Urban areas are almost always more expensive than rural areas. Longer commutes and using your car specifically for business can also raise your premium because it means more miles driven and, therefore, greater exposure to risk. Also, many people live in urban areas. Three-fourths of the U.S. population lives in metropolitan areas, and this is predicted to rise.

Most traffic accidents occur in urban areas. Typically, collision and personal injury claims are approximately 40 percent higher in urban areas. Property damage is approximately 30 percent higher as well, and over 70 percent of pedestrian deaths and injuries are most prevalent in urban areas. However, fatal auto accidents are more likely to occur in rural areas, where drivers tend to travel at higher speeds in open areas.

 checkpoint

List and describe factors affecting your auto insurance rates.

assessment 2.1

Think Critically

1. Why are there more crashes in urban areas than rural areas?

2. Why are some vehicles safer than others?

Make Academic Connections

3. **CIVICS**   Every time a state raises its speed limit, the highway death toll for that state rises. What political pressure do you think is put on state legislatures to raise speed limits? Why do you think the pressure to raise limits is stronger than the pressure to keep them at 55 mph? Write your thoughts.

4. **PHYSICS**   Research the law of inertia as it applies to moving vehicles. List three safe driving concepts inspired by an understanding of inertia.

5. **ENVIRONMENTAL STUDIES**   Why do you think most environmentalists believe sports utility vehicles (SUVs) are destructive to the environment? Do you agree or disagree with this belief?

 **Teamwork**

Write down the names of everyone you've known personally who has died in the past three years. Note the person's approximate age and the cause of death. As a group, make two simple bar graphs. Graph your list twice, once by age group and once by cause of death. Is there a pattern in the causes of death or in age?

Personal Auto Policies

2.2

goals

+ Discuss different types of coverage a personal auto policy provides.

+ Discuss different components of an automobile insurance policy.

terms

+ Personal Auto Policy
+ bodily injury liability
+ property damage liability
+ medical expenses coverage
+ Personal Injury Protection
+ comprehensive coverage
+ collision coverage
+ depreciation
+ declarations
+ endorsement
+ exclusions

Insurance Scene

Antonio drives a 1985 restored pickup truck. It handles like a barge, it burns a large amount of gas and oil, and its exhaust system is worn out. Even so, Antonio still loves that truck. He knows it will continue to run until the body rusts away underneath. It's time to renew his insurance policy. Should he continue to buy collision coverage just because he loves his truck? Why or why not?

GET YOURSELF COVERED

Now that you understand the risks involved in driving an automobile, you need to investigate various kinds of insurance coverage to compensate you in case of a loss, or anyone else to whom you might cause a loss.

Purchasing an automobile insurance policy is a serious undertaking. The policy is a legally binding contract between the insured and the insurer in which you, the insured, agree to pay set premiums to the insurance company. In exchange, the insurer agrees to pay for specific auto-related financial losses you might suffer during the term of the policy.

Different Uses, Different Policies

There are a variety of automobile insurance policies, depending on the vehicle and use of the vehicle. A luxury charter coach will require different coverages than a passenger car. A sales representative whose car is her "traveling office" will require different coverage than a retiree who walks almost everywhere. The coverages you need will help determine what type of policy you should purchase.

Whatever kind of policy you buy, you can adjust the different coverages to reflect uses and needs. If you drive an old car of little market value, for example, you can drop collision coverage entirely and use the money you save to buy better liability or medical coverage. Also, because your needs, uses, and risks change, you should review your automobile insurance coverage each year before you renew your policy.

The PAP Most people buy what is called a **Personal Auto Policy** (PAP) designed for personal use of a private passenger vehicle. A PAP covers not only you but other drivers named in the policy, usually other members of your family, who might drive your car. A PAP may or may not cover a

pickup truck or an SUV, but comparable coverage is available for these vehicles if they are used as passenger vehicles. A PAP contains four basic types of coverage, but you are not obligated to buy all coverages.

1. **Liability** Covers bodily injury and property damage you cause.

2. **Medical Expenses** Covers bodily injury sustained by you and your passengers.

3. **Physical Damage** Covers damage to your vehicle from collision and other events, such as theft.

4. **Uninsured/Underinsured Motorist** Covers you in case of an accident caused by someone not properly insured.

Liability Coverage

Liability is the most important coverage. It is so important that states set minimum liability requirements. Liability coverage compensates other people for any losses you or the other drivers named in your policy might cause. There are two kinds of liability coverage in every insurance policy—bodily injury and property damage.

Bodily injury liability covers physical injury to anyone in other vehicles involved in an accident that is your fault. It may also sometimes cover a passenger in your vehicle. It will pay medical expenses, funeral expenses, and possibly lost wages and compensatory damages for pain and suffering.

Property damage liability covers damage to other vehicles in case of an accident that is your fault. It also covers other property damage you might cause, such as damage to a fence, garage door, or other real property.

The Liability Question Your state minimum liability requirement is just that: a minimum. Many insurance experts suggest you buy as much liability

Green Car

Researchers continue to work on the development of a green, environmentally friendly vehicle. Technology plays a big role in the creation of such a vehicle. Hybrid technology (the combination of an electric motor and a gasoline-powered motor) and emission control technology (the elimination of auto pollutants) are essential to improving the environment. Technology also plays a role in the development of an alternative fuel for vehicles.

Think Critically   Why would insurance companies be interested in the development of a green car? How can you research the advantages and disadvantages of an environmentally friendly vehicle? What automotive technology other than that mentioned above is essential to improving the environment?

insurance as you can afford. This is suggested because if you cause a serious accident, medical bills, lost wages, and possible compensatory damages can soar into six figures very quickly.

In addition to the ethical issue of doing your best to right any wrongs you might commit, there are financial issues. If you are found to have been reckless or negligent, you can be sued for damages above the liability limit you carry on your insurance policy. Young people with few assets have less to lose in a lawsuit than an older person with property and an established career. However, if you are a minor, your parents may be liable for an accident you cause. If you are insured on your family's policy, your family will most certainly be liable. The issue of liability should be discussed with your parents and your insurance agent.

Medical Expenses

Medical expenses coverage pays for any physical injuries you or your passengers sustain while in the vehicle, even if you are not involved in a traffic accident. For example, if a tree falls onto your parked car and you are injured, you will be compensated. It may also cover any injuries you incur while you are a pedestrian.

Personal Injury Protection   Added medical coverage that will compensate you for lost wages is called **Personal Injury Protection** (PIP). It may also compensate you for damages regardless of who is at fault. This is a basic extension to your automobile insurance policy, and like any other policy option, it may raise your premium.

Review Your Health Plan   Some insurance experts suggest that, if you have a good health insurance plan, an auto policy's medical coverage only duplicates your health insurance. If this is the case, you should buy only minimal medical coverage on your auto policy. But if your health plan is not satisfactory, auto policy medical expense coverage may offer you valuable protection in case of an accident. This is another reason why you must be familiar with all of your insurance policies, whether medical or auto.

Physical Damage

Comprehensive and collision coverage are related but are often written separately in the auto insurance policy. Both coverages require the insured to pay a deductible before insurance payments are made. Insurance experts recommend you reduce your premiums by choosing the highest deductible you can afford. Remember, you only pay the deductible if you file a claim, but you pay your premium year after year.

Comprehensive coverage compensates you for physical damage to your car, including theft, vandalism, hailstorms, and other types of damage. It covers equipment, such as a stereo or gaming system, permanently installed in your auto. Detachable or removable equipment, such as an antenna, is usually excluded from this coverage, but you can buy separate coverage for such items. Comprehensive coverage generally does not cover collisions.

Collision coverage pays for damage to your vehicle in case of collision, no matter who is at fault. This includes not only collision with other vehicles in an accident, but also a collision with a tree, a fire hydrant, an animal, or other object. If a bank or other lender is financing your vehicle, the lender will require you to carry collision coverage, which is relatively inexpensive. If you neglect to purchase collision coverage, the lender may purchase it for you, probably at a large markup. Be sure you read and understand the terms of your auto loan or lease and follow through with all rules and regulations.

Determining Your Need   Both collision and comprehensive coverages must be considered in light of your car's market value. Every year you own your car, its market value depreciates. Depreciation is the reduction in the value of a car as it gets older. You've probably heard the saying, "Your car depreciates the minute you drive it off the car lot." Factors that affect depreciation are the number of miles driven, vehicle model, maintenance, consumer demand for the vehicle, and the maker's reputation for quality.

Your insurer will not pay more than your car is worth to have it repaired. For example, if your car is worth $2,500 and you incur $5,000 of damage, your insurer will usually declare your car totaled and give you a check for $2,500. Many people drop collision coverage, and sometimes comprehensive coverage, on an older car and put the money they save toward something else, such as a fund to buy another car.

Uninsured/Underinsured Motorist

A driver who is not insured is an uninsured motorist. A driver who doesn't carry enough insurance to cover your losses is an underinsured motorist. Uninsured/underinsured motorist coverages compensate you for an accident with such a driver. Of course, some accidents cause severe injuries, and even generous coverage will not pay medical bills in full.

Many people are confused by uninsured/underinsured coverages, and requirements vary from state to state. Some states require only medical expenses be covered, while others require coverage of property damage as well. The easiest way to be sure you are covered properly is to buy both coverages in equal amounts and buy them in the same amounts as your liability coverage. Some states will not let you buy more uninsured/underinsured motorist coverage than you yourself carry in liability. This is based on the principle that you cannot protect yourself better than you are willing to protect others.

No-Fault Insurance

In an attempt to reduce litigation and enable people to recover damages from their own insurance company no matter who is at fault in an accident, some states have passed no-fault insurance legislation. No-fault laws vary widely. If you live in a no-fault state, find out what you need to know before you buy auto insurance.

Currently, 12 states and Puerto Rico have no-fault insurance laws. Typically, the compensation involved in a no-fault accident is based on certain conditions related to the severity of injury. Some states have laws that require drivers to purchase a minimum amount of no-fault insurance for disability and litigation due to cases of fraud in the past.

PHOTODISC/GETTY IMAGES

Caveat Emptor

Do you know the phrase "caveat emptor"? It is Latin for "let the buyer beware," and it is ancient wisdom that holds true today. You should not buy insurance without being an informed buyer/consumer. Research your state insurance laws to know your legal rights and responsibilities. Research insurance company ratings. Read consumer literature for specific advice about how to make sure you meet your insurance needs and don't pay higher premiums than necessary.

Get at least three price quotes. You can obtain insurance quotes online from most companies. However, these quotes probably may not be as exact as you will get directly from an agent. To get a price quote, you must answer a number of questions about your driving history, the vehicle you wish to insure, and how it is used. You must answer these questions truthfully. In effect, when you get a quote, you are applying for insurance, and the company will apply various screenings, including a credit check, to see if you qualify.

Remember Your Discount When you get quotes for insurance, be sure to ask about available discounts to reduce the premium. These vary from state to state and company to company. Common discounts include the following:

- Multiple car

- Multiple line (home and car)

- Passive restraints (automatic seat belts, front air bags, side air bags)

- Good student grade point average (B or above)

- Certified driver training and defensive driving courses

- Accident-free driving history

- Anti-theft devices

- Antilock brake systems (ABS)

Remember, whatever price you are quoted is not legally binding until you have it in writing and the contract is signed by you and the agent.

 **checkpoint**

Name four basic types of coverage in a PAP.

_____

_____

READING A POLICY

Because there are differences in insurance policies and companies, it is critical that you read and understand the policy you are buying. Be aware that all insurance policies are written in legal language which may be difficult to understand. Don't be afraid to ask the insurance agent questions. Do your part by doing research, and expect the agent to do his or her job by explaining the policy's language so you know what it means.

The basic parts of an auto insurance policy include the following:

- Declarations

- Coverages

- Exclusions

- Conditions

- Definitions

The Application

If you've already asked for a price quote and shared personal information with a company, you've informally applied for insurance. But the formal document you read and sign is the actual *application*. At this point, you will also receive a standard policy you can read.

The different policy sections describing and defining coverages, options, exclusions, and conditions are included for future reference. Your individual

Insurance Math *Connection*

Your auto insurance premium is $1,000 every 6 months. This includes a $250 deductible. If you raise your deductible to $500, your premium will be reduced by 10 percent. If you increase your deductible to $1,000, your premium will be reduced by 20 percent. Calculate your 6-month premium for a $500 and a $1,000 deductible.

Solution

Multiply amount of premium by percentage reduction. Then subtract.

$500 deductible
$1,000 \times 0.10 = $100
$1,000 - $100 = $900   new 6-month premium

$1,000 deductible
$1,000 \times 0.20 = $200
$1,000 - $200 = $800   new 6-month premium

policy provisions specifying the amounts of each kind of coverage and the options you've purchased are also part of the policy.

The Declarations Page

The **declarations** page is individualized especially for you. It is the part of the policy you'll refer to most often. It lists important personal policy information: premiums, coverages, endorsements, deductibles, and liability limits. In addition to the insured's name, address, policy number, and the calendar period during which the policy is in effect, other specific information includes a description of the automobile, vehicle identification number (VIN), lender information (if necessary), garaging location (urban, rural, or suburban), and other drivers covered by the policy.

When you renew your policy each year, instead of sending an entire printed policy, the insurer usually sends a new declarations page along with printouts of portions of the standard policy that have been amended. The company will also include or attach endorsements to the new declarations page. In insurance terminology, an **endorsement** is an amendment to your policy that reflects any changes to the standard policy.

The Policy

A standard auto insurance policy is 20 pages or more. The *coverages section* of the policy details the standard coverages available for the kind of policy you've purchased: liability, medical payments, uninsured/underinsured motorists, property damage, collision, and comprehensive. Also listed in this section are the product options for various additional coverages you have chosen. Review the declarations sheet to make sure the amount of each kind of coverage you've purchased is correct. The coverages section will also list **exclusions**, or losses *not* covered by the policy.

The *conditions section* defines the insured's and insurer's duties that, under the terms of the policy, must be fulfilled. Premium payment schedules and steps to follow in filing a claim are included. The *definitions section* explains specific terms used throughout the policy. Examples of terms used in defined areas are as follows:

- "You" or "Your" refers to the "Named Insured" in declarations.

- "We" or "Us" or "Our" refers to the "insurer" (the insurance company).

- "Bodily Injury" refers to an occurrence of bodily harm, sickness, or disease, including death as a result.

- "Family Member" refers to a resident of your household related to you by blood, marriage, or adoption.

Not All Policies Are Alike   Policies differ between companies, and even between policies, so don't assume if you've read one policy you've read them all. Differences could occur in perils covered, persons injured, exclusions, definitions, personal injury protection, no-fault provisions, or other coverages or provisions of a policy. It is essential to read your policy carefully so that you are aware of your chosen coverages.

Cancellations

A policy cancellation may be requested by either the insured or the insurer. The insurer may cancel a policy if the insured fails to pay the premium, loses his or her driver's license, files too many claims, or misrepresents information during the application process.

The insured may cancel a policy at any time and for a variety of reasons, such as after selling a car or finding a cheaper policy. To cancel the policy, you must notify the insurer, preferably in writing. You might be due a refund for the remaining calendar period for which you've paid your premium. The cancellation process may differ from company to company. Consult your policy and follow the steps outlined by your insurance company.

 checkpoint

Briefly describe components of the declarations page.

_____

_____

_____

assessment 2.2

Think Critically

1. Why is liability the most important coverage?

2. Why might you purchase the minimum medical coverage?

3. Why do some people drop collision and comprehensive coverage?

4. Explain the meaning of caveat emptor.

Make Academic Connections

5. **RESEARCH**   Research the automobile insurance regulations in your state. Write a one-page report explaining four to five important automobile insurance regulations a new resident would need to know.

6. **CONSUMERISM**   List three reasons to buy insurance over the Internet. List three reasons why not to buy insurance over the Internet.

7. **TECHNOLOGY**   Visit the insurance department website of three states and critique (poor, good, or excellent) each one for usefulness of information, ease of use, and design. Fill in this table.

State			
Usefulness of information			
Ease of use			
Design			

 Teamwork

In pairs, role-play an insurance application interview between an agent and applicant. Choose the applicant's age and driving history.

2.3 Reporting Accidents

goals

+ Explain what to do in case of an accident.

+ List the steps involved in filing a claim.

terms

+ accident zones

Insurance Scene

Fidelia is an intern in neurosurgery at a prestigious hospital. Her finances are very tight now, but in a few years she expects her salary to grow. Fidelia walks to work or uses rapid transit and has had little time to drive anywhere. However, her insurance agent recommends she buy the highest auto liability coverage he offers. Is this a good idea? Why or why not?

IN CASE OF AN ACCIDENT •

If you're lucky, you'll never be involved in an auto accident. But chances are, even if you're never in an accident, you'll witness one. Or, you might come upon an accident that has just happened. No matter whether you're involved or not, here's what should be done, either by you or with the help of other people at the scene.

- **Help Anyone Who Is Injured** This is always the first priority. It is also your ethical and legal responsibility. Do not move the injured unless they are in further danger. Talk to them and keep them calm. If you know first aid, do what you can. Otherwise, keep them comfortable and possibly cover them with blankets or jackets while you wait for medical help.

- **Notify the Police** Make sure someone calls the police or 911. Provide accurate information about how many people have been injured, the location of the accident, how many cars are involved, and any other essential details.

- **Prevent Further Accidents** Turn on hazard lights, raise engine hoods, and use flares if they're needed and available. Direct traffic around the damaged vehicles, if necessary. You may need to move the vehicles if they are a hazard to other vehicles.

- **Preserve the Accident Scene** It is less important to preserve the accident scene than to prevent new accidents, but do it if you can. Leave the involved vehicles where they stopped and leave debris from the accident in place unless it creates a hazard. There are many areas where it is not

practical to leave vehicles in place. Many interstates now have areas called **accident zones** to which you are to move vehicles, if possible.

- **Record Information** If you are involved in an accident, be sure to record accident information. The drivers should exchange information such as names, phone numbers, addresses, driver's license numbers, and insurance information. If the drivers are not the owners of the vehicles in the accident, get the owners' names, their addresses, and names of insurance companies. List the names and addresses of any passengers. Note the time, location, and weather and road conditions along with the make, model, color, and license plate of any car involved in the accident. Get the names, addresses, and phone numbers of witnesses. Make a sketch of the accident scene. Identify your car as "A." Show names of streets or highways and directions of vehicles involved.

- **When the Police Arrive** Answer police questions truthfully and factually. Don't offer opinions or assign blame. Saying "The turn arrow lit up, and I entered the intersection to make a left turn" is different from saying "He ran a red light and hit me." For your own protection, make no statement about the accident except to the police. Be sure to note the officers' names and badge numbers. Ask where and when you can get a copy of the police report.

- **If the Police Ticket You** Sign the ticket. By doing so, you are not admitting blame. You are merely agreeing to appear in court. Even if you think you were at fault, do not say so to anyone. You are not avoiding responsibility. It may be that the other driver's actions contributed to the accident, and it would be premature to assume all the blame.

"communicate"

You are one of several witnesses to a serious accident. You are contacted by an attorney who asks you to write a short statement about what you saw. Write a description of what details to include in your report.

Be Prepared

Accidents can be life-or-death situations. Even minor accidents are highly stressful. It may be difficult under these circumstances to get the information you need. Your insurance company may give you an accident reporting packet to keep in your glove compartment. This packet contains forms asking for all the information you need. You can also find such forms on the Internet. Print them out and make your own packet.

✔ checkpoint

What are the most important things to do when an accident occurs?

_____

_____

AFTER AN ACCIDENT •

Report an accident promptly to your insurance agent or company. If the accident clearly was not your fault, and if the other driver carries sufficient insurance, you will not need to file a claim with your company.

Communicate with your insurer. Your insurer should know what has happened in case they have to become involved later for some reason. For example, if the other driver's insurer refuses to cover all your losses, they will help resolve the situation. Your insurer can provide advice on your rights when dealing with the other driver's insurance company, such as whether or not you have the right to choose the body shop that repairs your car.

COMSTOCK IMAGES/JUPITER IMAGES

Ethics in Action

A visitor backs into the fiberglass fender of Ethan's deteriorated 1972 VW Beetle parked at the museum where he works. The fender splits, and a security guard who sees the incident stops the visitor from driving away. The claims adjuster from the visitor's insurer sends Ethan to a body shop where he receives an estimate of $162.73 to fix the fender. After providing an estimate, the body shop owner advises Ethan that he'd be better off mending the fender with duct tape and using the money for something he cares about more than the car. Ethan takes the advice.

Think Critically

Did the body shop owner act ethically? Did Ethan act ethically? Explain your answers.

Filing a Claim

Sometimes you must file a claim. It might be that you are liable for an accident, or maybe you simply have a cracked windshield because a rock bounced up from a passing truck on the road. Generally, you will be expected to furnish the following information when filing a claim:

- Your name and the name on your policy (if different)
- Your home address and phone number
- Your policy number
- Your car's year and make
- Date, time, and location of accident/loss
- Injury information
- Whether your car is operable and its location
- Whether you were cited in the accident and, if so, for what offense

Consult your policy for specific details in reporting a claim. When you file, your insurer will tell you any additional steps you need to take. These steps will vary with the claim, the company, and the state in which you live. Be sure to consult available consumer information for your state and review your rights and responsibilities carefully.

When You're Liable for an Accident

If you read your entire auto insurance policy, you will discover that, when you purchase liability insurance, your insurer agrees to represent you if you are sued. The flip side of this agreement is that the insurer has the right to settle any litigation without your permission. Lawsuits are likely only if the sums involved are large and you have substantial assets.

PHOTODISC/GETTY IMAGES

Most of the time, the loss incurred in an accident is sufficiently covered and all bills are paid. However, if you're involved in accidents, your premiums are certain to rise. If you cause several accidents, your insurer may cancel your policy. Insurers vary as to how many claims they will pay before they decide the insured is too costly to keep as a customer.

When Losses Exceed Coverage Sometimes, especially when an insured carries only minimum liability coverage, accident losses exceed the amount of the coverage. The liable party's insurance company is only obligated to pay the amount specified in the policy. This is the kind of situation for which underinsured motorist coverage was developed. The injured party's losses not covered by the liability insurance of another's policy are then covered by his or her own underinsured motorist coverage. This helps alleviate additional financial loss.

When Losses Greatly Exceed Coverage If the injured party does not carry uninsured/underinsured motorist coverage, he or she may sue the liable motorist personally for the loss and perhaps for additional damages, such as lost wages and pain and suffering. This is more likely to occur if the amount involved is large and the liable motorist has enough assets. Even if the injured party carries uninsured/underinsured motorist coverage, his or her insurer may decide to sue the liable motorist personally to recover the amount paid to its insured. Again, this is only likely if the liable party has ample assets.

Large Losses Bring Lawsuits Lawsuits can happen even if a liable party carries substantial amounts of liability coverage. This is especially true in terrible accidents in which someone is disabled. The injured party may sue the liable party's insurer, which may decide to settle out of court for a large sum rather than risk losing the suit and being obligated to pay a larger sum. Under the terms of the policy, that is the insurer's right.

A Final Word There are any number of other possible outcomes, but liability is serious business. It is for this reason that insurance experts recommend buying enough liability coverage to protect all your assets, including probable future assets such as a large salary. That way, it's your insurer, and not you, who sustains the financial loss of a major claim.

✔ **checkpoint**

Where should you look for specific instructions about filing a claim?

assessment 2.3

Think Critically

1. Why should you try to preserve the scene of an accident?

_____

_____

2. Why should you get the names and addresses of witnesses of an accident?

_____

_____

3. Why should you carry sufficient liability coverage?

_____

_____

4. What happens when losses exceed coverage?

_____

_____

_____

Make Academic Connections

5. **RESEARCH** Using the Internet, find information about traffic accidents. Write a report explaining how experts reconstruct accidents from skid marks, debris placement, window shatter patterns, and so on.

6. **CONSUMERISM** Review your family auto and homeowner's/renter's insurance policies. Compare the two. Are the liability coverages for similar amounts? Look at the uninsured/underinsured motorist coverage. Does it match your liability coverage? Does anyone in your family remember how these amounts were chosen? From what you've learned about insurance so far, would you revise these policies? Make a presentation to your family.

7. **INSURANCE LAW** Some states have "comparative negligence" or "shared negligence" laws that distribute the liability for some accidents between drivers instead of assigning all the liability to one. Does your state have such a law? Find out and summarize it.

_____

 **Teamwork**

In a small group, discuss additional ways in which you can be prepared for an accident. Make a list and present your suggestions to the class.

chapter 2 assessment

Chapter Summary

2.1 Automobiles and Risk

A. Having automobile insurance does not keep you from having accidents, but it helps protect you from financial loss.

B. Insurance premiums vary according to individual risk factors, including age, gender, type of vehicle, geographic location, and driving history.

2.2 Personal Auto Policies

A. Most people are insured with a Personal Auto Policy (PAP) including four basic types of coverage: liability, medical expenses, physical damage, and uninsured/underinsured motorist.

B. Read and understand your insurance policy. The declarations page is a summary of coverages purchased, while the policy itself details the coverages and exclusions, conditions, definitions, and general provisions of the policy.

2.3 Reporting Accidents

A. The most important things to do in an accident are to help the injured, contact the police, and prevent further accidents. Gather insurance information from other drivers, obtain names and addresses of witnesses, and cooperate with the police.

B. When filing a claim with the insurer, make sure you provide details such as name, address, policy number, car year and make, date, time, location, and injury information. If you are liable for the losses from an accident and they exceed your liability coverage, there is a possibility you may be sued by the injured party.

Vocabulary Builder

a. accident zones
b. aggressive driving
c. bodily injury liability
d. collision coverage
e. comprehensive coverage
f. declarations
g. depreciation
h. endorsement
i. exclusions
j. medical expenses coverage
k. Personal Auto Policy
l. Personal Injury Protection
m. points
n. property damage liability
o. restricted license

Choose the term that best fits the definition. Write the letter of the answer in the space provided. Some terms may not be used.

_____ 1. Important personal policy information

_____ 2. Policy for personal use of a private passenger vehicle

_____ 3. Losses not covered by the policy

_____ 4. Covers injuries caused by the insured

_____ 5. An amendment to your insurance policy

_____ 6. A license that has specific requirements attached to it

_____ 7. Covers treatment for injuries to driver/passenger of insured vehicle

_____ 8. Coverage for damage to insured's vehicle in case of collision

_____ 9. Covers damage to vehicles and property of another

_____10. Coverage for damage to insured's vehicle other than by collision

_____11. The reduction in the value of a car as it gets older

_____12. Added medical coverage that may compensate you for lost wages

Review Concepts

13. List ways to reduce risk when you drive.

_____

_____

_____

14. Briefly describe how an auto insurance policy is a binding legal contract.

_____

_____

_____

15. What are some examples of different automobile insurance coverages? Why do people purchase different automobile insurance coverages?

_____

_____

_____

16. What can you do to reduce your insurance premium?

_____

_____

_____

17. Why should you carry sufficient automobile coverage?

_____

_____

_____

18. What are the four main coverages in a PAP?

_____

_____

_____

19. Describe various types of automobile discounts available to reduce premiums.

_____

_____

_____

20. List factors considered by an insurance company in determining insurance premiums.

_____

_____

21. What are the basic parts of an automobile policy?

_____

_____

22. List two reasons the insurer may cancel your policy.

_____

_____

_____

23. List two reasons the insured may cancel a policy.

_____

_____

Apply What You Learned

24. In addition to protecting your own interests, why is it important to buy liability insurance?

_____

_____

_____

25. Do you feel you have an ethical as well as a legal responsibility to obey traffic laws?

_____

_____

_____

26. Some people believe laws such as speed limits on rural highways infringe upon personal freedom. Can you think of reasons why it might benefit society to have such laws?

_____

_____

_____

27. Consumer wisdom dictates that by taking a higher deductible you save money in the long run. Describe disadvantages to a higher deductible.

_____

_____

_____

Make Academic Connections

28. **SOCIOLOGY**   Describe your life 10 years from now. Answer these questions: How old will you be? Where will you be employed? What is your job title? What type of vehicle do you drive? Where do you live? Are you married? Do you have children? How many vehicles do you own? After answering these questions, describe your automobile insurance needs. Check with an automobile insurance agent or go online to get a quote on an insurance premium based on your answers to these questions.

29. **RESEARCH**   Log on to an insurance company website and research the crash protection ratings of your dream car. Would you purchase this vehicle after reviewing the ratings? Explain why or why not.

30. **CONSUMERISM**   Open the *Yellow Pages* and look at the ads for attorneys. Carefully read the ads for attorneys specializing in accident and injury law. Would you feel comfortable hiring any of these firms to represent you in an accident? Why or why not? If you needed an attorney, how would you go about finding one? Do some research and write a short report.

31. **ADVERTISING**   Outline a marketing campaign for safe driving practices. Describe the audience you would target and how to reach that audience. Then either draw or write an ad for such a campaign.

32. **BUSINESS MATH**   Find a car loan calculator on the Internet. Enter the cost of the car, number of monthly payments, and current interest rate. Calculate the cost of each monthly payment, the payoff amount, and the total amount of interest to be paid based on the loan period and record them below.

33. **CONSUMERISM**   Research no-fault insurance. Does it sound like a good deal for the consumer? With a small group from your class, stage a debate about no-fault insurance.

34. **HEALTH**   Safety experts blame driver fatigue and lack of sleep for a large number of accidents. Research this topic and compile a list of natural ways you can make sure you stay awake and alert behind the wheel.

CHAPTER 3

Health Insurance

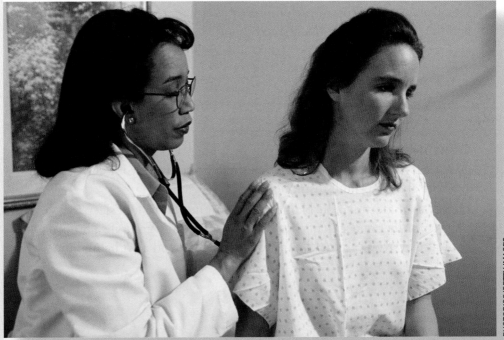

climbing the ladder

From Insurance Policy Processing Clerk to Medical and Health Services Manager

Freeman is completing his internship for a degree in business at Redfern University by working part time as an Insurance Policy Processing Clerk at McMaster Hospital. This internship has provided him with an excellent opportunity to gain experience in the field while completing his education. He is motivated to learn more and move up in a hospital setting.

It is essential that Freeman be organized and pay attention to detail as he processes and records new insurance claims and verifies the information provided. He also works to improve his communication skills to ensure he provides good customer service to clients.

His manager told Freeman that upon completing his degree at the university, the hospital would like to hire him on a full-time basis. His boss noted that Freeman demonstrates initiative and a concern for others through his work. Freeman has received excellent work evaluations, and the hospital would like to make him a part of the team. If he accepts the full-time job, the hospital will provide Freeman with on-the-job training and schedule his evenings free so he can continue his education.

Freeman's boss told him if he completes his on-the-job training and finishes his degree, he could work as a team leader of other information processing clerks or work toward a position as a Medical and Health Services Manager. Freeman investigated the possibility of the manager's position and found it to be an interesting possibility.

As a Medical and Health Services Manager, Freeman's responsibilities would include developing and maintaining records through a computerized system to store and process personnel activities; establishing goals, policies, and procedures for units; supervising and evaluating others' work; and maintaining communication between medical staff, departments, and governing boards.

All of these responsibilities will be demanding, but Freeman will double his salary in the new position. With the new responsibilities comes additional education. Freeman's boss strongly suggests he continue his education and obtain a master's degree to reach full salary potential in the management position. Freeman is seriously considering all possibilities to continue his employment with McMaster Hospital.

Upper Rungs to Consider

Freeman found his current position challenging and gratifying. However, this part-time employment is not completely preparing him for future job opportunities with the hospital. He is investigating other job possibilities in the area of hospital management.

Preparing for the Climb

It is essential to become a lifelong learner and continue your education in whatever setting is appropriate (employment, coursework, etc.). Are there responsibilities or projects you could undertake in your current setting that would give you experience for a job you would like to have?

3.1

goals

+ Describe the purpose of health insurance.
+ Discuss how to buy health insurance.

terms

+ law of large numbers
+ pre-existing condition

Health Insurance Overview

Insurance Scene

Chogan works as an accountant for a large dairy farm. His brother and cousin want him to go into business with them in a local delivery service they're starting. Their business plan looks solid, and Chogan is excited about the opportunity. However, Chogan has severe asthma, and his group insurance pays a large part of his annual medical expenses for doctor visits, supplies, and prescriptions. Because his asthma is a pre-existing condition, individual health insurance would be very costly. He can join a less expensive managed care plan, but his doctors aren't part of the plan. What are Chogan's choices?

WHY DO YOU NEED HEALTH INSURANCE?

At some point in your life you may need costly medical care. Even if you are normally healthy, you might become seriously ill or be injured in an accident. You might decide to have a child and incur costs for prenatal care, delivery, and hospitalization. Medical costs are high and continue to rise. Surgery, chemotherapy, or a few days in a hospital's intensive care unit can cause medical bills to skyrocket.

Health insurance, like other kinds of insurance, protects you against significant financial loss. Health insurance ensures medical care. Some health insurance plans, by providing their members with regular basic care at low cost, also help keep you healthy by detecting and treating medical conditions, such as diabetes, heart disease, or high blood pressure, before they become serious. Preventive measures such as regular checkups can help you maintain a healthy life.

How Health Insurance Works

Health insurance is complex and ever-changing. It is important to understand the basics of health insurance in order to protect yourself and your family. Time invested in understanding and analyzing the options available to you will pay off in terms of better coverage, better health care, and lower premiums.

In the past, the patient typically paid the provider—the doctor, pharmacist, or hospital—directly. As the cost of medical care rose, most

Americans began buying health care indirectly by buying health insurance. Depending on the insurance policy you buy or the health plan to which you belong, health insurance may cover some, most, or all of your medical expenses. Your health provider bills your insurance company. The insurance company pays certain amounts as regulated by your policy and options. You are responsible for paying any costs your insurance does not pay.

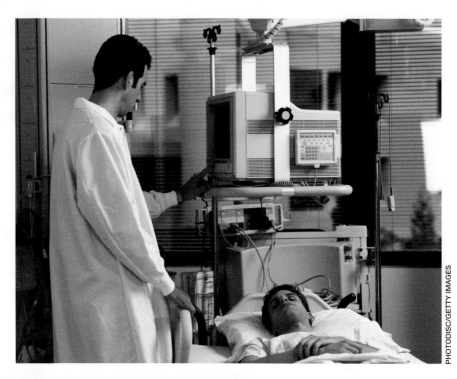

PHOTODISC/GETTY IMAGES

Law of Large Numbers

Health insurance companies, like other insurance companies, protect themselves against financial loss by spreading the risk of costly medical care among many customers over many years. This is the **law of large numbers**. Insurers will, depending on who is covered in any given plan, try to minimize losses and increase profits by insuring as many healthy and as few unhealthy people as possible. In some circumstances, insurers may refuse to insure individuals who are likely to need expensive medical care because of conditions requiring frequent or expensive treatment, such as kidney disease, or high-risk behaviors, such as intravenous drug use. Other insurers may insure higher-risk individuals but charge them more, sometimes much more, for their policies. Like any other type of insurance, typically increased risks result in increased premiums.

Pre-Existing Conditions   The more people need health insurance, the more likely they are to seek insurance. Most insurers ask new policyholders if they have been treated for any medical condition within the last six months. Any condition for which you have been treated in the past six months is called a **pre-existing condition**. Depending on the plan, the insurer may refuse to cover treatment for this particular condition for a year or more, charge more for the policy, or refuse to insure the person.

✔ checkpoint

What is the main purpose of health insurance?

_____

_____

interesting *facts*

The MIB Group, Inc., is a nationwide consumer reporting agency that provides reports regarding a consumer's eligibility for insurance, including information on a person's medical conditions. If you have ever applied for life, health, or disability insurance, your medical information is probably housed in this database. This information, however, is protected health information (PHI). Information may be disclosed without individual authorization if it will prevent/control disease, injury, or disability. ◾

HOW DO YOU BUY HEALTH INSURANCE? • • • • • • • • • •

Most Americans buy health insurance through one of two basic plans.

- **Group plans** A group buys insurance for everyone in the group.
- **Individual plans** An individual person or family buys insurance directly from an insurance company.

Group Plans

Most insured Americans belong to some type of group plan. Professional, religious, or other organizations can purchase group plans for their members, but health insurance is most often purchased through an employer. Employers are not required by law to offer health insurance. They offer health insurance as a benefit to help attract and keep good employees. Some employers may choose to offer different health insurance components to different employees. Employers may pay all, part, or none of an employee's premiums. They may also provide insurance benefits for the employee but not the employee's dependents.

Advantages of Group Plans Group plans are generally less expensive than individual plans. One essential advantage is that the insurance company must enroll anyone who belongs to or joins the group, even if that person or his or her dependent has a pre-existing condition that will be costly for the insurer to cover.

Disadvantages of Group Plans An employer may purchase a group plan that does not offer all options to meet all employees' individual needs. Another potential disadvantage is that, while an insurer is not permitted to drop individuals belonging to a group plan, it is permitted to drop the entire group. However, in this case, the employer typically finds another insurance company. But an employer does have the right to stop providing health insurance at any time as long as it stops providing it to all employees in the group and gives notice.

Individual Plans

People who are self-employed, or whose employers do not offer health insurance as a benefit, can buy health insurance directly from an insurance company. The cost of individual health insurance depends on your age, number of dependents if you're insuring the family, health condition, and policy options.

Advantages of Individual Plans Because you deal directly with the insurer, you can have the policy designed to cover your specific needs. For this reason many people buy an individual policy to bridge coverage gaps in their one-size-fits-all group policies. Some insurers offer discounts to individuals who have healthy lifestyles, such as nonsmokers.

Disadvantages of Individual Plans In general, individual plans are more expensive. Also, if you have a pre-existing condition, an insurer may charge more for your policy or refuse to insure you. If you are willing and able to pay, almost any condition can be covered.

The Bottom Line

Young people in entry-level jobs often do not see the need for health insurance. If they do not make a high salary, and if their employer does not offer insurance, they may not invest their time, energy, and hard-earned cash to pay for something intangible, health insurance.

Remember, neither medical care nor health insurance is a right. They are services you must purchase. A health provider is obligated to treat you if your life is in danger, but you will be billed for the treatment. If your life is not in danger, you will be asked to provide insurance information before you are treated. If you do not have health insurance and you cannot pay on the spot, you can be turned away by private health providers that are not required to care for the uninsured.

Almost always, no matter what your economic or health status, you can find health insurance that will cover at least some of your needs. Make sure your policy covers health maintenance for regular health care and includes coverage for catastrophic illnesses or accidents. If you had a biking accident and needed $50,000 in surgery and hospitalization, you would be very glad you were insured and able to afford the physical therapy to enable you to walk again.

PHOTODISC/GETTY IMAGES

✔ checkpoint

List two advantages of health insurance group plans. List two advantages of health insurance individual plans.

_____

_____

_____

_____

assessment 3.1

Think Critically

1. Describe how different health plans may influence an employee to choose one employer over another.

_____

_____

2. Describe how a low unemployment rate might influence employers to offer higher-quality health care plans to workers.

_____

_____

3. In contract negotiations, union leaders sometimes compromise on wage increases to keep members' group health insurance. Explain why.

_____

_____

Make Academic Connections

4. **PROBLEM SOLVING**   List different ways to lower your health risks so you can spend less money for insurance.

_____

_____

_____

5. **MARKETING**   Design a public service ad campaign to inform individuals your age about the importance of health insurance. Describe your target audience: Who are they? What do they care about? How do they spend disposable income? Describe a series of ads and relate information to each question. Explain which media (magazines, billboards, Internet, etc.) you would use to run your ad campaign.

6. **ART AND DESIGN**   Make a poster explaining how a healthy lifestyle reduces risk of chronic diseases such as obesity, heart disease, and diabetes.

 **Teamwork**

In groups write down everything you know about your family's health insurance coverage. Does your family have a group or individual plan? Do all of you see the same doctor? What different kinds of medical care are covered? Compare your answers with others in the group.

Health Plans

3.2

goals

+ Explain the basic types of health plans.

+ Discuss how to buy the best health plan for your needs.

terms

+ copayment

+ fee-for-service plan

+ managed care plan

+ health maintenance organization

+ primary care physician

+ preferred provider organization

+ point of service plan

Insurance Scene

Lee worked for a company that provided excellent health benefits. He selected a fee-for-service (FFS) plan because, for a single person, the premiums were competitive with the managed care options. When Lee married his wife, Kendra, they started a family right away. What kinds of questions should they ask themselves before choosing a family health plan?

A GUIDE TO HEALTH PLANS

In the past, medical insurance was reserved for large expenses such as surgery or hospitalization. When you needed a checkup or you were sick, you went to the family doctor and paid directly for the services. The doctor delivered babies, performed routine surgeries such as appendectomies or tonsillectomies, stitched wounds, and set broken bones. If you needed a specialist, you would be referred to one. If you needed inpatient care, you would be sent to a hospital.

Today, the practice of medicine is more complicated and expensive. Medical insurance often covers routine care, such as annual physicals, as well as major medical expenses. However, there are as many different insurance plans as there are insurers. Most plans, whether group or individual, can be divided into a few categories. Because every health plan is different, make sure you read the descriptions of coverages, exclusions, and deductibles very carefully.

Health insurance policies are binding legal contracts between the insured and insurer. You must always be truthful in your dealings with your insurer because falsifying information can void your policy.

Like most kinds of insurance, health plans involve premiums and deductibles, although some managed care plans may not have a deductible. Most plans also involve a small **copayment** you make at the time of service. If a deductible applies, you can lower your premiums by raising your deductible or by limiting your coverage in other ways.

Fee-for-Service Plan

A fee-for-service (FFS) plan is the closest thing to traditional medical coverage. For example, under an FFS plan, you may go to any physician, hospital, laboratory, or pharmacy you want. Basically, with a **fee-for-service (FFS) plan,**

PHOTODISC/GETTY IMAGES

you share the cost of the medical service with the insurer, usually at a 20/80 ratio after you satisfy your deductible. You pay 20 percent, and the insurer pays 80 percent. Most insurers designate a *reasonable and customary* fee for a service. If your provider charges more than the reasonable and customary fee, you will probably have to pay the difference in addition to your 20 percent. Because 20 percent of a large bill, such as that incurred during hospitalization, may still be an extensive amount of money, most FFS plans set a maximum amount you will pay out of pocket in any given year. Make sure you don't buy an FFS plan without a cap on what you will have to pay.

The big advantage of an FFS plan is its flexibility in choosing health care providers. The biggest disadvantage is its cost in premiums, the deductible, and possible out-of-pocket payments above the reasonable and customary fee. Most people end up paying more in FFS plans than in managed care plans. There is also more paperwork involved in submitting claims, because you manage your own care.

Managed Care Plan

In general, a managed care plan provides comprehensive medical care to all members, who pay a set premium. In theory, members receive almost all the care they need through the providers who participate in the health plan. Members make only a small copayment at the time various services are rendered. The principle behind managed care is economy through volume. Physicians and other providers agree to charge reduced fees for members of the managed care plan because they are guaranteed enough patients and know they will be paid for services.

As with any kind of insurance, some companies perform better than others. If you have any choice over which managed care plan you can join, research consumer satisfaction ratings first. There are three basic types of managed care plans as described below.

Health Maintenance Organization (HMO)

Health Maintenance Organizations (HMOs) are the most common and least expensive type of managed care plan. At times, HMO physicians may actually be employed by the plan, and their offices may be located under one roof. Other times, HMO providers are in private practice, and members visit them in their offices. In either case, each HMO member has a primary care physician (PCP) who serves as a gatekeeper to other services. The HMO will not pay for a visit to a specialist if the primary care physician has not referred the member to that specialist. An extra doctor visit may be necessary just to get the referral. Also, the specialist typically must be under contract or listed with the HMO. If you visit a provider outside the HMO, you must pay the entire fee out of pocket.

The advantage of an HMO, besides low cost, is that it may cover a wide range of preventive and health improvement services (such as cessation-of-smoking seminars) in addition to care when a member is actually sick. Also, there is less paperwork than with other health plans because claims are submitted by the provider. The main disadvantage of an HMO is the lack of flexibility because your choice of health care providers is limited. In general HMOs are perceived as providing good routine care and preventive services, which is all most people ever need. In the case of catastrophic or rare illnesses, though, HMO members may have difficulty receiving state-of-the-art care in a timely fashion. For example, a member may request to have a rare cancer treatment at a teaching hospital in another state but might be refused outright or might not be processed quickly enough to fully benefit the patient.

Preferred Provider Organization (PPO)

Preferred Provider Organizations (PPOs) combine the features of HMOs and fee-for-service plans. Under a PPO plan, physicians and other providers are listed in the PPO network. Health plan members can visit any provider in the network by paying a small copayment. Although the member may designate a primary care physician, a referral is not necessary if the member wishes to see any other physician in the network. If the member seeks a provider who is not in the network, the PPO pays a smaller percentage of the fee. You may have to pay up front and ask for a partial reimbursement.

"communicate"

Resolving a problem with an insurer may involve two or more telephone calls to the customer service center. What can you do before calling to make your call more effective?

Ethics in Action

Jenny loved animals and began volunteering at a wildlife center. Many local people brought orphaned and injured wild animals to the center. Only volunteers who had been vaccinated against rabies were allowed to work with raccoons, Jenny's favorite animal. However, a rabies vaccination costs about $600. It would cost twice as much for people who have already been bitten or scratched because they need additional shots. When Jenny called her insurer about being vaccinated, the insurer said that, because she is only a volunteer, the vaccination would not be covered unless she was actually bitten. Some of the volunteers told Jenny she should go ahead and pay up front for the shots, submit the claim, and fight to have it paid. Others told her to say she had been bitten by an animal that ran away, and then her insurer would have to pay for the shots.

Think Critically

What do you think about the advice given to Jenny? What do you think she should do?

PPO plans tend to cost more than an HMO, but less than an FFS plan. PPO plans are, however, fairly flexible. If most of your providers are in the same network, a PPO can be a high-quality and low-cost arrangement. One disadvantage is that PPO plans reserve the right to drop providers without notice, and you may suddenly find that the physician you visit regularly is no longer a preferred provider. You then have to choose between finding another physician or paying more to see your regular physician.

Point of Service (POS) Plan

Point of Service (POS) plans combine the features of an HMO and a PPO. Like an HMO, a POS provides a network of preferred providers, and you are required to select a primary care physician. The PCP usually refers you to other providers within the network. Like a PPO, you can choose to go outside the network for health care, but you will have to pay most of the cost, unless your PCP made the referral, in which case the POS will pick up the cost.

POS plans typically cost more than an HMO but less than a PPO. POS plans may offer preventive care and health improvement services.

 **checkpoint**

Describe one basic feature of each: FFS, HMO, PPO, and POS.

MATCHING A HEALTH PLAN TO YOUR NEEDS • • • • • • • • •

In health insurance, as in life, nothing is perfect. Even if a tight budget or lack of choice in the plans offered by your employer limits your options, you can probably still make your insurance work well for you. To do this, you must become an educated, persistent, and wise consumer. You can also purchase supplementary insurance to fill gaps in your coverage.

Group Plans

Begin asking questions about your options. Does your employer offer health insurance? Do you have a choice of plans? How much can you tailor each choice? Large employers tend to offer a wider variety of choices of health plans. If this is the case, the company's human resources department should be able to assist you in making wise decisions. Typically, human resources personnel can provide you with a summary, such as the table on the next page, allowing you to compare the different costs and coverages of the plans. If not, sit down, work through the information, and make a summary and comparison sheet yourself.

BENEFITS COMPARISON

This chart shows benefits provided under two health plans a large employer may offer. Each year, employees choose the health plan they want for themselves and their dependents.

Benefits	Preferred Provider Organization (PPO) Plan	Health Maintenance Organization (HMO) Plan
Annual deductible	Enrollee pays $50 per person/ $150 per family, except for diagnostic and preventive	No deductible
Annual maximum	$1,750 plan reimbursement per person; except as otherwise specified for orthodontia, nonsurgical TMJ, and orthognathic surgery	No general plan maximum
Dentures	50%, PPO and out of state; 40%, non-PPO (dental plan payment)	Enrollee pays $140 copayment, complete upper or lower
Endodontics (root canals)	80%, PPO and out of state; 70%, non-PPO (dental plan payment)	Enrollee pays between $100 and $150 copayment
Nonsurgical TMJ	70%; $500 lifetime maximum (dental plan payment)	70%; $1,000 annual maximum and $5,000 lifetime maximum (dental plan payment)
Oral surgery	80%, PPO and out of state; 70%, non-PPO (dental plan payment)	Extraction of erupted teeth: Enrollee pays between $10 and $50 copayment
Orthodontia	50%; $1,750 lifetime maximum (dental plan payment)	Maximum enrollee copayment per case: $1,500
Orthognathic surgery	70%; $5,000 lifetime maximum (dental plan payment)	70%; $5,000 lifetime maximum (dental plan payment)
Periodontic services	80%, PPO and out of state; 70%, non-PPO (dental plan payment)	Enrollee pays between $15 and $100 copayment
Preventive/ diagnostic	100%, PPO; 90%, out of state; 80%, non-PPO (dental plan payment)	100% (dental plan payment)
Restorative crowns	50%, PPO and out of state; 40%, non-PPO (dental plan payment)	Enrollee pays between $100 and $175 copayment
Restorative fillings	80%, PPO and out of state; 70%, non-PPO (dental plan payment)	Enrollee pays between $10 and $50 copayment

Look at Your Needs   When evaluating your health plan needs, it is helpful to list the different members of your household along with their medical needs, estimating the yearly cost of services for each family member. Does anyone have a chronic condition, such as allergies, requiring regular doctor visits? Does anyone need chiropractic care? What about orthodontia? Are you thinking about adding a new member to your household? As you compare your list of needs to the information you have collected on health plans, you can eliminate some options and concentrate on other options that seem to be the best fit for your situation.

Coverages to Consider

Not every plan will cover every health service. The list provided below begins with commonly covered services and moves toward more infrequently covered services. All plans cover some of these services. As you review your needs list, look for a plan that covers your particular needs. If you are planning to have a child, maternity and well-baby care will weigh heavily in your decision. If you take an expensive prescription drug, a plan that covers prescriptions for a basic fee may be essential for you.

Hospitalization	Rehabilitation facility care
Hospital outpatient services	Physical therapy
Physician hospital visits	Speech therapy
Office visits	Home health care
Skilled nursing services	Hospice care
Diagnostic tests	Maternity care
Prescription drugs	Chiropractic care
Mental health care	Preventive care and checkups
Drug and alcohol abuse treatment	Well-baby care
Contraceptives	Dental care
Fertility treatments	Vision care

As closely as you can, estimate the yearly cost for your household under each plan you are considering. Add the premiums, copayments for the estimated number of doctor visits, and prescription costs. Calculate variations on the cost, such as raising your deductible.

Don't Rely Only on Cost   Try not to use cost as your primary factor in choosing a health plan. It may be that for only a few hundred additional dollars a year, you could enroll in a plan that would give you much more flexibility and security. For example, you may be able to use a doctor of your own choice and have coverage for a particular need on your list. Only you can decide which factors are most important to you.

Individual Plans

If you are self-employed, or if your employer does not provide health insurance, and you cannot buy group insurance through a professional organization or another group, you will need to purchase an individual health plan. It will probably be more costly, but you may have more control over your medical care. With individual plans, you may be able to buy exactly

Computer Security

When people apply for insurance, they must provide personal and confidential information. Applying for insurance online raises privacy issues. Most companies use a Secure Socket Layer (SSL) system that encrypts information submitted online. Encryption technology protects information from being intercepted by another party while it is being transmitted. To protect information stored in a company's computers, firewalls are placed in the computer network to protect it from hackers who might try to steal information. User authentication systems further protect confidential information by allowing access only to authorized individuals.

Think Critically
What kinds of personal information do you think information thieves would like to steal? What precautions can you take to protect personal information?

the coverages you need and no more. Before buying, shop around and ask friends and family for their advice. State departments of insurance typically list insurers in your area. Remember to thoroughly investigate insurers through the state, through consumer satisfaction ratings, and through reputable ratings services. Get at least three price quotes for each type of plan you are considering.

One disadvantage to buying individual coverage is that you must provide evidence of insurability. During this process, you answer questions about your health and medical history and grant the insurer permission to check your medical records. You may also be asked to complete a physical. The insurer will apply its underwriting criteria to your application and decide your insurability.

Underwriting Factors Underwriters consider certain factors when deciding whether to insure an individual (and his or her family). These factors include age, gender, health, occupation, habits, and lifestyle. If you and your dependents are young and in good health, work at low-risk occupations, and are nonsmokers, the good news is that individual coverage may be surprisingly inexpensive. If, on the other hand, you are older and not entirely healthy, work at a high-risk job, smoke, or have a pre-existing condition, you may have more trouble finding coverage. When you do find coverage, it will be more expensive.

Generally Speaking

While every person's insurance needs differ, and choosing health insurance is an intensely individual activity, the following general guidelines may help you make wise choices as you consider health insurance options.

1. **Examine costs** Make sure you can afford the amount of insurance you are purchasing.

2. **Investigate coverages and restrictions** Review what coverages are available and be aware of pre-existing condition restrictions.

3. **Compare plans** Investigate plans to choose one that best meets your needs.

4. **Evaluate flexibility** Consider whether you can choose your own doctors/hospitals.

5. **Don't submit to pressure** Purchase what you need when you need it. Do not submit to pressure tactics.

If All Else Fails

Although many people are concerned they cannot obtain health insurance, the fact is that health insurance of some kind is almost always available if you look for it and are willing to pay for it. If you're employable, for instance, you can probably find an employer who makes group health insurance available to employees.

Many nonprofit or social service agencies make very basic group health plans available, sometimes temporarily, to people in bad economic circumstances. Many states operate a high-risk insurance pool for individuals who cannot obtain insurance any other way.

Insight to Insurers

Health plans, and the paperwork required, can be complicated. Thus, mistakes sometimes happen, and claims that should be covered are denied. You have a right to the coverage specified in your health plan, but it is up to you to follow up and ensure payment is ultimately provided. Keep your insurance information organized and handy. Then, if your claim is denied, call the insurer's customer service department. Usually one call will clear up the problem, but it is wise to document all calls and correspondence. Note the date, time, and customer service representative's name. If you are not satisfied, you should ask to speak to a supervisor.

If you are insured through your employer, you may also contact your human resources department. If the problem is that the insurer does not understand the medical necessity of a claim it denied, you should call the provider who filed the paperwork and request that the claim be refiled or discuss the claim with one of the insurer's medical specialists.

✔ checkpoint

What factors should you consider when selecting a group health plan?

_____

_____

assessment 3.2

Think Critically

1. List the benefits and drawbacks of each type of group health plan.

Fee-for-Service	Health Maintenance Organization (HMO)	Preferred Provider Organization (PPO)	Point of Service Plan (POS)
Benefits:	Benefits:	Benefits:	Benefits:
Drawbacks:	Drawbacks:	Drawbacks:	Drawbacks:

Make Academic Connections

2. **RESEARCH**   Using the Internet, find four websites with information about HMOs. Who owns/sponsors each site? What is the most important point provided on each web page? Is the information reliable? Why or why not?

_____

_____

_____

3. **ETHICS**   What ethical dilemmas do you think physicians who work for HMOs face?

_____

_____

_____

 ## Teamwork

Working in a group, use the coverages listed on page 70 to design a health plan for the members of your group. To keep costs down, you can select only 11 of the 22. How difficult was it to create a plan that met everyone's needs?

3.3 Supplementary and Transitional

goals

+ Explain how to continue being insured after leaving a job.

+ Discuss the role of supplementary insurance.

+ Discuss how Medicaid, Medicare, and Medigap programs work.

terms

+ COBRA

+ HIPAA

+ per claim maximum

+ lifetime limit

+ internal limits

+ Medicaid

+ Medicare

+ Medigap

Insurance Scene

Francisco worked for a dot.com company, but his position was terminated. He began to freelance from home, writing banner ads for the same company. Though his new freelance work no longer paid benefits, it was better than unemployment, and he could interview for new jobs whenever he wanted. Francisco continued his health insurance coverage through COBRA, though it cost him much more. Six months later, the dot.com company went out of business. What are Francisco's health insurance options?

LEAVE A JOB, STAY INSURED ●

To help make sure individuals are able to stay insured between jobs, while changing jobs, or in case of death or divorce, the federal government has passed two important laws—COBRA and HIPAA. They do not prevent loss of coverage in every circumstance, but if you meet the programs' eligibility criteria, you can stay insured on a short-term basis.

Consolidated Omnibus Budget Reduction Act (COBRA)

COBRA gives employees of companies employing 20 or more people the right to continue their group coverage at their own expense depending on circumstances such as:

• If you leave your job or are terminated for any reason (except gross misconduct)

• If you are divorced from the covered employee

• If your work hours are reduced below the minimum hours required for health insurance eligibility

• If you become eligible for Medicare

• If you become disabled

• If the covered employee of whom you are a dependent dies

Under COBRA, you must pay both your share and your former employer's share of your premiums, as well as any out-of-pocket expenses you normally would pay when you receive medical care. In addition, you will pay a small administrative fee. If your former employer goes out of business or stops offering group health insurance, your COBRA coverage ends even if the allotted time has not passed.

Check State Regulations and Up-to-Date Rules   COBRA is extremely complicated, and the rules change regularly. It is important to check the COBRA website for the most up-to-date information. Also, some states have set stronger regulations than the federal law. In some states, COBRA rights apply to companies with fewer employees than the federally mandated 20, so check with your state department of insurance as well.

Health Insurance Portability and Accountability Act (HIPAA)

HIPAA, the "portability" law, applies to all group health policies no matter what size, employer based or not. It covers individual policies sold by insurance companies or HMOs and, because it is a federal law, also covers self-insured plans that are not subject to most state regulations. As with COBRA coverage, some state laws may be more restrictive than the federal law, and in those cases, the state laws govern.

Under the rules of HIPAA, you do not take your group insurance with you if you change jobs, but you do take your eligibility with you—if, and only if, your new employer offers health insurance. So, you must be moving

PHOTODISC/GETTY IMAGES

from one job with insurance to another job with insurance. Under HIPAA, your new insurer must cover any family members who were covered in the last plan, and you cannot be rejected or charged higher premiums because of a family member's health problems. Also, if the new plan has a waiting period before it covers pre-existing conditions, you are credited for the time you were covered under your former plan. HIPAA does not mandate maternity coverage if the new plan does not cover maternity expenses. However, if the new plan does cover maternity, the insurer is prohibited from declaring pregnancy or prenatal problems a pre-existing condition.

Converting from Group to Individual Insurance   HIPAA also mandates some rights to coverage when you convert from a group to an individual plan. For example, if your new employer does not offer insurance or if you become self-employed, HIPAA rules may apply. If you have been

Insurance Math *Connection*

Jasmine has a fee-for-service (FFS) health plan that pays 80% of all her medical expenses once she meets her deductible. She is young and healthy and rarely needs to go to the doctor. Her premium will vary according to the deductible she chooses. Which deductible should she pick?

Deductible	Monthly premium	Annual premium
$100	$125	$1,500
$250	$100	$1,200
$500	$75	$900

Solution

To compare costs, first subtract the $900 annual premium from the $1,500 annual premium.

$$\$1,500 - \$900 = \$600$$

The policy with the $500 deductible is a sure savings of $600 on the annual premium. But Jasmine needs to consider her expenses if she needs medical care. With the higher deductible, she will pay $400 ($500 – $100) more a year before her insurance starts to pay for her medical care. The $500 deductible is still Jasmine's best choice. Even if she does get sick and needs to pay the entire $500 deductible, she will save $200 ($600 – $400).

covered for 18 months or more under a full-service health insurance plan or government health insurance, and if you meet a number of other qualifying conditions, you cannot be rejected for basic coverage or have pre-existing conditions excluded by an insurance company offering individual coverage.

Research Your Rights   Although you do have certain insurance rights under state and federal law, it is up to you to know and exercise your rights. Your state department of insurance is an invaluable resource, and so are the federal websites about health insurance. A number of consumer organizations offer useful information as well.

 **checkpoint**

What is the main difference between COBRA and HIPAA?

_____

_____

SUPPLEMENTARY MEDICAL INSURANCE • • • • • • • • • • • •

If you have high-quality health insurance, you should not need supplementary insurance. However, if your employer's group health plan is not adequate, you might consider buying additional coverage on your own. If you have an individual health plan that has one of the shortcomings discussed in this lesson, amend it.

Low Limits

Health insurance policies are written with dollar maximum limits. These restrictions refer to per claim limits, lifetime limits, and internal limits. A **per claim maximum** is the maximum amount of money the insurer will pay for any single claim. If you have a $50,000 per claim maximum and are involved in an accident that requires $50,000 worth of care, and then two years later require a $50,000 bone marrow transplant for leukemia, the insurer will pay both claims and your coverage continues.

Lifetime Limits   Instead of using a per claim maximum, most insurers write a **lifetime limit** on medical policies. This means that every dollar paid in claims reduces the amount available to be paid in the future. If your lifetime

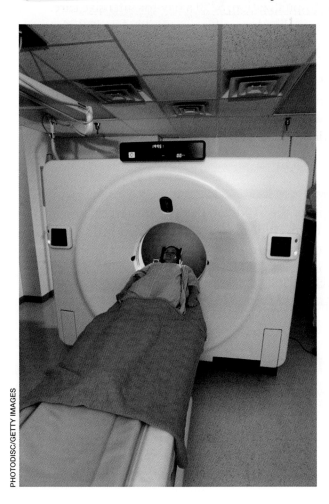

limit is $100,000, your accident and your transplant alone would consume your lifetime limit. Medical expenses can be astronomical. If a group plan's lifetime health benefits are only $100,000 or even $250,000, some experts recommend buying a personal major medical policy, also called an excess major medical policy, to increase the lifetime medical expenses to $500,000, $1 million, or more. This insurance will be used only if major expenses are incurred. Accepting a very high deductible makes the premium more affordable and does not drastically affect your out-of-pocket expenses.

flat world...

Allocation of Health Resources

In Canada, the government provides universal (national) health care for its citizens. Health resources are allocated so all citizens receive routine and emergency care. However, non-emergency surgeries, medical tests, and procedures such as cataract surgery or physical therapy are more difficult to obtain, even for the middle class. For most Americans, even basic health care is not considered a right. However, because the U.S. health care system is centered around people who have health insurance and can afford expensive,

non-emergency care, health resources are allocated toward these more expensive services. Meanwhile, millions of Americans are without medical insurance and must pay out of pocket for medical care, visit a clinic for low-income patients, or go without care.

Think Critically What are the advantages and disadvantages of a national health care system versus the health care system of the United States? Which system would you rather live under?

Internal Limits Some insurance plans specify amounts they will pay, for example $150 a day for hospitalization, $250 a day for intensive care. These are called **internal limits**. The insured is responsible for charges exceeding these internal limits, even if the total cost of the stay does not exceed the policy's limit. Medical costs rise so rapidly that these internal limits are quickly out of date, and a lengthy hospital stay might leave you with a sizable, out-of-pocket expense. If your health plan specifies such internal limits, you can purchase a personal major medical policy that will pay for expenses your health plan does not cover.

Insurance to Avoid

Policies that cover you only in very limited circumstances are not necessarily a wise choice. An example of this is "dread disease" insurance, in which you can buy large amounts of coverage in case you are diagnosed with cancer or some other specified expensive-to-treat disease such as encephalitis, spinal meningitis, and poliomyelitis. It would be better to put the amount of that premium toward a personal major medical policy that would cover expenses no matter what medical disaster might occur.

 checkpoint

Describe the difference between per claim maximum, lifetime limits, and internal limits.

_____

_____

_____

GOVERNMENT-PROVIDED HEALTH INSURANCE · · · · · · · · ·

A healthy population is a benefit to society. Health insurance is considered so essential that the federal government, in conjunction with the individual states, provides insurance for the citizens it deems most in need of assistance: the poor, the disabled, and the elderly. Both the Medicaid and Medicare programs are administered by the Centers for Medicare and Medicaid Services (CMS). These are also called *entitlement programs*.

The Medicaid Program

Medicaid became law in 1963 under the Social Security Act. Medicaid provides medical assistance for eligible individuals and families with low incomes and resources. Within broad federal guidelines, each state establishes its own eligibility standards; determines the type, amount, duration, and scope of services; sets the rate of payment for services; and administers the program. Therefore, Medicaid programs vary widely from state to state as programs and funding change.

The Medicare Program

Medicare is the nation's largest health insurance program, covering approximately 39 million Americans. Medicare provides health insurance for individuals age 65 or older, under age 65 with certain disabilities, and any age with end-stage renal disease (permanent kidney failure requiring dialysis or a kidney transplant). Most Americans over 65 take advantage of Medicare.

As you can imagine, Medicare is a very complex program. However, with so many people enrolled, a lot of information explaining Medicare is available. The federal government publishes the official handbook *Medicare & You*, which is available online at www.medicare.gov or by calling the agency. Many state departments of insurance also publish handbooks about Medicare, explaining state requirements and listing Medicare providers and insurers. Individuals should explore Medicare thoroughly before they are eligible to enroll.

Medicare Does Not Take Effect Automatically   You must apply for Medicare. If you do not apply, you will not receive the benefits. There is an open enrollment period of three months before your 65th birthday, when you become eligible. You apply for Medicare by calling your local Social Security office or the Social Security Administration.

Parts A, B, C, and D   There are several components to Medicare. Part A (Hospital Insurance) covers a percentage of inpatient care at hospitals. Part A also helps cover skilled nursing such as a nursing facility, hospice, and home health care if certain conditions are met. Part A is free to individuals who paid Medicare taxes while working. Part B (Medical Insurance) covers outpatient care and necessary doctor services. Part B also covers preventive services you may use to maintain your health. A monthly premium is charged for Part B. Part C (Medicare Advantage Plan) basically combines Parts A and B and generally offers extra benefits. Part D (Medicare Prescription Drug Coverage), as noted by the name, helps cover prescription drugs. At times, Part D is also combined with Parts A and B to create Part C. Both Parts C and D are approved by Medicare but managed by private insurance companies. Monthly premiums are charged for Parts C and D, and different copayments, coinsurance, and/or deductibles may be involved.

If You Don't Enroll, You'll Pay Anyway   Many health plans insist you enroll in Medicare upon eligibility. If you do not, they will not pay portions of bills that Medicare would have paid had you enrolled. Some employers and unions will reduce your retirement benefits if you do not join Medicare.

Medigap to the Rescue   The insurance industry has dealt with Medicare's shortcomings by developing a number of policies to cover expenses not covered by Medicare. These policies are referred to as **Medigap** or Medical Supplement Insurance and are sold by private insurance companies. Each plan is different but fills in the "gaps" not covered by the Original Medicare Plan such as coinsurance, copayments, or deductibles. Fortunately, most states have standardized these policies so that, although there are 12 policies to choose from, you can compare them relatively easily. Some states also have counselors who can assist you in making your choices.

Medigap policies cover only one person. Therefore, if you and your spouse both need policies, you must purchase two policies. Medigap policies do not cover all insurance needs. For example, long-term care, vision, dental, prescriptions, hearing aids, eyeglasses, and private nursing are not covered. However, most Medigap policies are guaranteed renewable. Therefore, as long as you pay the premium, the insurer can't cancel the policy. The open enrollment period for purchasing Medigap begins on the first day of the month you turn 65 and lasts for six months. If you do not apply during the open enrollment period, the underwriters may refuse you a Medigap policy, charge you a higher rate due to health problems, or postpone coverage due to a pre-existing condition.

checkpoint

Describe the difference between Medicaid and Medicare.

assessment 3.3

Think Critically

1. Why do you think the federal government started COBRA?

_____

_____

_____

2. Why do you think the federal government passed HIPAA?

_____

_____

3. Why might someone purchase supplementary medical insurance?

_____

_____

_____

Make Academic Connections

4. **ECONOMICS**   Many people are critical of entitlement programs such as Medicaid and Medicare, arguing they cost taxpayers too much money. Research what percentage of the U.S. federal budget goes to each program. Write a short report to summarize your findings.

5. **ANALYSIS**   By asking friends, family, or human resources personnel, obtain three copies of group health plan handbooks for different employers. Are there per claim limits, lifetime limits, or internal limits in the plans? Summarize and briefly critique each plan's limits.

6. **ORAL HISTORY**   Interview three friends, neighbors, or family members over the age of 65 about their experiences with Medicare. Ask them how their parents and their grandparents paid for medical care after retirement. Write a brief report telling the most startling things you learned.

7. **PUBLIC HEALTH**   People who are unvaccinated (measles, for example) or untreated (tuberculosis, for example) can spread disease to the rest of the population. Research the effect of childhood vaccinations on public health, the rise in cases of tuberculosis, or another similar topic of your choice, and present your information to the class.

 Teamwork

In small groups, discuss whether or not the government should provide health insurance for some segments of the population. Create a list of reasons supporting this policy and a list of reasons against it.

chapter 3 assessment

Chapter Summary

3.1 Health Insurance Overview

A. Health insurance offers financial protection against large medical expenses. Health insurance is based on the law of large numbers, meaning the high costs of a few insured are spread over many people.

B. Most people buy insurance through a group plan provided by their employer. People buy individual policies when their employer does not offer health insurance or they are self-employed.

3.2 Health Plans

A. Fee-for-service plans are most similar to traditional health care. Managed care plans keep costs down in part by offering members financial incentives to see providers within the plan.

B. In choosing a health plan, you must match the plan's coverages, referral procedures, and cost to the medical needs of your family.

3.3 Supplementary and Transitional

A. COBRA enables workers and their dependents to continue health coverage at their own expense after leaving an employer. HIPAA permits employees moving from one employer to another to maintain their insurance eligibility.

B. If an insurance plan is inadequate, a separate supplementary policy can be purchased to cover expenses the basic plan does not.

C. Medicare covers people age 65 and over and some disabled people under 65. Medicaid covers people who have low incomes.

Vocabulary Builder

Choose the term that best fits the definition. Some terms may not be used.

a. COBRA
b. copayment
c. fee-for-service plan
d. health maintenance organization
e. HIPAA
f. internal limit
g. law of large numbers
h. lifetime limit
i. managed care plan
j. Medicaid
k. Medicare
l. Medigap
m. per claim maximum
n. point of service plan
o. pre-existing condition
p. preferred provider organization
q. primary care physician

_____ 1. Physician who serves as the gatekeeper to other services
_____ 2. Health insurance for low-income families
_____ 3. Law that lets you pay to keep your health plan for a time after you leave your job
_____ 4. The portability law
_____ 5. The least expensive health insurance plan
_____ 6. Excludes coverage of any employee or dependents for a condition treated within the past six months
_____ 7. Similar to a PPO, but like an HMO you have a primary care physician
_____ 8. Small fee for services such as doctors' visits
_____ 9. Plan in which the insured shares the cost of the medical service at a specified ratio after a deductible is satisfied
_____10. Principle under which an insurer can cover enough people so the healthy individuals balance those with poorer health.

Review Concepts

11. Describe an employer's responsibility with regard to health insurance.

_____

_____

_____

12. Briefly describe how COBRA works when people are laid off.

_____

_____

_____

13. Summarize the advantages and disadvantages of individual insurance plans.

_____

_____

_____

14. Summarize the advantages and disadvantages of group insurance.

_____

_____

_____

15. What might an insurer do if an applicant for an individual policy has a pre-existing condition?

_____

_____

16. How do insurers use the law of large numbers to protect themselves against financial loss?

_____

_____

_____

17. Name three ways health insurance is like other insurance.

_____

_____

_____

_____

18. Discuss the principle behind managed care.

_____

_____

_____

19. Rank the four main types of health plans in terms of flexibility, from least flexible to most flexible.

_____

_____

20. Name the two types of health plans that are most likely to pay for preventive and health improvement services.

_____

_____

_____

21. List four factors underwriters consider in deciding whether to insure an individual.

_____

_____

_____

22. What are three ways a person who is difficult to insure might obtain health insurance?

_____

_____

_____

Apply What You Learned

23. Some people believe employers, especially large employers, should be required to offer group health plans to their employees. Do you agree? Why or why not?

_____

_____

_____

_____

24. Before health insurance was common, people who needed an operation but couldn't afford it either died or suffered painful and disabling conditions. This still happens if people do not know how to get help. Do you think the rising cost of health care could make this situation happen more often? Explain your answer.

_____

_____

_____

_____

25. Some people think it's their own business if they do not take care of their health. Others think they owe it to their family to take care of themselves. Still others point out that risky health behavior costs all society, not just the individual and family, by raising medical costs. What do you believe?

---

26. Many people do not feel that health care should be a for-profit business because the profit motive encourages providers to lower expenses or raise prices in ways that are bound to hurt patients. What do you think?

Make Academic Connections

27. **RESEARCH**   Using the Internet or the library, find out the mandated health benefits and health insurance laws of your state. Write a brief report describing benefits that must be covered, people who must be allowed coverage, length of time of restricted coverage for pre-existing medical conditions, and whether your state maintains a high-risk health insurance pool.

28. **MEDICAL HISTORY**   Using the library or the Internet, research the state of medicine a century ago. Physicians did perform operations, but some kinds of surgery were much more common than they are today, while many common procedures of today were unheard of then. Prepare a presentation of what you consider some of the most amazing information you find, or choose a common medical condition and describe in a report how it was handled then and now.

29. **CONSUMERISM**   Do an Internet search for cancer insurance. Be sure you look at consumer information sites as well as sites selling cancer insurance. Do some of the commercial sites selling insurance seem to be using scare tactics? Discuss their use of statistics. Discuss the ways in which benefits are paid. Would you buy any of these policies?

30. **CULTURAL HISTORY**   Using the library or the Internet, or by interviewing elderly people you know, write a short profile of American health at any time between 1880 and 1930. Concentrate on the foods people ate, how much and what kinds of physical exercise they engaged in, and what health problems concerned them the most. Or, if you know an elderly person who grew up in another culture, write a similar profile of that culture. End either profile with a personal response to that time compared to how you live today.

31. **CREATIVE WRITING**   Write brief character sketches of three different people. The first will not buy health insurance, the second cannot afford health insurance, and the third buys too much health insurance.

Insurance

CHAPTER 4

Workers' Compensation and Unemployment Insurance

4.1	Employer-Funded Insurance
4.2	Workers' Compensation
4.3	Unemployment Insurance

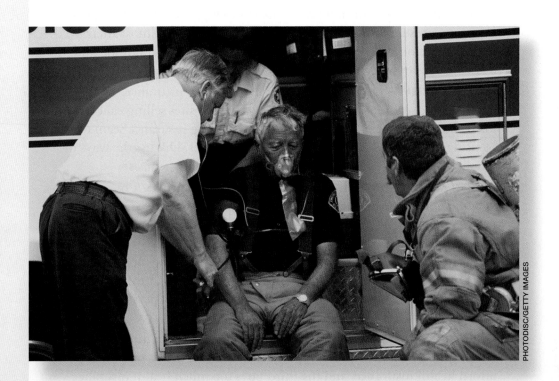

PHOTODISC/GETTY IMAGES

climbing the ladder

From Claims Examiner to Private Insurance Investigator

Antonio, a claims examiner, has been working in the insurance industry for five years. He enjoys applying his technical knowledge and human relations skills while working with clients and insurance companies during the claims process.

As a claims examiner Antonio interviews claimants and employers; obtains adequate and accurate information to support or deny the claim; resolves conflicts; processes and pays claims; and ensures that activities are consistent with corporate policies. These duties take time, and the information must be organized so there is clear evidence indicating whether a claim should be paid or denied. Specific claims-processing administration and management software is used to assist in making this determination.

Antonio has worked mainly with property and casualty insurance claims, but a coworker is working with workers' compensation and unemployment insurance claims. This has peaked Antonio's interest because the current case involves fraud by an employee.

As a claims examiner Antonio has in the past observed claimants, obtained reliable information from sources, and used deductive reasoning to determine claim results. He would like to apply these skills to other insurance areas. He has not had to deal with any fraud cases but is interested in the area.

Antonio was at an insurance career workshop when he learned of a position opening as a Private Insurance Investigator. He thought this may be his opportunity to use his skills to move into a new, exciting position. Antonio is pursuing the new job so that he can obtain and analyze information on those suspected of insurance fraud. For example, if an employee claims she is injured too badly to continue working, but in reality she is well and faking the injury, Antonio would report the information so that unemployment benefits would cease for that employee.

Performing research and learning about individuals' character is an essential part of the investigation process. Antonio is learning about new technologies such as special video equipment that can assist him in the investigation. One thing that he is nervous about is the possibility of testifying at hearings and/or court trials to present evidence. However, he is excited about performing undercover investigations to evaluate the honesty of employees.

Upper Rungs to Consider

Antonio found his current position demanding but wanted to move into more investigative types of positions in the insurance field. He has learned about a variety of tasks and technology involved and is working to increase his expertise in the field.

Preparing for the Climb

What if you decided you would like to be in a type of investigative position? Think about your current position in life, work, and school along with your current responsibilities. Are there responsibilities or projects you could request to begin learning the process and technologies involved in an investigation?

4.1

+ Explain the purpose of workers' compensation insurance.
+ Explain the purpose of unemployment insurance.

terms

+ repetitive stress injuries
+ workers' compensation
+ death benefit
+ Occupational Safety and Health Administration (OSHA)
+ unemployment insurance
+ claimants

Employer-Funded Insurance

Insurance Scene

Nguyen and Paolo were both chemistry majors with a strong interest in special effects for concerts and movies. They designed stage fireworks for a magician friend, and by word of mouth, more professionals began to ask for their help. Before they knew it, they were selling pyrotechnical effects to bands on concert tours. The business was wildly successful, and soon they needed to hire staff to handle paperwork and to label, pack, and ship the fireworks. List some of Nguyen and Paolo's considerations when purchasing workers' compensation and unemployment insurance for their employees.

RISK IN THE WORKPLACE •

The more time you spend in a given location, or engaged in a given process, the more you are exposed to whatever risks exist in that environment. Most adults in the United States spend 20 to 40 hours per week, or more, at a workplace outside the home. Some workplaces are dangerous due to the type of work performed. Factories, foundries, farms, refineries, mines, and similar worksites use heavy machinery, high electrical voltages, or hazardous chemicals that can pose an immediate danger to anyone on site. Long-term workplace exposure to certain chemicals or minerals, such as coal dust, can lead to debilitating and deadly diseases such as "black lung" disease. Laboratory technicians and hospital workers can be exposed to viruses and bacteria that can cause disease or infection. Other workers, such as taxi drivers or night clerks, can be targets for robberies.

Hidden Risks   Other jobs, such as data entry or shipping clerk, are not dangerous but may lead to **repetitive stress injuries**. These painful and potentially disabling injuries are caused by performing the same activity repeatedly for long periods of time. A common example includes a person employed in a position in which he or she sits at the computer and keys for long periods of time in a workstation that is not ergonomically correct. This person is in danger of carpal tunnel syndrome. This syndrome occurs when

a nerve running from your forearm to your hand becomes pressed or constricted at the wrist. Symptoms include numbness, pain, and weakness.

All employees are subject to random injuries that can occur anywhere: a finger slammed in a file cabinet, an ankle broken on a missed step, a hand scalded when the coffeemaker breaks, or other office injuries. Because they occur at work, for insurance purposes, these injuries are classified as work-related.

Workers' Compensation to the Rescue

Workers' compensation is insurance paid by the employer to provide employees with medical care, wage replacement, or death benefits if an employee is injured, disabled, or killed on the job. Before there were laws requiring workers' compensation insurance, workers were often injured, disabled, or killed or developed an illness due to a dangerous work environment. Prior to workers' compensation, employers were not required to provide compensation to the employee or his or her family. However, many employers did provide some death or disablement compensation. Generally, this compensation did not adequately replace the lost income and resulted in a hardship for the worker's family.

Not all states require employers to carry workers' compensation insurance. Consequently, there are varying regulations among the states in which it is a requirement. Some states require employers to have workers' compensation insurance if they employ one or more employees. Other states may not require it unless there are four or more employees. It is important to remember that the employers fund the entire cost of the insurance. Employees do not contribute to the fund.

Laws vary widely, but typically, in case of serious injury, workers' compensation will pay medical bills, a percentage of lost wages, and vocational retraining if an employee is unable to resume her or his former job.

Workers' compensation will pay a substantial **death benefit** to compensate survivors if an on-the-job injury results in death. However, an employee may be denied workers' compensation for a variety of reasons. Some reasons include willful misconduct, including intentional self-inflicted injury; being under the influence of alcohol or drugs; refusal to use safety equipment; and willful breach of any company policy.

Social Benefits of Workers' Compensation   High insurance premiums are a powerful incentive for employers to maintain the safest possible workplace. By rigorously following safety practices, employers can reduce workplace illnesses, injuries, and deaths and pay lower premiums. State and federal agencies such as the **Occupational Safety and Health Administration (OSHA)** set safety standards. These agencies further enforce safety and health legislation and focus on leadership, fair and effective enforcement, education and compliance assistance, and partnerships with state governments and private companies. These agencies reinforce worker safety standards by making periodic inspections, acting on reported safety violations, and fining employers found to have major or repeated violations.

Enabling ill, injured, or disabled workers' families to maintain an adequate standard of living benefits all of society. The eligible workers can receive the necessary medical attention and/or rehabilitation and, if possible, return to work in the old job or to another job for which they have been trained.

tech talk

Coal Mining

Coal mining traditionally is one of the world's most dangerous occupations. In 1925, in the state of West Virginia alone, 686 miners died. Today, fewer American coal miners die in accidents than in previous years. Technology, much of it mandated by safety regulations, is one reason mining is safer today. Roof bolts support the roofs of mine passages to prevent cave-ins. Sensors monitor gas and coal dust levels to prevent miners from being suffocated by toxic gases such as methane, or killed in explosions caused by bad combinations of gas and dust. The greatest improvements in safety have resulted from machinery that minimizes the presence of humans underground. Until the 1930s, coal seams were loosened with pickaxes and dynamite and then shoveled by hand and hauled out by ponies. With the introduction in the 1930s of large saws, drills, and conveyer belts to carry the coal, fewer men could mine more coal. Today, unmanned longwall mining machines follow coal seams deep into the earth, dig out the coal, and send it out on automated conveyer belts.

Think Critically   The coal mining counties are some of the poorest counties in the entire country. Mechanization and the closing of mines have led to the loss of many jobs in areas where there are few employment opportunities. How do you think unemployment benefits should be distributed in such circumstances?

✔ checkpoint

List two ways in which workers' compensation benefits society.

_____

_____

"communicate"

Contact a human resources manager in your town. Interview him or her about specific ways in which workers' compensation and unemployment insurance have helped his or her industry, or company, operate more efficiently, or have made it less efficient. Write a report to share with the class.

THE RISK OF UNEMPLOYMENT

In addition to potential injury, the workplace holds the equally devastating risk that, through no fault of your own, you may lose your job. When this

happens, the stakeholders who are impacted include you, your family, and society as a whole. For example, the cumulative impact of unemployment on the economy was obvious during the Great Depression of the early 1930s. Companies laid off workers. Unemployed workers could no longer buy goods and services. Consequently, the manufacturers who made cars, clothes, and other consumer goods were forced to lay off workers. Grocers, hardware stores, and other retailers began to fail as well. Physicians, hairdressers, mechanics, and other service providers learned to accept food and other forms of barter as payment because many consumers simply had no money. Many people also lost their homes and moved to other parts of the country in hope of finding work.

Social Security and Unemployment Insurance   In 1935, as part of the Social Security Act, U.S. employers were first required to carry **unemployment insurance**, which pays temporary benefits to eligible workers who have lost their jobs. The program is administered by each state within a framework of federal guidelines. Therefore, regulations vary widely among the different states.

In most states, the unemployment program is funded by employers, who pay both federal and state unemployment taxes based on their payroll.

State tax funds are recorded and deposited into a pool from which the state pays unemployment benefits to the **claimants,** unemployed individuals who meet the state's eligibility requirements. These benefits are typically about half of the person's salary. Benefits are usually paid for up to six months while the person actively searches for a job comparable to the one that was lost. Each state determines the unemployment tax an employer pays based on the industry the employer is in and the employer's record of former employees requiring unemployment payments. Employers who frequently lay off workers are taxed at a higher rate.

Social Benefits of Unemployment Insurance   As with workers' compensation, unemployment benefits help keep the ill effects of unemployment contained while the person deals with this temporary hardship and finds employment. These benefits help unemployed workers and their families continue to contribute to the economy by purchasing necessary goods and services. The benefits help decrease pressure on the unemployed worker while searching for employment and enable him or her to find a good, comparable job.

Unemployment insurance payments also serve as an incentive for businesses to plan hiring, firing, and layoffs with great care. Well-managed organizations pay less unemployment tax than employers that cannot precisely predict their staffing needs. For example, rather than hiring five permanent new workers to handle a temporary production demand and then laying them off a year later and paying their unemployment benefits, a savvy manager would either find a way to increase business long-term or hire temporary workers for the production needs. Employers that cannot balance their employment and production needs penalize themselves by paying higher unemployment taxes.

✔ **checkpoint**

Name two social benefits of unemployment insurance.

_____

_____

_____

assessment 4.1

Think Critically

1. Do you think many employers would pay for workers' compensation and unemployment insurance if they were not required by law?

_____

_____

2. Describe how workers' compensation and unemployment insurance are similar in purpose.

_____

_____

_____

3. Briefly describe how unemployment insurance is funded.

_____

_____

_____

Make Academic Connections

4. **LABOR HISTORY**   Research a strike, mining disaster, or other historical labor event of your choosing and review it as if it were a play. What are its themes? Who are its heroes and villains? Are the characters all good or bad?

5. **LITERATURE**   John Steinbeck's *The Grapes of Wrath* is considered the classic novel depicting the Depression era. Write a report discussing the labor issues discussed in the book.

6. **OCCUPATIONAL HEALTH**   Visit the OSHA website (www.osha.gov), particularly the OSHA fact page (www.osha.gov/as/opa/oshafacts.html). Did you realize how many American workers are injured, disabled, or killed on the job each year? Design a poster, or write a letter to the editor of your local paper, making the case for worker awareness of on-the-job safety.

 **Teamwork**

Imagine there is no workers' compensation and no unemployment insurance, and the chief wage earner in your household is badly injured or loses his or her job. Work in groups to decide what your household's options would be? Describe them in writing.

4.2 Workers' Compensation

Insurance Scene

Desiree made the best oatmeal cookies anybody in Virginia had ever tasted. She started selling them at a local farmer's market but quickly found she couldn't make enough of them in her home kitchen. She rented the kitchen of a neighborhood bakery three afternoons a week and hired her friends Meghan and Joachim to help. Desiree realized the big ovens and mixers were somewhat dangerous and wondered whether she needed to buy workers' compensation coverage to protect her friends. She also wondered if it was required by law in Virginia if she had only two employees. Where should Desiree start looking for answers to her questions?

MAKING WORKERS' COMPENSATION WORK • • • • • • • • •

There is a federal Office of Workers' Compensation Programs within the U.S. Department of Labor. However, each state sets standards for employers within its state. Workers' compensation laws vary from state to state. In some states, small employers with just a few employees are exempt from the workers' compensation requirement, and large, stable employers are permitted to insure themselves.

In some states, employers can purchase workers' compensation coverage from any insurance company, while in other states, an employer is required to purchase coverage through a state agency. Some states have a state workers' compensation pool, similar to a high-risk medical insurance pool, for employers who find it difficult to buy insurance because they perform extremely dangerous work or have a poor safety record. In Texas, workers' compensation is voluntary for most employers, although there is a state commission that assists those who choose to provide workers' compensation.

What Workers' Compensation Covers

The workplace can be dangerous, and employees can develop an illness or be badly injured, disabled, or killed. Workers' compensation is designed to deal with life-changing accidents and their consequences.

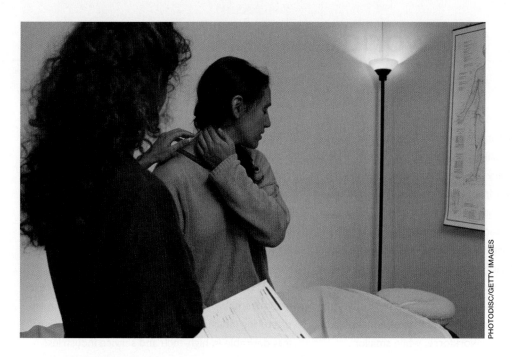

Workers' compensation coverage varies with state requirements and the type of policy. When you suffer an injury covered by workers' compensation, your medical expenses should be covered. If you are out of work for more than a few days, a percentage of your lost wages may also be covered. Lost wages benefits are usually about two-thirds of your income, unless your income was so high that you would exceed your state's payment limits, in which case the payments are less. The payments are tax-free. Workers' compensation will also cover a certain amount of vocational training if you are unable to return to your old job. If you die as a result of your injury or occupational disease, your survivors would receive death benefits.

If your injury leaves you permanently disabled, you may be eligible for a lump-sum payment or long-term benefits. If you are unable to earn as much as before your injury, contact your state or local workers' compensation office about long-term payments. If you are completely and permanently disabled, you may be eligible for Social Security benefits.

No-Fault Insurance   In **no-fault insurance**, the parties involved in a claim agree not to assign liability (fault), but to resolve the problem in a way both find acceptable. In workers' compensation, the employer agrees to buy insurance to cover virtually all injuries that occur on the job, whether they are literally work-related or not. For example, if you twist your ankle by stepping off the handicap ramp on work premises, your medical expenses and occupational therapy are covered, as well as a percentage of wages lost because of the injury. Your employer holds your job for you until you return. If the accident includes loss of a limb that prevents you from performing your job, the employer could use **adaptive technology**, which would allow you to continue to perform your job and meet expectations. For example, if the accident left you without the use of your left hand, there are adaptive technologies to assist you. If the situation does not allow for adaptive technologies to correct the situation, you may be trained for another position.

flat world...

American workers who hate job hunting might envy Japan's policy of so-called "lifetime employment." The policy has two basic elements: (1) the employer refrains from laying off/dismissing full-time employees for management reasons and (2) employees do not take another job until they reach retirement age. In reality, only about one-third of Japan's workforce, primarily men who work for large companies, enjoy the stability of lifetime employment. There are some disadvantages to this policy. During economic downturns, large companies concentrate on maintaining their workforce, while smaller companies must let workers go. As a result, job hunting is extremely difficult and stressful because no one is hiring. There are disadvantages for the economy as well. Lifetime employment was useful in building Japan's heavy manufacturing industries. However, the practice discourages the risk-taking and innovation essential in today's high-tech and service industries.

Think Critically
How did the practice of lifetime employment help Japan build its heavy manufacturing industries? Why is lifetime employment less desirable in high-tech and service industries?

In turn, by accepting the workers' compensation benefits, you cannot sue your employer for damages unless the environment was known to be hazardous and the employer failed to address the issue. If this is the case, you may have the option of suing the employer for negligence, but if you also filed for workers' compensation, your legal case might be weakened.

Eligibility: Who's Covered, Who's Not

Remember, in some states some employers, usually small ones, are not required to carry workers' compensation. Also, not all classes of workers are covered even in states in which workers' compensation is required. In different states, workers exempted from coverage include business owners, independent contractors such as consultants, plumbers, or painters, "casual workers" such as a student who works occasionally, domestic workers in private homes, agricultural workers, and unpaid volunteers.

Injuries Not Covered   State laws differ, but in general you would have trouble receiving workers' compensation benefits for the following:

- Injuries inflicted upon yourself

- Injuries suffered while under the influence of alcohol or illegal drugs

- Injuries suffered in the course of a fight that you started

- Injuries suffered while disobeying orders or violating employer policy

- Injuries suffered while committing a crime

- Injuries suffered while not on the job

Notification of Workers' Compensation Rights Employers must notify employees of their right to compensation for work-related injuries, diseases, and death. Employers must also inform employees that they cannot be fired for filing a claim and that workers' compensation insurance premiums are not deducted from the workers' pay. Most employers satisfy this requirement by displaying a poster from the state in a common area such as the cafeteria or work room.

✔checkpoint

Name two instances in which workers might not be eligible for workers' compensation.

interesting *facts*

Many experts recommend that homeowners add an optional workers' compensation clause to their basic homeowner's or renter's policy, just to be on the safe side. It will protect you in case the neighbor girl who shovels the driveway breaks her arm, the painter's assistant cuts his scalp falling off a ladder, or the babysitter burns his hand opening the microwave popcorn. ■

FILING A WORKERS' COMPENSATION CLAIM •••••••••

Maybe you're a stone worker and a block of granite is dropped on your foot. Or, after 20 years breathing dust in a cotton mill, your chronic cough turns to a painful wheeze. Or, attending a work-related seminar in Florida, you go for a swim during your free time, and you are attacked by a shark and require 30 stitches. What should you do?

First, Notify Your Employer If your injury is an emergency, of course you should get medical attention immediately. As soon as possible, you should notify your employer of the injury. Your state law sets a time limit within which you must report an injury. The limit varies from 2 to 30 days,

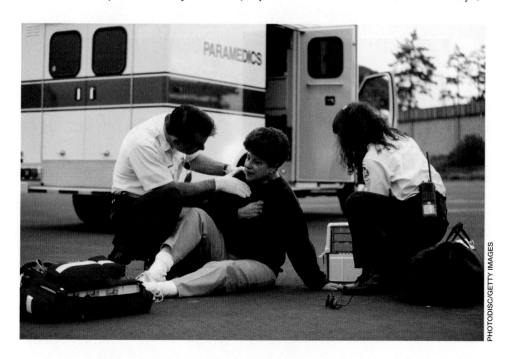

PHOTODISC/GETTY IMAGES

NET Bookmark

Workers' compensation rules and regulations vary from state to state. If you were injured on the job, are you covered by workers' compensation in your state? How could you find out everything you needed to know? The best way is to check out your state's website, which will explain workers' compensation. Access www.cengage.com/school/pfinance/insurance and click on the link for Chapter 4. Then click on your state's link. List five questions you would want answered. Find the answers to your questions and share your answers with the class.

www.cengage.com/school/pfinance/insurance

so you need to know your state limit, or report promptly. In the case of the chronic breathing problem, the time limit would date from the time you saw a doctor who linked your health problem to your work.

Second, Follow Doctor's Orders   Depending on your injury, where it happens, the terms of your employer's workers' compensation coverage, and the size of your employer, you might see an emergency room doctor, your own doctor, or the company or insurance company's doctor. Be sure to follow the doctor's instructions. If you don't follow instructions, it could be grounds for denying workers' compensation coverage. If you need to take time from work, or refrain from some of your normal work assignments, the doctor should note this in writing.

Third, File Your Claim   Whether your employer is insured through a private carrier or the state or is self-insured, the employer is required to have forms available for you to file your claim. Complete the forms truthfully, make a photocopy, keep and file the copy, and submit the claim according to instructions.

Always, Document Everything   Make copies of all correspondence with the insurer, all health providers, and your employer. Keep a log of the dates, times, and content of all conversations and meetings. When you have a telephone conversation, be sure to write down the name and title of the person to whom you talk.

PHOTODISC/GETTY IMAGES

Dealing with Denial

Sometimes a workers' compensation claim, or part of a claim, is denied by the insurer. This happens if the circumstances are open to different interpretations. For example, in the case of the shark bite, people might disagree about whether it is work-related. A claim might be denied if the debilitating nature of the injury, or whether the injury even exists, is open to interpretation. Chronic pain and disability resulting from whiplash is easy to dispute because it cannot be seen. A claim resulting from an arm mangled in machinery is unlikely to be disputed. The most critical factor in a denied claim is expense. An expensive claim involving disability payments open to interpretation is more likely to be denied than an inexpensive claim.

In Case of Denial, Know Your Rights   If your claim is denied, know what your rights are in your state. Obtain a copy of your state's workers' compensation laws. Even in Texas, where workers' compensation is not required, if

PHOTODISC/GETTY IMAGES

your employer does carry workers' compensation, you have certain rights. Your state workers' compensation agency will have caseworkers who can answer your questions and help you understand your rights. They will guide you through the denial and, if necessary, appeal processes.

You Have the Right to Appeal
If your claim is denied, you have the right to appeal. If your claim was denied on medical grounds, you may need to get a second medical opinion for which the insurer might have to pay. Your first appeal is to the insurer. If the claim is still denied, you can appeal to the state workers' compensation office. To appeal the denial of a large claim, especially one

involving disability, you may want to hire an attorney specializing in workers' compensation.

What steps should you follow in filing a workers' compensation claim?

assessment 4.2

Think Critically

1. List three benefits that workers' compensation might cover.

_____

_____

2. Why do you think workers' compensation pays lost wages benefits as well as medical expenses?

_____

_____

3. List three factors that might lead to denial of a claim.

_____

_____

Make Academic Connections

4. **OCCUPATIONAL HEALTH**   There are a number of lung diseases caused by exposure to fine particles of coal dust, asbestos, chemicals, and other substances. Research a lung disease and write a report discussing its symptoms and how it affects the patient's ability to work and quality of life.

5. **ERGONOMICS**   Ergonomics, the design of equipment to increase productivity and reduce worker fatigue and discomfort, is a controversial subject. OSHA published ergonomics standards in 2001, applying to all general industry employers. Approximately 2 million U.S. workers each year are affected by work-related musculoskeletal disorders (back injuries that may be prevented if ergonomic standards are followed). With a classmate, research ergonomic risk issues with a job of your choosing. Both of you should be prepared to discuss your findings.

6. **MEDICAL ETHICS**   Workers' compensation advocates argue that it is a conflict of interest for a physician who has been retained by an insurance company to evaluate occupational injuries. Research the issue and write your own opinion.

 **Teamwork**

In a small group, make a list of different jobs you've had, or volunteer work you've done. List the risks you encountered for which you may have needed workers' compensation. Compare your lists with other groups.

Unemployment Insurance 4.3

Insurance

goals

+ Describe employers' unemployment insurance responsibilities.

+ Explain how to file for unemployment insurance benefits.

terms

+ base period
+ reasonable cause
+ lockout
+ Social Security number
+ fraud

Insurance Scene

Rosarina was a freelance botanical illustrator who lived in Boston. One day a new client, a publisher who was expanding his business, offered her a job as illustrations manager. The company was located in an isolated, though beautiful, area in the Ozark Mountains of Arkansas. If she accepted the offer, Rosarina would have to give up her apartment, leave her friends, and start a new life. The publisher assured her the business was profitable and the position was secure. Rosarina moved, rented an old farmhouse, and rode her bike to work almost every day. She loved her work and grew accustomed to country life. But after 14 months, the publisher stunned everyone by announcing he needed to lay off half of the staff members. There were no jobs within 80 miles. What does Rosarina need to do to receive unemployment? Why is it in society's interest to discourage employers from laying off workers?

MAKING UNEMPLOYMENT INSURANCE WORK ● ● ● ● ● ● ●

The Federal-State Unemployment Compensation Program pays benefits to unemployed workers who meet certain eligibility requirements. The program has two main objectives: to give economic relief to workers and their families and to promote economic stability. Unemployment insurance promotes economic stability by maintaining individual purchasing power during periods of unemployment, and by giving employers a financial incentive, through the system of unemployment taxes, not to lay off workers.

Although administered under the Employment and Training Administration of the Department of Labor, each state sets unemployment insurance standards for employers and employees within its borders. The unemployment insurance program is funded through a system of federal and state taxes that in most states are paid entirely by the employer. A few states deduct small amounts of unemployment tax from employee wages. There are no exemptions, even for small employers. An employer with even one eligible employee will pay state unemployment taxes.

Who Is Eligible?

Individuals are eligible for unemployment insurance benefits if they meet these general criteria.

- Individuals must meet their state's requirements for wages earned, or time worked, during the **base period**, a time period used to determine eligibility, typically four quarters (one year).

- Individuals must be unemployed through no fault of their own. This definition varies from state to state.

- Individuals must be able to work.

- Individuals must be available for work.

- Individuals must be actively searching for work.

Who Is Not Eligible?

State regulations vary widely, and are open to interpretation, but these general criteria hold from state to state.

Individuals Who Quit Their Job Voluntarily   If you leave voluntarily, you are not eligible for unemployment benefits. However, if you are forced to leave because of unreasonable, illegal, or unsafe job conditions, or harassment by the employer or other employees, your unemployment claim may be accepted. You would, however, need to prove you acted reasonably and legally and notified the employer about the problem, and that the employer did not attempt to correct the situation.

Individuals Who Are Fired for Reasonable Cause   **Reasonable cause** is a basis for firing to which no reasonable person would object. Examples of reasonable cause include gross misconduct, on-the-job use of alcohol or controlled substances, theft or other crimes, or refusal to follow instructions. Some states list criteria such as "careless or shoddy work" as a reasonable cause for termination, or being fired. "Careless or shoddy" might be open to interpretation if an employee wished to appeal denial of benefits.

Individuals Involved in a Labor Dispute   If you belong to a union and are on strike, you are not typically eligible for unemployment. However, one way you may be eligible in this situation is if the employer withheld work from employees by closing down during the labor dispute. This is called a **lockout**.

Ethics in Action

Nathaniel disliked DaNae, the only woman in the department. Although he was not DaNae's direct supervisor, he complained about her to Alberto, the operations director. Alberto had always thought DaNae didn't pull her weight, so he told Nathaniel to keep a log of her shortcomings on the job. Nathaniel made note of every time DaNae came in a few minutes late. He ridiculed her work and noted she could not take criticism when she defended herself against his comments. Three months later, Alfredo was told to cut costs by laying off two people. He immediately thought of DaNae. Harry was the only other person in the department with the same job description. Perfect. Alfredo thought DaNae could not sue for sex discrimination if he also laid off a man. He gave DaNae and Harry two weeks' notice. They both applied for unemployment benefits. When DaNae's and Harry's unemployment paperwork came through, Alfredo decided to contest DaNae's eligibility, writing that DaNae had been a tardy, incompetent, and insubordinate worker.

Think Critically

Do you think Alfredo's actions were ethical? Do you think they were legal? If you were DaNae, what would you do?

Seasonal Employees in the "Off" Season   You are a seasonal employee if, for example, you work for a ski resort every winter, but the ski resort closes during the off season. During the off season, you cannot receive unemployment benefits. However, if one winter there is not enough snow, and not enough skiers, and the resort lays you off when you would normally expect to work, you may be able to receive unemployment benefits if you meet the requirements. Farm workers, some professional athletes, and teachers are also not able to draw unemployment during the off season.

Employer Responsibilities

Workers who have been terminated must be notified by the employer of their possible eligibility for unemployment benefits. Most employers post a notice from the state in a common area to fulfill this requirement.

After a terminated employee files for unemployment, the state unemployment office sends paperwork to the employer to verify the employee's wages, dates of employment, and reason for termination. This provides the background information for the unemployment claim made by the employee.

Contesting Eligibility   An employer may contest or challenge a former employee's eligibility for unemployment benefits. Employers have an economic incentive to do so because the number of former employees who collect unemployment directly affects the amount of state unemployment

PHOTODISC/GETTY IMAGES

taxes the employer pays. The employer may be completely justified in contesting eligibility. For example, if an employee was fired for a reasonable cause, he or she is not eligible for unemployment benefits. The employer should document the termination of an employee by producing relevant documents from the worker's personnel file.

An employer cannot go back and create documents after the fact. Nor can an employer, wishing to create a legal case to fire an employee in the future, enforce rules selectively or hold performance reviews for that employee alone. If a worker is written up for tardiness, for example, all tardy workers must be written up. An employer has the right to fire any employee for any nondiscriminatory reason, without just cause. However, if an employee is fired without just cause, he or she cannot be denied unemployment payments.

✔ checkpoint

List four categories of employees who are not eligible for unemployment benefits.

FILING AN UNEMPLOYMENT CLAIM • • • • • • • • • • • • • • • •

Perhaps your employer lost its largest client and must reduce the payroll. Perhaps the corporate office decided to cut the workforce by 20 percent to reduce finances. Perhaps you were the only male neonatal unit nurse and your female coworkers harassed you until, despite your complaints to management, you were so miserable you decided you had just cause to quit. In all these instances, you have committed no gross misconduct, you're out of work through no fault of your own, and you believe you are eligible for unemployment benefits. What should you do?

File Your Claim   Contact your local state unemployment insurance agency as soon as you lose your job. In some states you can file by telephone or online. When you visit the office, phone the office, or access the office online to file, you must furnish the following information:

- Your **Social Security number**, which is your primary identification number used by government. Some states require it printed on an ID.

- The names and addresses of your employers for the last 18 months, plus the dates you worked for each.

- Proof of your immigration status if you are not a U.S. citizen.

Remember, if you withhold information or do not tell the truth when filing a claim, you not only may be refused benefits, but you also may have

Insurance Math *Connection*

Every state uses a different formula to calculate a claimant's unemployment insurance weekly benefit amount. Here is one state's method. The weekly benefit amount is calculated using the wages a claimant earned during the previous year. This year is called the base period. The claimant's wages for each quarter of the base period are given separately. The highest-paid quarter is divided by 26 and rounded down to the next lowest dollar to calculate the weekly benefit.

Antoine worked for Sayer's Landscaping during the base period, earning a total of $15,762.37. During the four quarters of the base period, he earned $2,673.47; $4,836.32; $6,224.81; and $2,027.77. What is his weekly benefit amount? What is his monthly benefit?

Solution

High Quarter Wages ÷ 26 = Weekly Benefit Amount

$6,224.81 ÷ 26 = $239.42, weekly benefit rounded down to $239

$239.00 × 4 = $956.00, monthly benefit

to pay back benefits you have collected. You could also face prosecution for **fraud**, which is deception for the purpose of unlawful gain.

Your Former Employer Verifies After you file, the state unemployment insurance agency will send notice to your former employer requesting verification of the information you gave. This is usually a formality, but if you think your former employer might contest your eligibility, consider what information you need to challenge the employer. If your former employer contests your eligibility, the unemployment insurance agency will schedule a hearing to resolve the dispute.

If the hearing officer decides against you, you have the right to appeal. There will be another hearing and another decision. If your claim is still denied at that time, you can appeal to a review board.

Your Benefits: How Much and for How Long?

If all goes smoothly, it should take two or three weeks to receive benefits, but this time will vary. Some states have a brief waiting period before you can file or collect. Every state uses a different formula, some more complicated than others, to calculate unemployment payments. Generally speaking, your payment is approximately half of your former pay. If you maintain your eligibility while you are unemployed, you can usually receive benefits until you find a job, but for no longer than 26 weeks. Many times, the unemployed do not qualify for full 26-week benefits. In times of high unemployment when jobs are hard to find, a state may decide to extend the benefits period for its residents. Funds from the federal unemployment tax are used for this extension, which typically lasts 13 or 20 weeks.

Maintaining Your Eligibility When you receive benefits, you must meet certain requirements to maintain your eligibility for unemployment payments. Again, these requirements are defined differently from state to state. If you fail to meet any of your state's requirements, your payments may be canceled. General eligibility requirements include the following:

PHOTODISC/GETTY IMAGES

- You must be able to work.

- You must be available for work.

- You must be actively looking for work each week, and you may have to document where you have applied for work.

- You must be looking for full-time employment.

- You must be registered with the unemployment office, and you must respond when contacted. You must report to the office on the date and at the time scheduled.

- You must not refuse any suitable job offers—work that you are qualified for, located reasonably near where you live—without good cause.

- You must report all earnings from other sources while drawing benefits. Your benefits may be adjusted to reflect what you earn.

Job Training and Placement In addition to paying unemployment benefits, state unemployment offices offer career counseling, training, and job placement programs. When you file for unemployment, you may be required to register for these programs. The extent and quality of these services vary from state to state.

Eligible Individuals Can Be Disqualified If you fail to fulfill all the state requirements, you can be disqualified. If you think you have been disqualified wrongly, you have the right to appeal the decision, and to re-appeal.

 checkpoint

Name four of the requirements for maintaining your unemployment insurance eligibility.

_____

_____

_____

assessment 4.3

Think Critically

1. Why do you think it is necessary to give your Social Security number when filing for unemployment benefits?

_____

_____

2. Name the five criteria individuals must meet to be eligible for unemployment insurance benefits.

_____

_____

_____

3. Name two ways in which the unemployment insurance program promotes economic stability.

_____

_____

Make Academic Connections

4. **RESEARCH**   Visit a local office of the state unemployment insurance agency. Pick up print material describing your state's insurance eligibility requirements or job training and placement services. Summarize this information in a written report or a short oral presentation.

5. **JOURNALISM**   Make an appointment with a public information officer of your state unemployment insurance agency. Interview the officer on the topic of what students need to know about unemployment insurance. Write a service piece for your school newspaper or website.

6. **CULTURAL HISTORY**   Research the popular music of the Depression to find songs dealing with poverty and unemployment. Analyze the lyrics. Create a poster using images and short pieces of text.

 Teamwork

Unemployment insurance pays approximately 50 percent of the wages you earned at your last job. Working in groups, answer these questions: If you needed to get by on unemployment benefits, how would you cut your living expenses in half? Would you be able to save any money? Compare your answers with other groups.

chapter 4 assessment

Chapter Summary

4.1 Employer-Funded Insurance

    A. Workers' compensation insurance, required by government regulations and paid for by employers, pays medical expenses for employees who have a job-related illness or are injured/disabled on the job. It also covers a percentage of lost wages and pays death benefits.

    B. Unemployment insurance assists those who lose their job through no fault of their own. Unemployment benefits provide payments to help individuals/families continue to contribute to the economy.

4.2 Workers' Compensation

    A. Workers' compensation is no-fault insurance. It covers all workplace injuries and occupational diseases, with the exception of those incurred as a result of reckless or illegal acts by the employee.

    B. When filing a workers' compensation claim, it is important to follow the rules and keep detailed documentation.

4.3 Unemployment Insurance

    A. Unemployment insurance pays a percentage of an eligible person's lost wages up to a specified number of weeks while the person looks for another job. Individuals are not eligible if they quit voluntarily, were fired for reasonable cause, are involved in a strike, or are seasonal employees in the off season.

    B. The requirements for maintaining unemployment insurance eligibility include being able to work, being available and actively looking for full-time work, registering with the unemployment office, reporting at the date and time scheduled, not refusing suitable job offers without good cause, and reporting other earnings.

Vocabulary Builder

Choose the term that best fits the definition. Write the letter of the answer in the space provided. Some terms may not be used.

a. adaptive technology
b. base period
c. claimant
d. death benefit
e. fraud
f. lockout
g. no-fault insurance
h. Occupational Safety and Health Administration (OSHA)
i. reasonable cause
j. repetitive stress injury
k. Social Security number
l. unemployment insurance
m. workers' compensation

_____ 1. Insurance that covers employee workplace injuries
_____ 2. Caused by performing the same activity repeatedly
_____ 3. Temporary benefits paid to eligible workers who lose their jobs
_____ 4. Time period used to determine unemployment eligibility and payment amount
_____ 5. Worker eligible for unemployment insurance
_____ 6. An agency that sets safety standards
_____ 7. When both parties in a claim agree not to assign liability
_____ 8. Enables a disabled person to perform work
_____ 9. Deception for the purpose of unlawful gain
_____10. Compensation paid to survivors

Review Concepts

11. List four different types of workplace hazards.

_____

_____

_____

12. Explain how workers' compensation insurance premiums provide an incentive to employers to maintain a safer workplace.

_____

_____

13. Explain how unemployment insurance taxes provide an incentive to employers to carefully manage hiring and layoffs.

_____

_____

_____

14. In dealing with workers' compensation and unemployment insurance, with which level of government do employers and employees work most closely (federal or state)? Why?

_____

_____

15. Workers' compensation is a form of what category of insurance? Explain why.

_____

_____

16. List four instances in which you might have trouble receiving workers' compensation for an injury that happened at work.

_____

_____

_____

_____

17. When might an injured employee be eligible for Social Security benefits? Provide an example.

_____

_____

18. When might a state decide to extend the unemployment benefits period for its residents beyond the usual 26 weeks?

_____

_____

Apply What You Learned

19. Why do you think employers are required to notify employees of their workers' compensation and unemployment insurance rights?

_____

_____

_____

20. Why do you think the states set time limits as to when a workplace injury must be reported?

_____

_____

_____

21. What is the single most interesting thing you've learned about workers' compensation and its history? Explain.

_____

_____

_____

22. Discuss the differences between workers' compensation and unemployment insurance.

_____

_____

_____

_____

_____

23. If the individual states write regulations and administer their own workers' compensation and unemployment insurance programs, why do you think the federal government needs to oversee the state programs? Do you think federal oversight is necessary or unnecessary?

_____

_____

_____

_____

_____

_____

Make Academic Connections

24. **RESEARCH**   Using the Internet or other means, research unemployment statistics for your state. Answer these questions: How many people receive benefits in a year? What is the average length of time recipients are on unemployment before they find another job? What percentage of unemployed individuals use benefits for the entire period? Prepare a short report.

25. **COMMUNICATION**   Create a fictional scenario about a serious workplace accident. Assume you saw the accident happen and you are now writing an account of it for insurance purposes. Write this account as clearly, concisely, and objectively as you can, without making suppositions or drawing conclusions you cannot support.

26. **FILM CRITICISM**   Several movies based on real people and events contain issues of workplace safety and industrial contamination: *Silkwood* (1983), *A Civil Action* (1998), and *Erin Brockovich* (2000). Two movies that touch on workplace conditions but are more concerned with labor issues are *Matewan* (1987), also based on actual events, and *Norma Rae* (1979). Research one or more of these movies and write a review. Be sure to discuss safety and contamination issues.

27. **BUSINESS MATH**   Calculate the weekly benefit amount for these unemployment recipients who live in a state where the weekly benefit amount equals the high-quarter wages divided by 26, rounded down to the next dollar.

    a. Annette's quarterly totals at her insurance sales agent job were $3,847.09; $2,894.89; $3,721.23; and $4,234.98.

    _____

    _____

    b. Wei's quarterly totals as an insurance statistician were $5,984.23; $6,109.87; $6,009.36; and $6,059.56

    _____

    _____

28. **PSYCHOLOGY**   Some states' workers' compensation regulations permit coverage of work-related mental or emotional illness. Other states will only cover psychiatric illness brought about by a work-related physical injury. Insurance coverage for mental health is an important issue. Research the mental health coverage in a sampling of states and develop a presentation based on your findings.

29. **BUSINESS ETHICS**   Some insurers and employers have become aggressive about not paying workers' compensation disability benefits. Their argument is that many workers are committing insurance fraud, claiming to be disabled when they really are not. A sizable investigation and surveillance industry has developed to try to document workers who falsely claim they are disabled. Investigators may use vans mounted with video cameras to follow people around. Is this fair investigation or invasion of privacy? Research this issue and report your findings.

5

Retirement Plans

5.1	Insure Your Retirement
5.2	Types of Plans
5.3	Plan for Retirement

COMSTOCK IMAGES/JUPITER IMAGES

climbing the ladder

From Employment Interviewer to Personal Financial Advisor

Geoffrey is an employment interviewer in the human resources department at Spruill Technologies. His responsibilities include posting positions, qualifications, and promotion opportunities, as well as verifying resumes, checking references, and explaining employment benefits. He enjoys learning about new benefits and retirement options, as he is personally planning his own retirement.

Geoffrey is only 22 years old, but he understands the importance of early retirement planning. His high school education has served him well thus far in his career, but he realizes to move forward in reaching his career goal of becoming a personal financial advisor, he will need to continue his education.

In his current position, he enjoys interaction with individuals and provides excellent customer service. Geoffrey is also in charge of facilitating benefit workshops for all new hires to help employees understand their benefit packages. His personal interaction skills along with his communication, language, and grammar skills are essential to his position.

He has won the Employee of the Month Award twice due to his ability to effectively communicate complex information to applicants. This information includes explaining annuities, 401(k)s, the pension plan, and other options for retirement, as well as insurance and tax deductions.

To reach his goal of becoming a personal financial advisor, Geoffrey has enrolled in the Finance Program at Northside University. All of his classes meet one night per week. He knows it will take a few years to complete his degree on a part-time basis, but he is willing to put forth the effort to achieve his career goal.

He has talked to several personal financial advisors and researched position announcements to learn what is expected in the career. Geoffrey looks forward to an increased salary, of course, but knowing he will be able to continue interacting with people by helping them choose retirement options also appeals to him.

To help him prepare for his future career, Geoffrey has asked for more responsibilities in his current position. Additional responsibilities include researching and recommending 401(k) investment strategies to help employees reach financial security in retirement. These additional duties will give him experience that can be applied to his new position.

Upper Rungs to Consider

Geoffrey is smart to use his current position to learn as much as he can to help him move toward his career goal. Although he enjoys his current job, he knows he needs to strive for a higher-paying position to save more for retirement. Thus, he will continue his education to improve his chances of working in a field he enjoys while earning more money.

Preparing for the Climb

As noted, a career in financial planning involves research and analytical skills along with good communication and language skills. These are good skills for any job. Are there things you can do now to improve your skills in these areas?

5.1

Insure Your Retirement

Insurance Scene

Martez Chamblee is a recent college graduate with a degree in Insurance and Finance. He has two job opportunities. Boltman Insurance Company offers a minimal benefits package, but the annual salary is $5,000 higher than the second job opportunity. The second job, Racey Financial Services, offers an outstanding benefits package, including a 401(k) and stock options, but it pays less. If you were to help Martez decide which job to accept based purely on the combined worth of the salary and benefits package, which job would you recommend he take and why?

LIFE EXPECTANCY: THE NEW FRONTIER • • • • • • • • • • • •

Retirement as many people hope to enjoy it today is a period of life devoted not to earning a living but to active leisure—"the golden years." Retirement American style requires wealth. Throughout human history, there has never been such a large, prosperous middle class as now exists in the United States and other industrialized nations.

Even if they could afford to, relatively few people in the past lived long enough to retire. Without antibiotics, vaccines, and modern sanitation, people in early history could easily die of a simple cut if it became infected. Measles, influenza, smallpox, cholera, typhoid, dysentery, and other contagious and infectious diseases regularly swept through human settlements. Complications of childbirth killed many women. A diagnosis of pneumonia or tuberculosis was a death sentence for an entire town. People who lived to old age were the exception, not the norm, and most people did not have reason, even if they had financial resources, to plan for "the golden years."

Money: Don't Retire Without It

If you knew you were going to die before you stopped earning a living, or if you knew you could keep working until you died, then you wouldn't need to plan for retirement. If you lived in a culture where it was taken for granted your children would care for you in your old age, you might not need to plan your retirement so carefully.

Today the average American lives 18 years in retirement. Therefore, a sizable portion of our population lives 20 or more years after retiring. Many of these seniors remain active, traveling, engaging in vigorous exercise, or perhaps embarking on a second career. Most retirees want to live in their own homes and pursue interests they didn't have time for when they were working and raising families. This requires a substantial amount of money. That's why people pay into retirement plans: to ensure that when they stop working, they will have enough money to live where they want, do what they want, and pass on some financial resources to their children.

PHOTODISC/GETTY IMAGES

Thinking about Tomorrow

A retirement plan, like insurance, transfers risk. You buy health insurance when you're healthy to protect yourself financially in case you become seriously ill or injured. Similarly, you pay into a retirement plan when you're young in case you live long enough to retire from work and are no longer receiving a paycheck. As with health insurance, you can buy into a retirement plan on your own or through an employer. Many people do both.

The basic idea behind a retirement plan is that you, and/or your employer, make payments into your personal retirement account or a pension fund. The money is invested and earns interest. Your share of the pension fund or retirement account grows because of the payments being deposited, plus what it earns in interest. Because the money is in a retirement fund, it is **tax-deferred**—that is, you don't pay the taxes until the money is distributed, usually upon retirement. When you retire, you receive the accumulated funds. Some retirement benefits are distributed to you in a lump sum. Others may be distributed according to various payment schedules. You pay taxes on the money when you receive it.

Your Retirement Fund Belongs to You   You buy insurance for health protection, and whether or not you receive benefits by using the insurance, what you paid in premiums is never seen again. In a retirement plan, you do get your money back. If you die before the fund is distributed, your beneficiaries receive the money that was paid in, plus some or all of the earnings on the money to that point, depending on the terms of the plan.

flat world...

Retirement Packages Abroad

In many foreign countries, employers do not provide workers with any form of savings or retirement packages, only wages. Employees must plan for future expenses by saving part of their monthly take-home pay. In contrast, many U.S. employers, unions, and professional associations require employees to contribute to some kind of savings or retirement plan to help protect family assets and prepare for future medical emergencies. Millions of U.S. full-time workers, ages 18–64, are enrolled in some kind of retirement plan with matching funds provided by the employer.

Think Critically Why might you choose to work for a company in another country that did not provide savings or a retirement plan instead of a U.S. company that provides these options? How would you plan to protect family assets and to pay for medical emergencies?

Thinking about Today

One of the advantages of paying into a retirement account is that your payments are made in pre-tax dollars. At income tax time, this means your taxable income is reduced, and you will pay less income tax—federal, state, and local. For example, if your wages total $45,000 and you have paid $8,000 into your retirement account, your taxable earnings are $37,000, not $45,000. At the 25 percent tax rate, that saves you $2,000 in federal income tax, plus savings on your state and local taxes. There are maximum amounts you can personally contribute in combination with your employer's contribution.

The contribution you make to your retirement account grows (if you have invested wisely) for 20, 30, 40, or however many years until the funds are distributed to you in retirement. The fund's earnings are not taxed during this time because the tax has been deferred. When the funds are distributed, you must pay taxes. However, when you retire, you will more than likely be in a lower tax bracket and will pay fewer taxes than you would have at the height of your earning power. Therefore, the government encourages you to save now for your retirement later. The combined value of the tax reduction and tax-deferred earnings from long-term investment is an extremely powerful financial tool.

Name two ways in which retirement plans are similar to health insurance.

EMPLOYER RETIREMENT PLANS ● ● ● ● ● ● ● ● ● ● ● ● ● ● ● ● ● ●

Many employers, particularly larger employers, offer retirement plans. Employers can do this for a reasonable cost, which is determined by the number of employees. The larger the group of employees, the lower the cost to both employers and employees. This is similar to other types of insurance.

Employers offer retirement benefits, like all benefits, to attract skilled employees. Offering retirement benefits is not required but is considered a positive social benefit. The retirement plans help employees save for the future to assist them in providing for themselves and their families after retirement. Of course, the company plans are considered a business expense and reduce taxable income for the employer. Depending on the employer and how badly it wants to attract employees to certain positions, the employer may offer no retirement benefits, a single plan, or a number of different types of retirement plans. Depending on an employee's particular situation, some plans or combinations of plans will work better than others.

Advantages of Employer Retirement Plans

Like group health plans, employer retirement plans, because of their size, provide employees opportunities for a better return on their retirement investment than they might be able to get individually. The savings vehicles have likely been screened for soundness. Employer plans might also offer investment and savings vehicles—401(k)s, 403(b)s, SEP-IRAs, or employee stock options—not available to an individual outside the company. A large employer's plan typically offers options for employees to diversify their retirement accounts. Employees can likely put some money into options with a modest but low-risk return and some in stocks or mutual funds that have a higher risk but might yield a higher return.

PHOTODISC/GETTY IMAGES

Your income needs should be lower during retirement because your children will be self-sufficient, work-related issues such as commuting and meal expenses will be reduced, mortgages may be paid off, and you will be in a lower tax bracket. ■

Payments you make into your retirement account are automatically deducted from your paycheck, which encourages saving. Also, most employers offering retirement plans make matching payments (contributions) into the employee's account. For example, an employer may contribute 3 percent of your salary to match your 6 percent contribution. Employer contributions dramatically increase the return on your contribution. Some retirement plans, such as pension funds and SEP-IRAs, are funded entirely by contributions from the employer.

Government Protection   Although employers are not required to establish retirement plans, they are strongly encouraged. **ERISA**, the Employee Retirement Income Security Act of 1974, protects retirement plan participants. ERISA sets and enforces minimum standards to ensure employee benefit plans are managed in a fair and financially sound manner for the benefit of participants and their beneficiaries. The act ensures that participants receive promised benefits, that funds are protected under the terms of the law, and that no employees are unfairly denied benefits. Employers are also required to provide participants with a Summary Plan Description, the plan's rules and restrictions in writing, and other documents.

The provisions of ERISA are enforced by the **Pension Benefit Guaranty Corporation (PBGC)**, a federal corporation, and the Internal Revenue Service. Approximately 45 million American workers and retirees are protected by PBGC. Remember that ERISA protects only employer-sponsored programs. If you purchase or are contributing to retirement savings plans on your own, these plans are probably not covered by ERISA. Therefore, you must investigate and be careful when buying into commercially available savings vehicles or retirement accounts.

Disadvantages of Employer Retirement Plans

Employer retirement plans may have disadvantages. There are typically many components of retirement plans over which you do not have control. For example, you do not control how much the employer contributes and the types of savings options within the plan. Carefully review a company's retirement plan before accepting a job.

Sometimes You Can't Take It With You   It is important to remember not all employer-sponsored plans are transferable. Traditional pension plans, for example, are not transferable. If you leave one job with a pension plan, your company retirement benefits stay with that employer. Changing jobs often may result in your having no or few retirement funds if you do not have other retirement options.

Many employers who fund pension plans reward employees who have longevity with the organization. The distribution of funds to the pension plan may be based on years of service as well as salary. Usually employers require employees to become vested in a plan. **Vested** means you have worked for the employer a certain number of years. For example, if full vesting is defined as working five years for the company, you would be 20 percent vested after the first year of service, 40 percent vested after the second year, and so on.

If you change jobs after having been employed for a set period of time, you may be vested in the plan. It may then be possible to leave your retirement funds behind with the employer but still draw from that retirement fund at a later date, typically normal retirement age.

Sometimes You Can Take It With You   Some retirement plans permit you to take the funds you contributed and any interest earned on those funds if you leave the company. However, if you leave before a designated number of years, you will receive none of the contributions made by the employer. Other retirement plans permit you to transfer your funds into a different plan when you leave the company for another job. Investigate your retirement plan completely and be aware of any restrictions.

Buying an Individual Plan

If you are self-employed, you may need to buy an individual retirement plan. You may also work for a small employer who does not provide a retirement plan. Even if you have a group plan through your employer, it

may not be completely diversified and portable, so you may wish to purchase additional retirement protection.

Certain kinds of plans—traditional pension plans, 401(k), 403(b), or SEP-IRA— are not available to individuals. Most people buying individual retirement

plans open an IRA (Individual Retirement Account), buy an annuity or annuities, or invest in stocks through a mutual fund structured for retirement purposes.

 checkpoint

Describe how employers benefit by offering employees a retirement plan.

_____

_____

_____

assessment 5.1

Think Critically

1. Why do you think retirement plans are considered a positive social benefit?

_____

_____

_____

2. Why is it important for retirement plan contributions to be pre-tax?

_____

_____

_____

3. List four kinds of retirement plans that are not available to individuals.

_____

_____

Make Academic Connections

4. **ANTHROPOLOGY** Research ways people in different cultures handle old age. Choose a culture you find particularly interesting and write a report or prepare an oral presentation. What insights into your own culture does learning about the other culture give you?

5. **COMMUNICATION** Interview three workers who have different job descriptions and work for different employers. Ask each one about the employer's retirement benefits. Determine specific benefits offered, the employee's personal opinion of the benefits, and what should be changed, if anything. Write a one-page report about your findings.

6. **ORAL HISTORY** Interview two elderly people, over age 80 if possible, about their grandparents, great-grandparents, and other elderly people-from their past. Ask your interviewees to compare their health, activity levels, financial situation, living situation, and general quality of life with those of the elderly people they knew. Condense the interviews or write a one-page report about insights you have gained about aging.

 Teamwork

Work in groups to discuss people you know who are currently employed and people who are retired. Make a list of living expenses for each group. How do expenses differ? Is one greater than the other?

Types of Plans

5.2

goals

+ Describe the basic types of employer-sponsored retirement plans.
+ Describe retirement plans available to individuals.

terms

+ diversify
+ pension plans
+ 401(k)
+ rollover
+ 403(b)
+ SEP-IRA
+ annuity
+ IRA

Insurance Scene

Janet Smith has been a stay-at-home mom for the past seven years. Her husband is self-employed. They have been paying a high rate for individual health insurance and need to begin contributing to a retirement plan. Janet is in the market for a job with a good benefits package. Before she actively seeks employment, she needs to learn more about retirement plan options so she can determine which benefit package fits her needs best. What are these options?

Employer-Sponsored Retirement Plans

There are several ways to save for retirement. No one plan is best for every person. Individuals have different savings goals depending, for example, on whether they have children, a spouse, or other dependents. People also have different investment styles. At one extreme, some people choose to invest their retirement savings in high-risk, but potentially very lucrative, stocks or mutual funds. At the other extreme, there are people who contribute all their savings into risk-free, but low-yield, vehicles and leave the funds there for an extended time.

Neither extreme is the smartest way to save for retirement. The high-risk stocks may never earn a penny and might even lose all the money invested. Low-yield earnings will be safe but might lose ground to inflation, even though the principal will increase substantially over 20, 30, or 40 years. Therefore, as a smart consumer, you must investigate all options for investing.

Learn about Investments

When you choose to contribute to a retirement plan, you are making a critical step in investing for your future. You should not do this without knowing how any more than you would drive a car out on the highway without having learned how to drive. Basic information about principal, interest, and yield must be understood. You need to know about stocks and mutual funds, bonds and bond funds, Treasury bills, certificates of deposit (CDs), money market accounts, and more. You must be aware of and understand service fees, management fees, and finance charges and how these are deducted from your investment. Perhaps most important of all, you

need to realize that investment and savings vehicles are products that make money for the people and institutions selling them to you. These institutions are for-profit organizations, and their own financial welfare is essential to their success. Explore all options to make sure the investment is one that meets your needs now and in the future. To do this, you need to be an educated and savvy consumer.

Diversify

Ideally, the funds you save for your retirement should be invested in such a way that they are safe from risk and yield a high return. Unfortunately, with investments, you can rarely have it both ways with the same type of savings or investment vehicle. Certificates of deposit, for example, are completely safe if the institution that issues them is insured through the Federal Deposit Insurance Corporation (FDIC), but they often yield a small percent of interest. However, you may earn a high percent of interest on high-risk stock, but if the stock market drops, you may lose money. Therefore, when investing, it is important to diversify, or spread risk among many types of investments.

Retirement plans differ among employers. A company with 2,000 employees will be able to offer more benefits than a company with 20 employees. The best employer retirement plans offer you options in how your retirement funds are invested. You can then decide how to diversify the money in your account among investments for growth, income, and capital preservation.

Basic Employer Plans

Some types of retirement plans are only available through an employer. These plans are *tax-deferred*, meaning you pay no taxes on them until they are distributed or withdrawn. Tax-deferred funds reduce your taxable income. Tax-deferred savings plans are an important investment tool the government gives citizens to encourage saving for retirement.

Pension Plans

At one time, pension plans were the most traditional type of retirement plan. They are not as common today because of the expense to the employer. They are also called *defined-benefit plans*, because it is determined ahead of time how much you are going to be paid. In such plans, after you have become vested by working for the employer a certain number of years, you have earned the rights to the benefits accumulated. At that point, the employer guarantees you a certain amount of income every year in retirement, determined by a formula that includes your years of service and your salary. Employees do not contribute to a pension plan.

The Downside to Pension Plans Generally, with pension plans, all the investment decisions are made by the employer or whomever the employer hires to manage the plan, and you have no input. A pension plan may be managed jointly by the employer and a union or professional association. The biggest drawback is its lack of transferability. If you leave the employer, you leave your retirement fund behind. In today's workplace where employees change jobs more frequently than in the past or are downsized by the employer, this can be a significant issue for employees. If you have been with an employer many years, you might feel as if you are stuck and can't leave because you would be losing too much money. If a company is bought out or restructured, there is no guarantee the pension agreement will stay the same. Changes can be made. In fact, the employer has the right to reduce the pension at any time as long as you are notified.

401(k) Plans

A **401(k)** is an employer-sponsored *defined-contribution plan* offered by corporations to its employees, which allows employees to set aside tax-deferred income for retirement purposes. In 1978, the Revenue Act introduced the 401(k) as a new way to save. The name "401(k)" refers to the section of the Internal Revenue Code that provides details about the plan. Both the employer and the employee can make contributions to a 401(k). Contributions are made in pre-tax dollars, so taxes are deferred until funds are withdrawn. Employer contributions are optional, but most employers make contributions to participating employees' accounts. The contribution ranges from 25 to 100 percent of the employee's contribution. For example, a company might contribute 3 percent when you contribute 6 percent (50 percent of your contribution). Taking advantage of an employer's contribution as you contribute increases your earnings.

tech talk

Online Services

Employees may now view payroll information, as well as employer benefits, and enroll in or change some benefit programs online. Employees can diversify funds by making changes to 401(k) investment choices and also request loans. Websites have checklists for employees to use to review current market data and select general benefits, insurance plans, and retirement savings options. Online access allows employees to rate existing services and rate the quality of information provided about compensation and benefits.

Think Critically Do you think employees would prefer to use online services versus traditional human resources services? Why or why not? How can these online services assist the employer?

"communicate"

Employees can change the status of their benefits packages based on the changing economy and their personal circumstances. As an employee, you want to make a major change in your monthly savings contributions to your 401(k) plan. Write a memo to the human resources department communicating the changes you wish to make.

The Economic Growth and Tax Relief Reconciliation Act (EGTRRA) of 2001 was key legislation in reducing tax rates and simplifying retirement plan rules for IRA, 401(k), 403(b), and pension plans. In 2008, for 401(k) plans, employees under the age of 50 could contribute $15,500 annually, and those age 50 and older could contribute $20,500 annually.

Other advantages of the 401(k) are that the funds are transferable when you leave your employer, as long as you choose a direct rollover. A **rollover** is a transfer of the funds into a retirement plan offered by your new employer or into a rollover IRA you've opened on your own. It is important to follow the rules for rollovers carefully to avoid taxes and penalties.

Loans and Early Withdrawals Some plans permit you, once you have enough money invested in your 401(k), to take out a loan against your own funds and then repay it, with interest. Basically you are making a loan to yourself. However, it is best to leave your money in your 401(k) because your money is not growing for you if you take it out.

The 401(k) is designed to be paid out to you between age 59½ and age 70½. You may choose to have the benefits distributed at age 59½, but must begin withdrawing at age 70½. There are exceptions to this rule if you become disabled. You will pay a penalty for early withdrawal (before 59½) as well as taxes on the extra income. It is best not to withdraw your 401(k) savings early because you may need the funds for retirement.

The Downside to 401(k)s One disadvantage to a 401(k) is that it is somewhat expensive for the employer to initially set up the plan for employees. Therefore, 401(k) plans are typically only offered by larger employers. Another disadvantage is the early withdrawal penalties. It can be costly to access your 401(k) savings before age 59½. Also, the benefits are not guaranteed. If the investment options you choose do poorly, you can actually lose money. However, most people will invest for 20 to 40 years, minimizing fluctuations in the stock market. Historically, stocks have outperformed all other forms of investment, and the compounding effect of consistent contributions over a long period of time can be quite dramatic.

403(b) Plans

A **403(b)** plan is a tax-deferred retirement plan designed for employees of certain nonprofit institutions, including health care, religious, scientific, and educational institutions and organizations. The 403(b) plans are often referred to as "401(k)s for nonprofits," but there are some differences. Employees typically choose 403(b) plans to supplement a pension. The maximum amount an employee can contribute is increasing over the years, as with a 401(k).

SEP-IRA

SEP-IRA, Simplified Employee Pension Individual Retirement Account, is a retirement plan set up by employers to which only employers can contribute funds. Individuals who are self-employed may also set up and contribute to SEP-IRAs. Financial institutions may require the employee to establish a traditional IRA which will be labeled as a SEP-IRA, so that the employer may contribute to the account. Employers make tax-deductible contributions to SEP-IRAs on behalf of the employees. The employees, as with other retirement plans, do not pay taxes on the SEP-IRA funds until they withdraw the funds.

Other Advantages to Employer-Sponsored Plans

In addition to the advantages already discussed, an employer retirement plan also offers the following benefits:

- Access to professional financial planners at no additional cost

- Periodic assessments and updates regarding the status of accounts

- Employee educational seminars

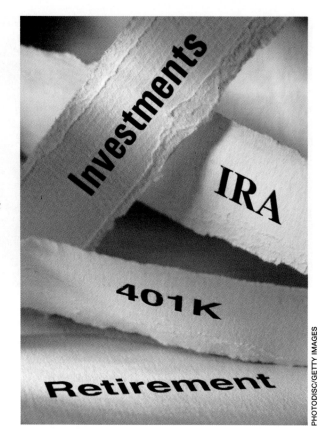

PHOTODISC/GETTY IMAGES

✔ checkpoint

Describe three important factors of a 401(k).

_____

_____

_____

INDIVIDUAL RETIREMENT PLANS ● ● ● ● ● ● ● ● ● ● ● ● ● ● ● ●

If you are self-employed, or if your employer does not offer retirement benefits, you can buy into tax-deferred retirement savings plans on your own. Annuities and IRAs are set up for this reason.

Annuities

Many employer retirement plans offer an annuity option. However, individuals may buy annuities on an individual basis as well. An **annuity**, like other insurance, is a legal contract with an insurance company that provides for either a lump-sum payment or a series of payments. In exchange for payment of premiums, the insurer promises to pay you a certain amount of money, in a lump sum or through periodic payments, for a specified period.

PHOTODISC/GETTY IMAGES

Annuities are popular products that, if carefully chosen, can help reduce current taxable income, provide future income for retirement, and accumulate cash reserves for emergencies. Earnings are tax-deferred as long as you do not withdraw funds from the account before the annuity matures. Annuities are generally available for purchase in two basic types: *fixed* and *variable*. All annuities have advantages and disadvantages to consider when making purchasing decisions.

Annuity features vary among insurers. Therefore, it is essential to research any annuity thoroughly before you make a purchasing decision. The research process gives you the perfect opportunity to comparison shop. It is critical to investigate a company's ratings and the agent's knowledge and experience before you invest in the long-term relationship of an annuity. Buy only from an experienced, reputable agent with a top-rated company.

Fixed Annuity   Sometimes called a *fixed rate annuity*, this type of annuity offers a stable return based on current interest rates. Annual yields are guaranteed for a specified period of time. The insurer guarantees you will earn a minimum rate of interest during a fixed amount of time agreed upon by both of you. The principal is guaranteed by the insurer, and payments may be made over a certain period, such as 20 years, or an indefinite period, such as your lifetime.

Variable Annuity   Variable annuities provide an opportunity for investing in a wide range of stocks, bonds, mutual funds, and other securities where earnings may increase or decrease over time. Buying a variable annuity enables you, the investor, to manage your own investments if you want, moving money from one source to another based on your tax needs. Some variable annuities have a fund manager to make those decisions. In either case, a variable annuity shifts the risk of the investment to you, meaning you might do very well, or you might lose money on your investment. The amount of periodic payments will be determined based on the performance of your investment. Variable annuities should be researched carefully before you buy.

Defer Your Annuity   Annuities can be set up for immediate payment, but typically annuities are purchased by individuals who want to guarantee a future minimum income during retirement. For retirement plan purposes, *deferred annuities* are typically purchased because payout is meant for the future. Both fixed and variable annuities may be deferred, so don't be confused by the terms "variable deferred annuity" or "fixed deferred annuity."

Individual Retirement Accounts (IRAs)

An **IRA**, or Individual Retirement Account, is another type of savings plan designed to help individuals save for retirement. There are two basic types: traditional IRAs and Roth IRAs.

Traditional IRAs

Anyone younger than 70½ who has earned income can open an IRA. Traditional IRAs are tax-deferred retirement funds that permit you to contribute up to a certain amount of earned income. The federal government imposes contribution limits on IRA accounts. In 2008, $5,000 was the annual limit for individuals age 49 and below, and $6,000 was the annual limit for those age 50 and above. After 2008, the limit for contributions will raise in increments of $500 depending on inflation. Taxpayers age 50 or over may also make "catch up" contributions of $1,000 or less.

Deductibility Criteria   IRAs may be tax-deductible depending on several factors such as income and tax-filing status. If you do not participate in an employer-sponsored retirement plan and your income is low enough, you can deduct your entire IRA contribution and reduce your year's taxes. If your income falls into a higher category, you can deduct part of your contribution. If your salary is too high, you cannot take the tax deduction, but your IRA can still grow, tax-deferred until the funds are withdrawn, at which time they are assessed as income and taxed.

Rollovers, Withdrawals, and Distribution   IRAs are easily transferred between financial organizations and rolled over into a new account. Distribution must be taken between the time you are 59½ and 70½. Early withdrawal before age 59½ is heavily penalized (typically 10 percent) except in cases of hardship, such as death, disability, or loss of your job, in which case you are not penalized but must still pay taxes due.

Roth IRAs

In 1997, Congress passed the Taxpayer Relief Act, which provided more flexibility and options for saving, such as the Roth IRA. Roth IRAs are similar to traditional IRAs but with several distinct differences.

- Contributions are not tax-deductible

- Income limits are higher

- You do not have to withdraw funds at age 70½, and you can continue to contribute to a Roth IRA after you are 70½ if you have earned income.

- Principal contributions can be withdrawn at any time without penalty. However, earnings withdrawn before an initial five-year holding period and before the recipient reaches age 59½ will be penalized.

The most dramatic feature of a Roth IRA is that it reverses the traditional defer-taxes-until-retirement formula. You pay taxes on the funds you invest in your Roth IRA. You do not pay taxes on the distribution, so the earnings are tax-free.

Comparing Retirement Plans

When choosing which type of retirement plan to open, research each type for changes in contributions and withdrawals based on current U.S. tax laws. The chart below demonstrates features to review. Amounts provided are subject to change yearly.

	401(k)	Traditional IRA	Roth IRA
Who sets up?	Employer	Individual	Individual
Taxes	Contributions tax-deferred; distributions taxed.	Contributions are tax-deductible (limited by income and participation in pension or 401 plans); distributions are taxed.	Contributions are taxed; distributions are tax-free.
Income Limits*	Typically none	Single: Full Contribution—$53,000 Single: Partial Contribution—$63,000 Married: Full Contribution—$85,000 Married: Partial Contribution—$105,000	Single: Full Contribution—$101,000 Single: Partial Contribution—$116,000 Married: Full Contribution—$159,000 Married: Partial Contribution—$169,000
Contribution Limits	Under 50: $15,500; 50 or over: $20,500; Employee and employer combined contributions must not exceed 100% of employee's salary or $46,000, whichever is less.	Under 50: $5,000; 50 or over: $6,000; Limits are total for traditional and Roth IRA contributions combined.	Under 50: $5,000; 50 or over: $6,000; Limits are total for traditional and Roth IRA contributions combined.
Matching Contributions	Yes	No	No
Distributions	Can begin at 59½; must begin withdrawing at 70½ unless still employed.	Can begin at 59½; must begin withdrawing at 70½.	Can begin at 59½ if contributions have been in the account for at least 5 years; no forced distribution.
Early Withdrawal	10% penalty plus taxes.	10% penalty plus taxes.	Principal allowed, but penalty on earnings.
Transferability	Rollover to another employer's 401(k) or traditional IRA.	Rollover to another financial institution's IRA.	Rollover to another financial institution's IRA.

*For a traditional IRA, these income limits apply if you are participating in an employer-sponsored retirement plan. If you do not participate in such a plan, often no income limits or much higher income limits apply.

 **checkpoint**

Describe the differences between traditional and Roth IRAs.

_____

_____

_____

assessment 5.2

Think Critically

1. Why should you be careful when buying an annuity?

_____

_____

2. List two benefits of IRAs.

_____

_____

3. List two benefits of 401(k)s.

_____

_____

Make Academic Connections

4. **RESEARCH**   Using the Internet, media center, or other research sources, investigate the Taxpayer Relief Act of 1997 and the Economic Growth and Tax Relief Reconciliation Act of 2001. Answer the following questions in a one-page report. Do you think these acts helped taxpayers? Why or why not? How do they affect you? What do you believe is the single most important regulation in each act?

5. **STOCK MARKET**   Some companies offer preferred stock as an employee retirement benefit. Is this an effective retirement planning mechanism? Using the Internet or business reference, identify two companies offering stock benefits. Track the price of the stocks for one month and report your findings.

6. **CONSUMERISM**   Variable annuities are coming under fire from consumer groups who feel some insurers are selling products without adequately informing buyers of risks involved. There is also concern over high management fees and expenses. Research this issue and write a brief report, or if you prefer, make a poster explaining to consumers what they should know before they purchase a variable annuity.

 **Teamwork**

In groups, make a list of features that would be of importance in a retirement plan, such as availability of funds for loans. Compare your list with that of other groups. Which features are most popular? Discuss why.

5.3 Plan for Retirement

Insurance Scene

Aubrey Wintermeier, 38 years old, is analyzing his retirement plan. He is thinking about starting his own business and leaving his present employer. However, he will have to leave his retirement fund. He would still earn interest on the fund but could no longer contribute to it, nor would the employer contribute to the fund. Aubrey understands he would not make much money in the beginning when his new business is getting started, and the risk may cause him a meager lifestyle in retirement. He wants to review his projected Social Security benefits to determine whether he can afford to leave his employer and take a chance on a new career without facing retirement with little income. How can Aubrey find out what his projected Social Security benefits will be?

SOCIAL SECURITY BENEFITS •

Social Security is a federal insurance program providing aid to those who are eligible for benefits, including the retired, the disabled, or the widow/widower or child of someone deceased who is eligible for benefits. Social Security was signed into law in 1935 and has become an important component in the American way of life. You are eligible to receive Social Security retirement benefits if you have worked 40 quarters (ten years) at jobs for which Social Security tax was collected on your wages and have reached retirement age according to the Social Security guidelines. For example, if you were born in 1955, the retirement age is 66 years and 2 months; however, if you were born in 1960 or later, the retirement age is 67. You are also eligible if you were married for ten years or more to a spouse now deceased who was eligible to collect Social Security.

The amount of your Social Security benefit reflects your work history. It is calculated using the Average Indexed Monthly Earnings (AIME), which is based on an average of the 35 years you earned the most. Generally speaking, the more paid into your Social Security account, either because you paid for many years or because your wages were high, the more you will receive. However, there is a maximum benefit limit. Social Security should be only one component of your retirement plan because the average yearly benefit at full retirement is approximately 40 percent of your annual salary.

To calculate your estimated Social Security benefits, the following guidelines are provided on the Social Security Administration website.

Step 1   Add each of the worker's highest 35 years of earning up to the year the worker reaches age 60. Then, average that number by dividing by 35.

Step 2   To calculate the AIME, divide the number in Step 1 by 12.

Step 3   Apply the following formula to the AIME.

- 90 percent of the first $627, plus
- 32 percent of the AIME over $627 through $3,779, plus
- 15 percent of the AIME above $3,779.

In 2008, the Social Security tax for both employers and their employees earning up to approximately $100,000 was 6.2 percent each. Therefore, a total of 12.4 percent of your wages is paid as Social Security taxes. If you are self-employed, you are responsible for the 12.4 percent Social Security tax yourself because you are the employer and employee. You can contact the Social Security Administration to find out how much you've paid into Social Security throughout your working life and calculate your estimated benefits upon retirement age. When you turn 40, the Social Security Administration automatically sends you a statement outlining your expected benefit amount based on your working life to date.

Longevity Creep   Currently most people begin to collect Social Security benefits at age 65, but if you retire earlier, you may choose to receive a reduced benefit beginning at age 62. This reduced benefit is approximately 80 percent of the full benefit amount. Due to the large number of retirees and increased longevity after retirement age, the age at which retired workers are eligible to receive full benefits has gradually increased to age 67 for those born after 1959. Social Security benefits are paid beginning at your designated retirement age and continue as long as you live. At your death, if you are survived by a spouse or ex-spouse eligible to continue collecting your benefits, that person can do so unless he or she is already collecting Social Security in his or her own right.

PHOTODISC/GETTY IMAGES

How Much Will It Pay?   Even if you receive full benefits by waiting until full retirement age, your Social Security benefits may only be about 40 percent of your total earnings. However, the percent of earnings depends on your earnings over the 40 quarters. Social Security is not designed to provide total retirement income. It is intended as a supplement to savings

PHOTODISC/GETTY IMAGES

Many people do not understand how Social Security works. Access www.cengage.com/school/pfinance/ insurance and click on the link for Chapter 5. Review this website to brief yourself on facts about Social Security. Review topics such as what you need to know about Social Security while working. After reviewing the site, what are some things you think are important and could share with others to help them understand Social Security?

www.cengage.com/school/pfinance/insurance

and a pension or retirement plan. Also, remember that if your income is high enough, your Social Security income is taxable.

Will Social Security Be There for You?   Two of the most important features of a retirement plan are security and predictability. A successful retirement plan is usually thought to include savings, assets, a pension/401(k) plan, and Social Security. It is essential to make plans to insure yourself and your family so you will have enough money in retirement. Remember, Social Security funding will be challenged by the large group of aging baby boomers. There will be more people at retirement age; therefore, you must set financial goals and make decisions without relying on Social Security. Sound financial planning now will provide alternative means of income in later years to compensate for reductions or changes made to Social Security benefits. Base your plan on the assumption you will live to be 100.

✔ **checkpoint**

In your own words, describe briefly how Social Security is calculated.

_____

_____

Ethics in Action

Nisha has planned for her retirement by contributing to a company annuity plan that has accumulated a large sum of money. Under the terms of the annuity, she can borrow against it for home improvement loans without a penalty. Nisha actually wants to borrow the money to buy a car. She knows this loan won't show up on her credit report.

Think Critically

Is Nisha acting ethically in misrepresenting her reasons for withdrawing money from her account? How could her actions change her annuity status in the future?

AN ECONOMICALLY SECURE RETIREMENT

Have you heard the saying "Good things come to those who wait"? This may be true in some aspects of life, but it won't get you far in retirement. Waiting too long to save for retirement is likely to lead to working longer or pinching pennies all through your 50s or 60s in a last-ditch effort to build your retirement fund.

Even in your teens, begin to develop a retirement strategy. Learn the basics of personal finance and begin your savings plan. Personal finance knowledge will not only help you plan for retirement but also help you become a wise consumer before you buy a car or get a credit card. Remember, before you can make complex investments, you need to know how to plan. And before you can plan, you need to develop financial skill: You need to know how to save.

Start Saving as Soon as Possible

It may be difficult to try to save for your retirement if you're struggling to pay college tuition, build a business, buy your first home, or start a family. But if you begin in your late teens or early 20s and put $10 a week into your retirement fund (savings account), and keep putting it there for the next 30 or 40 years, you will have accumulated an impressive total because of the power of compound interest. Saving money early is the single smartest thing you can do to help secure your retirement.

Compound interest, which is interest paid on the ever-increasing total of principal and interest, is an effective tool for saving. The weekly amount you save is not necessarily as important as the fact that the money compounds for three or four decades. Start saving early, and your retirement savings will surpass those of your peers who put away much more a week, but do not start saving seriously until their late 30s or 40s. If, as your earning power grows, you deposit larger amounts into your account, and keep doing so, you can accumulate a sufficient amount for retirement.

Insurance Math *Connection*

Compare simple interest and compound interest to see why investments grow so dramatically over time. Harold lends $1,000 to Fred, who agrees to pay Harold back in five years at 10% interest. How much money does Harold lose by loaning $1,000 to Fred instead of investing it and earning 10% interest compounded annually?

Solution

The formula for calculating simple interest is

$$\text{Principal} \times \text{Rate} \times \text{Time} = \text{Interest}$$
$$\$1,000 \times 0.10 \times 5 = \$500$$

Fred pays Harold back his $1,000 principal, plus $500 interest, so Harold has $1,500.

If Harold had instead placed $1,000 in a savings vehicle paying 10% interest compounded annually, the formula would look like this.

$$\text{Principal} \times (1 + \text{Rate})^{\text{Time}} = \text{Future Value}$$
$$\$1,000 \times (1 + 0.10)^5 = \text{Future Value}$$
$$\$1,000 \times 1.10^5 = \$1,610.51$$

Since the principal was $1,000, the interest earned was $610.51. Compound interest yields a 22% higher return over the same time period ($610.51 compound interest compared to $500 simple interest).

Factors to Consider

Remember, you must make wise decisions early in life regarding projected savings for retirement. You must investigate savings for retirement and the cost of education for you and your dependents.

Estimate how much you will receive from your pension or other retirement plan, Social Security, savings, and investments. You do not want to outlive your assets because life expectancy rates are on the rise, as shown in the chart. To provide for economic security, you will need a minimum of 60 percent, and as much as 100 percent, of your pre-retirement income to live

U.S. Life Expectancy by Decade		
Year	*Males*	*Females*
1980	69.9	77.5
1985	71.1	78.2
1990	71.8	78.9
1995	72.4	79.0
2000	73.8	79.5
2005	74.6	80.0
2006	74.7	80.1
2007	74.9	80.1
2008	75.0	80.2
2009	75.2	80.3
2010	75.3	80.3

comfortably. An income that will keep pace with inflation is especially important after you retire. Start assessing how to provide for a more secure retirement by

- Participating in health/wellness programs

- Reviewing long-term care options

- Staying abreast of financial trends

- Saving

interesting *facts*

For every ten years you delay saving for retirement, you will need to save three times as much each month to catch up. ■

What about Early Retirement?

Many people fantasize about retiring early, but the reality may not be as pleasant as the fantasy. Early retirement may not be strictly voluntary, but may occur under pressure. Because businesses are constantly cutting costs, restructuring, and downsizing to increase profits, employers offer "early retirement" packages as incentives to encourage older, highly paid employees to retire sooner than planned. Incentives offered by employers might include a **severance payment**, which is a lump sum of perhaps a year's salary or other designated amount and post-retirement medical coverage. Even though these incentive packages are expensive, in the long run, the employer will save money.

Factors to consider when contemplating a voluntary early retirement, or evaluating an early retirement package, include the following:

- Fewer working years in which to save

- More years over which to stretch retirement savings

- The psychological impact of not working

- Possible changes in Medicare/Social Security benefits

- Loss of health/dental insurance

- Need to reduce living expenses

- Retraining for a job that could provide part-time income

PHOTODISC/GETTY IMAGES

How Much Do You Need?

The sooner you begin planning your retirement, the better off you will be. Use this worksheet to give you a basic idea of the savings you'll need when you retire.

Sources of Annual Income	Amount in Dollars	Example
What is the annual income you want after retirement?	$	$90,000
Social Security	$	$19,200
Pension plan from employer	$	$46,000
Part-time job	$	$12,000
Other	$	$ 5,000
Total expected income	$	$82,200
Annual savings needed	$	$ 7,800

The difference between your annual desired income and your total expected income is how much you need to save each year to reach your desired retirement income.

Whether or not to take early retirement is not an easy decision. You must analyze your financial resources and estimate what your expenses might be after you retire. Consulting with a financial planner to guide you through the decision-making process is a wise choice. Calculate the amount you can expect to receive after you retire and the difference between that amount and the early retirement amount (based on receiving reduced benefits from Social Security and other retirement plans due to early retirement or early withdrawal)—how will that difference decide your future lifestyle?

 checkpoint

Why is taking an early retirement a difficult decision?

assessment 5.3

Think Critically

1. List four factors to consider when planning for retirement.

2. Why should you start saving for retirement at an early age?

3. Why is the age at which you are eligible to receive full Social Security benefits being increased?

4. List four components of an economically successful retirement.

Make Academic Connections

5. **SOCIAL HISTORY**   By the 1930s, the problem of poverty among the elderly had become severe. Visit the Social Security Administration's "Brief History" pages (www.ssa.gov/history). Write a report, create a poster, or make a presentation about poverty among the elderly.

6. **COMMUNICATION**   Interview two or three people who are self-employed. Ask how they are planning for retirement. Write a report on your findings.

7. **CREATIVE WRITING**   Some people don't retire at all. They may love their jobs and want to keep working, or they may not be able to afford to stop working. Write a story about a person who doesn't intend to retire.

 **Teamwork**

As a group, explore the power of compound interest. Imagine someone saves $50 a month in an account paying 5 percent interest compounded annually. How much money has accumulated after one year? After 10? After 20? After 30? After 40? Compare the total to that of someone who saves $100 a month for 20 years.

chapter 5 assessment

Chapter Summary

5.1 Insure Your Retirement

A. It is necessary to start saving money and choosing investments in early adulthood to ensure financial security in retirement. Tax-deferred retirement plans are powerful investment tools.

B. Workers should take full advantage of available employer-sponsored group retirement plans. Workers to whom employer plans are not available should investigate individual retirement plans.

5.2 Types of Plans

A. Defined-benefit plans, such as pension plans, and defined-contribution plans, such as 401(k)s and 403(b)s, are only available from employers. SEP-IRAs are also only available from employers.

B. If an employer does not offer retirement benefits, individuals can purchase various kinds of annuities and IRAs.

5.3 Plan for Retirement

A. Social Security benefits, combined with savings, investments, retirement plan benefits, and other assets form the basis of a sound retirement plan.

B. In planning for retirement, it is important to consider individual needs, goals, and assets and to start saving early.

Vocabulary Builder

a. AIME
b. annuity
c. compound interest
d. diversify
e. ERISA
f. IRA
g. Pension Benefit Guaranty Corporation (PBGC)
h. pension plan
i. rollover
j. SEP-IRA
k. severance payment
l. Social Security
m. tax-deferred
n. vested
o. 401(k)
p. 403(b)

Choose the term that best fits the definition. Write the letter of the answer in the space provided. Some terms may not be used.

_____ 1. Retirement savings plan in which the employer can match the employee's contribution

_____ 2. Taxes are not paid until money is distributed

_____ 3. Sets standards for employer-sponsored retirement plans

_____ 4. Interest paid on the ever-increasing total of principal and interest

_____ 5. Enforces ERISA standards

_____ 6. Individual retirement plan

_____ 7. Contract with an insurance company to provide a lump-sum payment or a series of payments

_____ 8. Transfer of funds from one tax-deferred plan to another

_____ 9. Government program to assist in retirement

_____10. The right to keep benefits you have accumulated after working a certain number of years

_____11. To spread risk among many types of investments

_____12. Average indexed monthly earnings

_____13. A lump sum of perhaps a year's salary or other designated amount offered to employees as an incentive to take early retirement

Review Concepts

14. Why is retirement a recently developed concept?

15. Why should employees contribute pre-tax dollars to a retirement plan?

16. Why might employer contributions to a retirement fund be referred to as "free money" for the employee?

17. Describe three differences between a traditional IRA and a Roth IRA.

18. Name two factors in calculating a pension benefit.

19. What is the main factor in calculating Social Security benefits?

20. What does it mean to be vested?

21. Why does inflation threaten your retirement?

Apply What You Learned

22. Why do you think Congress thought it was necessary to pass the Employee Retirement Income Security Act (ERISA)?

23. Describe ways to compare retirement options such as pensions, IRAs, annuities, 401(k)s, etc.

24. Describe a situation in which you might not choose to participate in your employer's retirement plan.

25. Describe why you should be cautious when buying a variable annuity.

26. Describe ideal retirement plan options from an employee's point of view.

27. Why would saving for retirement be even more important if you were going to put three children through college?

28. Why would you want to buy an annuity with a deferred payout instead of an immediate payout?

29. Why can a large employer offer more benefits than a company with only a few employees?

30. Why should you diversify your retirement investments?

31. Why might an employer offer you early retirement?

_____

_____

_____

32. Should you rely solely on Social Security for retirement? Why or why not?

_____

_____

_____

Make Academic Connections

33. **PUBLIC HEALTH**   In some countries, life expectancy is actually drop-
    ping rather than rising. What are the social implications of shorter life
    spans? Could the same phenomenon happen in the United States? Is
    there a common cause of decreasing life spans in different parts of the
    world? Choose a country, and using the library or the Internet, research
    this issue. Explore reasons why life expectancy is dropping and write a
    report, create a presentation, or make a poster describing your findings.

34. **RESEARCH**   Using the Internet, media center, interviews with ben-
    efits coordinators, and other research sources, choose one type of annu-
    ity, IRA, 401(k), or other benefit that may be included in a retirement
    plan. Create a one-page listing of the pros and cons of that benefit.
    Also, define and describe the benefit. Find other students in the class
    who researched the same benefit. Compare findings and as a group
    create an electronic presentation and present your findings to the class.

35. **EMPLOYMENT**   Search the Classified Ads section of the newspaper.
    Find ten employment ads that mention benefits offered. List these
    benefits, calculate which benefit was mentioned most often, second
    most often, and so on. Enter your data into a spreadsheet. Have other
    students add to your spreadsheet until you have an accumulation of all
    students' findings.

36. **PERSONAL FINANCE**   In groups of three, choose three or four stocks
    you think would be good ones to purchase now to help prepare for
    retirement. Keep track of the stocks for the rest of the term. Assum-
    ing you would have purchased $500 of each stock, what is the result?
    Create a one-page document explaining which stocks you chose and
    why. Also discuss the amount of money you would have gained or lost.
    Finally, conclude by stating whether you think the stock market is a
    good or bad investment for retirement and why.

37. **BUSINESS MATH**   Using the Internet, search for a "Retirement
    Calculator." Enter the information asked for to determine how much
    money you need to have upon retirement. Assuming you will not
    retire until you are 68 years old, how much do you need to save every
    year between now and age 68?

Insurance

6 Renter's and Homeowner's Insurance

6.1	Risks at Home
6.2	Basic Policy Types
6.3	Coverage and Claims

PHOTODISC/GETTY IMAGES

climbing the ladder

From Field Representative to Loss Control Specialist

Jake worked in a variety of business and manufacturing careers prior to accepting a field representative position with the Walton Insurance Company. His degree in management has served him well in past employment and currently provides him the opportunity to serve as a liaison between the insurance company and the agents and brokers.

As the field representative for Walton, he utilizes his strong interpersonal and management skills. He serves as an important resource for the company itself and the agents. Good communication skills are essential to his success.

He must be able to communicate effectively with those selling the company's products (agents and brokers) to ensure they understand the company's policies and practices. By educating the agents and brokers, conflicts among the company, policyholders, and the sales force are avoided.

Jake's position requires a lot of travel, which is becoming less appealing to him now that he has a family. Thus, recently, he has begun to investigate other career choices in the area of manufacturing and insurance. Although his bachelor's degree is in management, he has 15 years of experience in manufacturing and an additional 10 years of experience in the insurance industry. Through his experience, he has analyzed many situations in which loss occurred and ways it could have been avoided.

Therefore, he has decided to pursue a position as a loss control specialist. In this position, he would work for an insurance company to help minimize accidents and losses in the manufacturing industry. It would make good use of his insurance and manufacturing backgrounds. Jake would conduct a thorough examination of work areas and machinery and recommend safety procedures.

Such positions are at times labeled as safety engineers. Safety is a key issue in all industries, especially when insurance is involved. Jake may work with industrial firms or even public institutions to help prevent accidents and loss. Jake's ability to analyze situations and judge the potential for loss is essential to success in this type of position.

He is confident in his abilities and experience and is excited about the possibilities. He will begin applying for loss control specialist positions with his current company and other, larger insurance companies.

Upper Rungs to Consider

Jake finds his current position as a field representative rewarding and enjoys the interaction with others, but he is ready for a change. He continues to carry out the duties in his current job, enabling him to improve his analytical and communication skills.

Preparing for the Climb

Many careers demand analytical and communication skills. Are there things you can do now to improve your analytical and communication skills to help prepare you for a future career?

PHOTODISC

6.1

Risks at Home

Insurance Scene

Joe and Fernando are seniors in college and have decided to live in an apartment off campus. They have a couch, chair, two beds, their clothes, three televisions, DVD player and 200 DVDs, stereo system, desktop computer, laptop computer, kitchen items, and two bikes. They have talked about buying renter's insurance but would rather use the money for other things. If you were Joe or Fernando, would you buy renter's insurance? Why or why not?

RISK-FILLED HOMES

You've heard the saying "A man's home is his castle." Even life in a castle has risks, and if homeowner's insurance had been available to kings and queens who lived in castles, they would have bought it.

Because insurance is intangible—you do not actually see what you are getting—some individuals are not motivated to purchase insurance. Risks are intangible, too, and many times are not realized until you experience a loss or survive a close call.

Your home and its contents may not be at risk from an invading army or an outbreak of the plague, but they can meet with a variety of modern **perils**, or sources of danger that result in loss. Your home can burn down, blow up, be blown down, or be washed away. A tree can fall on it, or a vehicle could crash through the wall. Thieves can empty your home of all the appliances and antiques you own, or vandals can destroy your home and belongings. And if your home is so badly damaged you must move out for a period of time, there's the expense of lodging and meals.

Don't forget the issue of liability. You are legally responsible for injuries that occur on your property or that are caused by you, members of your household, or your pets. A pizza delivery person could break his or her leg tripping over a skateboard on the front steps. Your dog could bite a toddler who runs to pet it. A friend's child may drown in your pool. Fortunately, homeowner's and renter's insurance can help protect you from the financial consequences of any of these misfortunes.

Homeowner's Insurance

Homeowner's insurance, like other insurance, is a binding legal contract between you, the insured, and the insurer. It is designed to protect you, your home, and belongings if they are damaged or destroyed. The term *home* includes condominiums and mobile homes, as well as single-family houses. Protection is provided against losses caused by fire, water damage, storm, theft, and other perils.

DIGITAL VISION/GETTY IMAGES

Homeowner's insurance does not just protect what you own. It also protects anyone named in the policy—your spouse, children, other residents, household employees, guests, and visitors. A good homeowner's policy should cover medical expenses, personal injury, loss of use, and liability claims as well as property damage.

Homeowner's insurance provides coverage not only for the structure itself but also for detached structures such as a garage, tool shed, or in-ground pool located on your property. Homeowner's insurance also covers your personal property away from home, such as a camera or luggage that is stolen while you're on vacation.

What's Not Covered   Coverage may be limited or excluded on objects that are prone to damage or that tend to result in liability claims, such as boats or all-terrain vehicles. In insurance, an *exclusion* is a particular loss that is specifically not covered. Coverage is also limited on valuable or one-of-a-kind items such as jewelry, art, or other collections. Such property is dealt with in one of two ways to increase the limits and coverages. You might purchase an *endorsement*, which is an amendment to a policy

flat world...

Insuring a Second Home Abroad

The life span of Americans is lengthening. Many Americans live 20 years or longer after they retire. They may choose to purchase second homes or retirement homes outside the United States. Insurance companies based in the United States may or may not be permitted to write insurance policies in different countries. Standard insurance policies and named perils vary from country to country, as do local natural hazards. Coverages readily available in the United States may not be available abroad. For example, in Greece, the standard perils may include only fire and lightning. If you own property in Greece, an endorsement must be purchased at an additional premium for all of the following: explosion, earthquake, flood, riot/civil commotion, malicious damage, vehicle impact, and weight of snow or avalanche.

Think Critically   If you wanted to purchase a home in another country, how would you investigate that nation's insurance requirements?

written to cover unique items or special circumstances. You might also schedule each item separately, which means you will insure it for a specific value of its own.

Certain natural disasters in areas prone to them, such as hurricanes in Florida and earthquakes in California, are also excluded from standard coverage in those areas and require special coverage. Also, property used for home-based businesses cannot be covered on a homeowner's policy. If you run an accounting business from home, you cannot expect your computer and filing cabinets to be covered. If you have an alterations business at home, you cannot cover the sewing machine on your homeowner's policy. You would need to buy a separate business policy.

Homeowner's Insurance Is Not Optional   Although insuring your home is not required by law in all states, it will more than likely be required by your mortgage company, which will purchase insurance for you if you neglect to do so and pass the cost on to you. The coverage that the mortgage company buys will probably only protect the home itself, not your personal property. Always buy your own insurance to protect what you cannot afford to lose.

Renter's Insurance

Renter's insurance protects individuals who live in a house, mobile home, condominium, or apartment that is owned by another person. Renter's insurance protects against theft, loss of personal property, and loss of use. It is similar to homeowner's insurance except that it does not cover the dwelling itself. The owner of the property is responsible for obtaining homeowner's insurance to cover the dwelling. Renter's insurance is relatively inexpensive.

People tend to routinely buy homeowner's insurance, but for some reason do not automatically buy renter's insurance. Both types of insurance are equally important.

Tenants may not realize they are leaving personal belongings open to risk when they don't purchase renter's insurance. Many renters believe the landlord has insurance that covers the renters too. This is a false assumption, which leads to a false sense of security. You must purchase renter's insurance to protect yourself against loss. Your belongings are only as safe as the most careless tenant in, or visitor to, your apartment building.

The absent-minded neighbor upstairs who leaves the bathwater running, the tenant who lets the kettle boil dry, the smoker who falls asleep after working a double shift—all represent a potential threat to you and your belongings.

What's Covered, What's Not   Personal possessions such as furniture, clothing, books, DVDs, and other media and electronics are covered under renter's insurance, as is loss of use and medical payments. Personal liability coverage is an option under renter's insurance, but it will result in a higher premium. Because you do not own the rented property, renter's insurance coverage does not extend to the structure, but it is important to note that you are responsible for damage to the structure of your rented property. If your lonely beagle gnaws the woodwork when you leave the apartment, your renter's insurance will not compensate your landlord for the damage, but you are still responsible for it.

checkpoint

Why is it important to purchase renter's or homeowner's insurance?

interesting *facts*

In 2008 there were approximately 75 million dogs in the United States. Emergency rooms see approximately 1,000 Americans per day due to dog bites. Homeowner's insurance pays over $300 million per year for dog bite claims. Owning a dog may make getting renter's or homeowner's insurance more difficult or costly. ▪

REDUCE RISK •

Although you need to buy insurance, there are many other things you can do to protect yourself against a loss and resulting physical damage. Even if your insurance covers all your expenses, it is extremely disruptive to live in a motel and eat every meal out for a week while workers scrub and repaint your walls due to the smoke damage from a grease fire you caused through your own inattentiveness. Some risks, such as tornadoes, simply cannot be prevented, but others, such as electrical fires from improper use of appliances, can be greatly reduced or eliminated by being knowledgeable and careful and by following rules for use.

Increase Security

It is essential to develop good security habits. One simple example is to lock your doors and windows when you leave your home or go to bed. Millions of burglaries occur in the United States and approximately half happen without force. This indicates that these burglaries happen easily through unlocked doors and windows. Also, don't hide the key under the doormat or above the doorframe. This is too obvious and sets you up for loss.

Install strong external doors and deadbolts that must be locked with a key. Consider installing a burglar alarm or a whole-home protection system that monitors fire and interior motion as well as doors and windows. This will also result in a deduction in your homeowner's insurance premium.

Frank Johnson is a general contractor. He carries his tools in the back of his truck in a locked tool chest. One day he was shopping for supplies in a home improvement store. When he returned to his truck, he discovered his tool chest had been broken into and his tools were gone. He did not have business insurance and knew his homeowner's insurance policy would not cover the loss because the tools were used for his business. To collect insurance, he lied to the insurance company, telling them the tools were stolen from his garage and that they were used at home and not for business purposes.

Think Critically

How will Frank's actions affect his insurance policy? How will his actions affect others?

Whether or not you have a burglar alarm, keep your home well lit and trim shrubbery around doors and windows so thieves won't be able to hide while attempting to break into your house. Secure sliding doors with a heavy dowel or a device made for that purpose.

Don't Let Your House Look Vacant When you're away even for a couple of days, put variable timers on house lights so they click on and off at different times every night. Stop the mail and newspaper or have someone pick them up for you. Better yet, have a trusted friend or family member come in and check your house while you're gone. They can adjust the curtains and move porch plants and furniture around. If you're away a week or more in the summer, arrange to have the lawn mowed.

Protect Small Valuables The jewelry box on your dresser is not a safe place to keep your great grandma's diamond necklace. It is the first place a burglar will look. If you have extremely valuable or heirloom jewelry you rarely wear, consider putting it in a safety deposit box at the bank for safekeeping. Antique coins or other irreplaceable or uninsurable objects fall into the same category. If you do wear or use these items regularly, find a good hiding place somewhere in your home or, more importantly, buy a safe for your home.

Reduce Water Damage

Flood damage in the United States grows steadily worse as floodplains are drained and filled and former farmland and natural areas are developed. Paved roads and concrete parking lots do not absorb precipitation but send it rushing into the nearest stream. Make sure you aren't buying a house in or near a floodplain or floodway. Even a small creek or a dry ditch can become a roaring torrent, flash flooding in a sudden or heavy rainfall.

Beware of buying a house with a driveway that might channel water straight into the basement. If you are considering buying a house that has a basement sump pump, do some research into the frequency of flooding in the neighborhood.

Check Your Pipes   Know where the main water valve in the house is located. Test it to be sure it works. If frozen water pipes burst, for example, you will want to be able to turn the water off quickly. Insulate water pipes to help prevent freezing. See that each sink and toilet has cutoff valves installed, so if the fixture springs a leak, you can turn off the water to the fixture without turning off the main water valve. Examine all valves, water handles, and faucets for corrosion.

When You Are Away from Home   Turn off the taps to your washer in case a hose breaks and water flows the whole time you're gone. Get someone reliable not just to watch the house, but to go in and check to make sure the power is on and everything works, especially in the winter. Imagine the damage caused if the pipes to your third-floor bathroom were to freeze, break, thaw, and then send water running down the walls and through the floors for a week while you're on vacation.

Reduce Fire Risk

Fire kills. So does smoke. You can't be too careful in preventing fires. Install smoke alarms near the kitchen and in all areas where people sleep. Change the battery every year and test the devices regularly. You may also choose to install a carbon monoxide alarm near the furnace and any gas-fired appliance such as a water heater. Have a master electrician examine your electrical system and update your service if necessary. Unplug heat-producing appliances such as space heaters and toaster ovens when not in use.

Smoke, even if it doesn't injure anyone, can ruin every rug and piece of fabric and upholstery in your home. When you have something cooking on the stove, set a timer so you don't forget to check it. Make sure you have your furnace inspected

regularly, and check the filters on a regular basis. Forbid or discourage smoking in your home.

Housekeeping Matters

Eliminate dangerous clutter in your home such as piles of newspapers, old paint, and unused chemicals such as fertilizer, paint thinner, or paint stripper. Paper can burn, and chemicals can become unstable and possibly explosive with age. Store gasoline and gasoline-powered equipment, and any other substance that might explode or corrode through its container, in a detached, locked storage area if possible.

When you need toxic or inflammable substances for a project, buy the smallest amount you need and dispose safely of the rest. Be careful with cleaning substances as well. Even common substances such as chlorine bleach and ammonia can seriously injure a child, a pet, or you. Always read labels and follow directions.

 checkpoint

List three ways to protect your home against losses from theft, fire, and water damage.

assessment 6.1

Think Critically

1. What is the difference between an exclusion and an endorsement?

2. List three types of property commonly excluded from homeowner's coverage.

3. Discuss the differences between renter's and homeowner's insurance.

Make Academic Connections

4. **PROBLEM SOLVING**   Mario lived in New Orleans and his house was destroyed by a hurricane. He moved away for two years but is now reconsidering rebuilding on his property. Use key terms in this section to describe what he should consider before rebuilding.

5. **SAFETY**   Many fire victims die of toxic gases given off by smoldering upholstery materials. Research and prepare a presentation about which materials to look for and which to avoid when buying furniture.

6. **ENVIRONMENTAL ISSUES**   There is intense disagreement between supporters of flood control by means of manmade dams, channels, dikes, and levees and supporters of "natural" flood control who seek to remove dams and leave floodplains undeveloped. With two or three classmates, research the issue and present a debate. Be prepared to argue either side.

7. **PROBABILITY**   It is impossible to eliminate risk from life. Research the frequency of different categories of homeowner's claims. Select a category you find interesting and discuss in a report whether or not the risks your own home faces are typical. For example, do you live in an area more or less prone to particular natural disasters, or do you own a breed of dog statistically shown to be more likely to bite?

 Teamwork

In small groups, discuss the statement "Insurance fraud is not a victimless crime." Give examples of insurance fraud.

6.2

Basic Policy Types

+ Discuss the basic coverages of homeowner's and renter's insurance.

+ Describe the basic policy types.

terms

+ replacement cost

+ loss of use

+ personal liability

+ umbrella policy

+ actual cash value

+ inflation guard clause

Insurance Scene

Jaine and Willis are purchasing their first home. They have two children, two cars, a boat, and a coin collection. The home they want to buy has a detached garage and shed. The house is located in a nice neighborhood, and a creek runs through the property. Which type of homeowner's policy should they buy? Explain your choice. Should they purchase any endorsements? If so, which should they buy? Explain why.

IT'S A PERILOUS LIFE •

The different coverages available in any homeowner's or renter's policy are written to cover loss from certain perils, or causes of loss. Some policies only cover losses stemming from *named perils*, which are causes of loss specified in the policy. Other policies will cover losses from any peril not excluded in the policy. The most common named perils are listed below.

- Fire or Lightning
- Windstorm/Hurricane/Hail
- Explosion
- Riots
- Damage Caused by Aircraft
- Damage Caused by Vehicles

- Smoke Damage
- Theft
- Vandalism
- Glass Breakage
- Property Damage

Flood damage is typically purchased separately from a homeowner's policy. Endorsements can be purchased for earthquake damage, except in earthquake-prone areas, where earthquake coverage is separate and, of course, more expensive. The same is true for hurricane coverage. No policy covers losses resulting from war or nuclear accident.

Basic Coverages for Homeowner's or Renter's Policies

Within every homeowner's policy, coverage falls into four main categories—the dwelling itself, detached structures, contents or personal property, and loss of use. Renter's policies cover the last two categories. Be sure you know exactly which perils are covered in your policy and the dollar amounts of the coverages you purchase. Do not assume every loss is covered. Be a wise consumer and know what you are buying.

The Dwelling Itself   Dwelling coverage compensates you for damage to or destruction of the house, cabin, condominium, or mobile home that you live in, as well as any attached structures. This coverage is not found in a renter's policy. You can buy different dollar amounts of coverage, within reason. For example, you cannot insure your small three-bedroom ranch for $5 million.

Many insurance companies require you to purchase coverage amounting to at least 80 percent of the value of your home. However, you probably want more coverage, enough to completely rebuild the dwelling. **Replacement cost** is the current cost of replacing or rebuilding without any deduction for depreciation. You can purchase insurance for 100 percent of the replacement cost and also purchase excess dwelling coverage. The excess coverage may pay as much as 120 percent or 150 percent of the value of the policy to rebuild your home. This additional coverage will protect you from possible building supply shortages or an increase in building costs. Sometimes this coverage, or similar coverage, is called *guaranteed replacement cost*.

Detached Structures   This coverage compensates you for damage to or destruction of detached structures, such as a storage shed, gazebo, greenhouse, or detached garage. It also covers in-ground pools and fences. A typical cost of insuring other structures is approximately 10 percent of the total amount of coverage. The more structures you insure, the more it will increase the cost of your premium.

Contents or Personal Property
Contents coverage protects against damage to or destruction of building contents: appliances, clothing, furniture, and other personal property. The typical limits on coverage are 50 to 70 percent of the value of the dwelling itself, but it is possible to buy a greater amount of coverage if your possessions are valued at more than that amount. Objects of particular value such as computers, jewelry, furs, or cameras are covered collectively by category for a certain amount, and you can increase the amount of coverage for a particular category. For example, you might insure all your jewelry for $2,500 but need $10,000 of coverage for camera equipment.

PHOTODISC/GETTY IMAGES

tech talk

E-Insurance

More and more insurance companies are offering services on the Internet as a way of bringing in new customers. The Esurance website enables you to compare its auto insurance rates with rates from other top companies. It offers 24/7 customer service and also allows you to manage your policy and claims online.

Think Critically   What other features and information do you think insurance companies should provide online? Why?

Extremely valuable, unique, or irreplaceable personal property, such as fine jewelry, art, and other collectibles, will not be covered unless an authorized appraisal is made and a special endorsement is purchased. This is referred to as *scheduled coverage* because items are listed separately at an appraised value. Sometimes such items are covered under a special policy called a *floater*.

Loss of Use   Coverage for loss of use is sometimes called *additional living expenses*. Loss of use refers to your home or rental property being uninhabitable due to a loss. Expenses for loss of use may include the cost of a temporary rental home or hotel room, meals, and parking. Typically, this type of coverage pays for living expenses incurred to maintain a normal lifestyle. You will be provided coverage for expenses such as room and board, up to a previously set amount. This insurance is typically capped at 20 percent of your home's coverage, depending on whether you carry homeowner's or renter's insurance, but some insurers will let you purchase more coverage. For example, if you normally pay rent of $800 per month, but during the time your apartment building is under repair, you pay $1,000 per month for a motel kitchenette suite, your insurance should cover the difference of $200.

There are limits to additional living expenses covered. Payments for these expenses will only be provided for a reasonable amount of time, ideally the time it takes to make your home or rental property livable again. The total amount of payable living expenses may also be limited by your policy.

You cannot expect the insurer to pay for meals and lodging at expensive restaurants and luxury hotels while your two-bedroom, one-bath home is being repaired. Some policies may pay you up front for these expenses, but others will reimburse you only after you have paid the additional expenses. Be sure to keep and organize your receipts!

Personal Liability Coverage

Personal liability coverage protects policyholders from claims or judgments made against them for the following:

- Damage to the claimant's property caused by you or a member of your household, including your pets

- Physical injury to the claimant that occurred on your property

- Physical injury to the claimant caused by you or a member of your household, including pets

Coverage may include medical payments, funeral expenses, legal fees, and settlement costs up to the limits set by your policy. For example, suppose your friend Earl teases Godzilla, your large tomcat, and Godzilla severely bites and scratches his arm, sending Earl to the hospital and leaving him with permanent nerve damage to his hand. Earl might sue you for damages as well as expenses on the grounds that his profitable car customization career has been cut short. Personal liability coverage pays regardless of fault. Although property coverage includes a deductible, there is no deductible for liability insurance.

Personal Umbrella Policies

A special type of liability insurance, called an **umbrella policy**, can be added to your coverage if the same insurer handles your renter's or homeowner's and auto insurance. It acts like an umbrella because it sits on top of your auto and homeowner's or renter's insurance to provide extra protection.

Umbrella liability insurance is a separate policy typically sold in increments of $1 million. It costs approximately $200 to $300 annually for $1 million worth of coverage. However, rates for this additional coverage vary according to the risks you and your family incur. If you keep poisonous snakes as pets or have dangerous hobbies such as race car driving, or if you have an in-ground pool with a diving board, such a policy will cost you more than if you have a very low-risk lifestyle.

PHOTODISC/GETTY IMAGES

An umbrella liability policy can provide coverage for unusual and expensive losses, including being sued for mental anguish, libel, slander, defamation, and false arrest. It will also cover losses exceeding the liability limits on your automobile and homeowner's or renter's policies.

Home Business Insurance

Your homeowner's policy will not cover most losses incurred while running a business out of your home. Most home business owners are uninsured or underinsured and do not realize it. Be sure you buy business insurance to cover your home-based business activities.

What are the four basic coverages in a homeowner's policy?

POLICY TYPES BY THE NUMBERS

Fortunately for insurance buyers, homeowner's policies are somewhat standardized and are numbered so it is easier to understand exactly what kind of policy you are buying. This also helps you more easily compare policies offered by different companies. There are eight types of policies.

In general, the different policy types cover different groups of perils or cover them in different ways. It is important to decide what policy type is right for you and to know exactly what is in a particular policy. Be aware that specific details of these policy types differ from insurer to insurer. Also, policies may be categorized differently in your state.

Homeowner's 1 (HO-1), Basic Form This basic homeowner's insurance is typically the least expensive. Most HO-1 policies protect your home and possessions against 11 different perils. It provides security for the insured against damage by fire/lightning, glass breakage, windstorm/hurricane/hail, explosion, riots, damage caused by aircraft, damage caused by vehicles, smoke damage, vandalism, property loss, and theft. It also provides liability coverage for people who are not members of your household who are injured on your property.

Homeowner's 2 (HO-2), Broad Form   Sometimes called *Homeowner's Basic Plus*, most policies of this type provide the coverage in Homeowner's 1 (HO-1) and add 6 additional coverages for a total of 17 total perils. Some of the common additional coverages include damage such as a roof collapse caused by the weight of ice, snow, or sleet; collapse of any part of your home; damage from hot or frozen water pipes; damage caused by falling objects; heat or air conditioning explosion; and damage caused by electrical surges to appliances (except televisions). The specific perils covered by a broad form are listed in the policy, and those not listed are excluded. The HO-2 policy may also include living expenses due to loss of use.

Homeowner's 3 (HO-3), Special Form   This is a commonly purchased homeowner's insurance policy because it is more comprehensive and provides a wider range of coverage than HO-1 and HO-2. It not only protects you from specific perils, it protects you against all perils unless they are listed as excluded perils. The excluded perils typically include floods, wars, and earthquakes. The more perils covered by the policy, the more expensive the policy.

PHOTODISC/GETTY IMAGES

Replacement cost may be included in the policy for an increased premium. In all policies, it is important to know whether replacement is for *replacement value* or *actual cash value*. **Actual cash value** is defined as current cash value considering *depreciation*, its decrease in value because of age and wear. Actual cash value is much less than replacement value. For example, if your dining room set initially cost $1,400 and it is destroyed, the insurer would only compensate you for what the used dining room set would now be worth, maybe $600. But it would still cost you $1,400, perhaps a bit more, to replace your table and chairs with a comparable set.

Homeowner's 4 (HO-4), Renter's Form or Contents Broad Form   This policy typically includes coverage for 17 named perils that may cause damage to the personal property of the tenant. It is often referred to as the HO-2 policy for renters of rooms, apartments, or houses. Furniture, clothing, and other personal property damaged by smoke, fire, lightning, theft, and other perils are covered. This policy typically provides liability insurance of at least $100,000 for injuries to others in the rented dwelling. It does not insure the dwelling itself. The premium will differ from company to company

and depends on factors such as the crime rate in the area and the age of the apartment or rented structure.

Homeowner's 5 (HO-5), Comprehensive Form   The HO-5 is the most complete type of policy. Therefore, it is the most expensive and is not often sold. It includes replacement cost and covers practically all hazards except flood, earthquake, war, and nuclear attack. There are requirements you must meet before you can purchase the comprehensive form of insurance: the home must be equipped with smoke detectors; the home must have been built after 1950 and be in decent condition; a dead bolt must be installed on outside doors; and a hand-held fire extinguisher must be located in the home.

Homeowner's 6 (HO-6) Condominium or Unit Owners Form   This policy is a modified HO-2 policy to provide coverage for the same 17 perils for people who own a condominium. It covers personal property and building additions or alterations to the inside of the unit. Additional coverage can be purchased to cover property and liability related to the condominium association's common ownership. The owners' association typically carries insurance to cover the structures themselves and common areas.

Homeowner's 7 (HO-7) Manufactured Homes Form   The HO-7 insurance policy is specifically for mobile homes—technically called manufactured homes. It is similar to other policies protecting against loss of personal property, the manufactured home itself, and structures on the property.

Homeowner's 8 (HO-8) Modified Coverage Form   The HO-8 insurance policy is designed for older or historic homes in which the replacement cost would be much higher than the market value of the home. This type of policy is well suited for homes that have depreciated extensively. This type of policy provides *functional replacement*, which is cheaper than replacement cost. Covered perils are listed in the policy, and liability and medical payments are included in the coverage. Repairs, rather than rebuilding, are typically covered.

Generally Speaking

It is essential to review your policy annually to make sure you have adequate coverage. Many policies now include an **inflation guard clause**, which increases the policy coverage each year based on the changes in building costs in your area.

Remember, no matter which policy type you choose, it will exclude losses caused by certain perils. In these cases, you'll simply have to avoid the risk or deal with the loss some other way as noted below.

- **Water damage from flooding** You can sometimes buy flood insurance from a private agency that is part of the federal government's flood insurance program.

- **Sewer or drain backup** If a developer builds a subdivision nearby and overloads the existing sewers, which back up into your house, you'll have to prove your case and sue the developer for damages.

- **Power failure originating off your property** If you have electric heat and the main power lines snap in an ice storm, causing your water pipes to freeze and break, you may be out of luck. Next time, turn off your main water valve and empty the pipes before they freeze.

- **Neglect in protecting property at time of loss** If you leave your home during a hurricane and it is looted, the theft may not be covered.

- **War, nuclear attack, or nuclear accident** Don't buy a house too close to a nuclear facility. The federal government may step in to help displaced homeowners, but your insurer won't.

- **Loss caused by intentional action by the insured** You're not allowed to burn your house down to collect the insurance. If you have an argument and throw your china into the fireplace, that's not covered either.

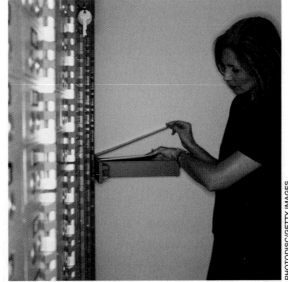

PHOTODISC/GETTY IMAGES

Document, Document

Inventory your belongings. Take pictures or make a video and save receipts. If your cashmere coat is burned in a fire, you will need to prove it actually was a cashmere coat, not ordinary wool. Keep the documentation in a place other than your home, for example, in a safety deposit box.

 checkpoint

Discuss the reasons why more homeowners buy HO-3 policies than HO-1.

_____

_____

assessment 6.2

Think Critically

1. Explain the difference between policy type and policy coverage.

_____

_____

_____

2. List and describe at least three homeowner's insurance policy types.

_____

_____

_____

3. List and describe at least three typical homeowner's insurance policy coverages.

_____

_____

4. Give an example of when loss of use coverage may be necessary.

_____

_____

_____

Make Academic Connections

5. **PROBLEM SOLVING**   If everything in your apartment or home were destroyed, would you be able to afford to replace everything immediately? What would be your first priority for replacement? Second, third, fourth, fifth priority? What would be your last priority? Explain how you determined each item's priority for replacement.

6. **SAFETY**   Has your family ever had a fire drill? If not, organize one. Determine how everyone should get out of the house from different rooms and practice. If your family already does this, find a friend whose family doesn't and organize a drill for them. Write a memo discussing what you did.

 **Teamwork**

In a small group, discuss why it is important to know exactly what is covered in your insurance policy and why you should not assume everything is covered.

Coverage and Claims

Insurance Scene

Ray and Suzanne are thinking of buying a second home in California. They know the house suffered $30,000 worth of damage in a 2005 earthquake. They are concerned whether they can afford to insure the house to cover a future earthquake loss. Where do you think they can find the information they need?

goals

+ Describe the factors affecting the policy you buy.
+ Explain the steps involved in filing a claim.

terms

+ natural risks
+ settlement recourse

KNOW YOUR NEEDS WHEN YOU BUY • • • • • • • • • •

Before buying homeowner's insurance, you should do your homework, asking yourself the usual questions about a potential insurer's ratings and reliability and researching average premiums for your area. You should also know what natural risks, such as earthquakes, storms, and floods, you face as a homeowner in your region. If they are an issue, you need to buy appropriate insurance.

You must know the new home's current market value. When you choose your insurer, the agent may visit your new home or do a drive-by inspection. The agent may also have an estimator do this and estimate the replacement cost to rebuild your home. If you have a question about the process, or if you disagree with the insurer's estimate, be sure to speak up, citing your research findings.

There are a number of ways to estimate the value of your possessions to make sure you know how much insurance to buy. An accurate but extremely time-consuming method is to determine the replacement cost of everything you own and add it up. There are also a number of different formulas to use, such as adding up the replacement cost of every major appliance and other important possession you own, then doubling that figure for a total. This formula will help you choose one of the coverage options the agent offers you, usually 50 to 70 percent of the value of your home or 30 to 50 percent of your manufactured home. If you have an inventory of your most costly possessions, the agent can help you decide the appropriate coverage needed.

The Application Process

When you apply for homeowner's insurance, the agent will ask questions about your new home and your lifestyle. A number of factors besides the

interesting *facts*

In California, an insurance company that sells residential property insurance is required by law to offer you earthquake insurance, although you are not required to buy it. ■

replacement cost of your home will affect your premium. These include the following:

- **Type of construction** Brick houses cost less to insure than frame houses.

- **Age of structure** Newer homes cost less to insure than older homes.

- **Local fire protection** The distance from your nearest fire station makes a big difference. Homes in rural areas, especially rural areas with volunteer fire departments, are more costly to insure for fire. Your insurer may also ask how close your home is to the nearest fire hydrant.

- **Amount of coverage** The more coverage you buy, the higher your premium. Insuring your contents for replacement cost rather than actual cash value, for example, will cost more because the insurer will have to pay more to settle your claims.

- **Claims frequency** If you have a history of filing claims often, your premiums will increase.

- **Size and makeup of the household** The larger the number of people in a household, the higher the likelihood of claims being filed.

- **Neighborhood** Insurers are not permitted to "redline," or refuse coverage to people just because they live in certain neighborhoods. But insurers are permitted to charge higher premiums in neighborhoods where more claims are filed.

- **Smoke alarms and fire extinguishers** These items reduce the risk of a bad fire.

- **Home security systems** A burglar alarm or whole-home protection system reduces losses from theft.

- **Tiedowns for mobile homes** Tiedowns secure the mobile home to the ground or foundation and reduce damage in windstorms.

DIGITAL VISION/GETTY IMAGES

Reduce Your Premium   As with other kinds of insurance, raising your deductible will reduce your annual premium. Deductibles for the standard homeowner's insurance policy typically start at $250, but you can increase or decrease the deductible amount. Of course, the actual savings depends on your insurance company and other factors. But generally speaking, raising your deductible to $500 may reduce your annual premium approximately 10 to 15 percent, and raising it to $1,000 may reduce the premium approximately 25 percent. If you do not file many claims, raising your deductible will save money in the long term.

Insurers typically offer a number of discounts to reduce your premiums. Typical discounts are listed below, but not every insurer will offer all.

- Homeowner's and automobile insurance purchased from same insurer
- Fire resistant structure, interior sprinklers, or smoke detectors
- Tiedowns for mobile homes
- Insured who is 55 years of age or older and retired
- Original owner
- New home
- Nonsmoker
- Security system

Don't Count the Lot
Keep in mind that it is not necessary to include the cost of the land your home sits on when you calculate how much insurance you should buy. Even if your home were completely destroyed, the land on which to rebuild should remain—unless there is a landslide or an earthquake, in which case your insurance would not cover the loss anyway.

PHOTODISC/GETTY IMAGES

✔ checkpoint

List three ways to decrease your renter's or homeowner's insurance premium.

IN CASE OF LOSS

When the time comes to file a claim, there are certain steps to follow. Depending on what has happened, you might change the order of the steps. If your loss is the result of a crime, you should also call the police before you do anything else.

Imagine that a deer has crashed into your living room through one of your triple-paned patio windows and out through another. There is deer blood and broken glass all over your carpet. Sharp hooves ripped your sofa cushions as the deer leaped around the room. The curtains are ripped and the curtain rod is bent. Some glass figurines on the mantel were knocked over and broken. Your dog has cut all four paws while chasing the departing deer out the window. It's 3:00 in the morning and ten degrees below zero. Steps to follow are described below

Make Emergency Repairs You wipe the dog's feet to make sure no more glass sticks to her paws. You use tarps and duct tape to cover the broken windows until the glass company can come. You start picking up and vacuuming bits of glass. Even if you could make a permanent repair, you should not do so until the insurance claims adjuster has seen the damage.

Call the Police If there has been a theft or other crime, call the police. Although no crime is involved in this scenario, you decide the deer was enough of a disturbance that the police ought to know about it. Also, the animal might be badly injured and become involved in some other incident. Remember that if you've had a theft or loss from a crime, you need the police report for insurance purposes.

Call the Appropriate Company You should call your insurer and report the loss. You also would need to call the glass company, carpet cleaning or replacement company, and your veterinarian.

List the Damage and Review Your Policy At daylight, when you can see better, you make a list of damages: the windows, the curtains and rods, four sofa cushions, and five glass figurines—family heirlooms, but not particularly valuable. The carpet needs cleaning and there's a little blood smeared on the wall as well. You get out your policy. You have a $1,000 deductible, which you will easily meet because of the size of the windows. You confirm everything is covered at replacement value. The only questions about coverage are the glass figurines, because you don't know how much they're actually worth, and the vet bill, because you think the dog will need stitches.

Make Arrangements with Insurer Your agent calls back at 8:00 that morning and tells you to go ahead and have a glass company

make a temporary repair. The adjuster calls soon after and makes an appointment to review the damage. The glass company makes an emergency visit and hammers up plywood. You take the dog to the vet to get stitches.

The adjuster comes at noon to survey all of the damage. You walk through the house with the inspector, pointing out all areas damaged. You talk to the insurer about having the figurines repaired instead of replaced, because their value to you is sentimental and not monetary. She agrees to pay for repair on the condition that the repairs not be museum quality, just simple repairs. She tells you to call local art restorers for repair costs before you do anything. However, she does give you approval to have the glass company replace the windows. She also gives you approval to buy new curtains and a rod from the catalog where you purchased them and new sofa cushions from the department store where you bought the sofa. She advises you to call any cleaning service you want. If they can't get the stains out of the carpet and off the wall, the insurer will pay to re-carpet and re-paint.

Get More Than One Bid for Repair or Construction Technically, you must get more than one bid for repair or construction, but if the insurer knows a company and trusts its bids, it may approve the costs based on just one bid. If the insurer is unhappy with the bid, you may be asked to get more bids. Good insurers try to make life easier for their customers and will not make more demands on your time than they must. Of course, the more money involved, the more particular the insurer will be.

Keep Records of All Contacts with Insurer By this time, you've started a file and a log. You start calling art restorers and two days later present the estimates to your agent, along with the estimate from the glass company, which is substantial. Floor-to-ceiling triple-paned windows are expensive, and the insurer will pay handsomely even after your high deductible. You congratulate yourself on having purchased replacement cost coverage.

Insurance Math *Connection*

Alfredo and Tonya pay $536 a year for their home insurance. Their deductible is $250. They could raise their deductible to $500 and decrease their premium by 12 percent each year. One day Tonya realizes they have lived in their home for ten years and have never filed a claim. How much money could they have saved over the past ten years by raising their deductible to $500?

Solution

Percent decrease × Annual premium = Annual savings
      0.12   × $536   = $64.32
Annual savings × Number of years = Total savings
    $64.32   ×   10   = $643.20

Don't Agree to a Settlement Until You Are Satisfied   The glass figurines turn out to be common and worth less than $200, but the lowest bid to repair them is more than $400. It would be cheaper to buy new, but your great grandmother carried these in her trunk from Ireland. The agent asks what you want to do. You really want these figurines, not others. You ask about the dog's vet bill of $300. The agent says that technically the dog is not covered, but if you'll pay the vet bill, the insurer will pay to repair the figurines, and you agree.

Save All Receipts   You and the agent also agree that you will pay all the expenses and the insurer will reimburse you. You make copies of the receipts as you pay them and send the originals to the insurer. Before the week is out, your windows have been replaced, the curtains are in the mail, and the new sofa cushions have been ordered. The carpet and wall have been cleaned to your satisfaction. Your claim has totaled more than $7,000, but you have paid only $1,300, which includes your $1,000 deductible.

Settlement Recourse

Not every claim is settled as easily as this one. If you and the insurer cannot agree on acceptable terms, you do have options. **Settlement recourse** is the systematic process of disputing a settlement.

First, discuss the settlement with the insurance company. Make sure you have provided all details and receipts in a timely manner and be polite but firm. If you are still unsatisfied with the insurer's decision, follow the procedures stated in your policy to dispute the settlement. If this still does not result in a satisfactory settlement, contact the consumer division of your insurance company, the National Insurance Consumer Helpline, or your state insurance commissioner.

 checkpoint

In your own words, describe the steps involved in filing a claim.

assessment 6.3

Think Critically

1. Why would you choose to insure for actual cash value rather than replacement cost?

_____

_____

2. How could the addition of a sunroom to your home and inflation each year increase the replacement cost of your home, while the actual cash value of your home decreases?

_____

_____

_____

_____

Make Academic Connections

3. **CONSUMERISM** Use the Internet to compare the premiums for renter's insurance to homeowner's insurance for the same coverage. Compare at least three companies. Present your data in a spreadsheet.

4. **GEOLOGY** While the U.S. earthquakes you hear the most about occur mostly around the Pacific Rim states—California, Oregon, Washington State, and Alaska—earthquakes can occur anywhere. The most dramatic series of earthquakes in U.S. history occurred near New Madrid, Missouri, in 1811 and 1812, damaging buildings as far away as Cincinnati, Ohio. Visit the U.S. Geological Survey at http://www.usgs.gov to research the likelihood of an earthquake in your area. Create a presentation or write a brief report.

5. **CIVIL RIGHTS** Using the Internet, research the illegal process of "redlining." Some banks, mortgage companies, and insurers have in the past made a practice of not making home loans or writing homeowner's policies in certain neighborhoods, even if potential customers living in those neighborhoods qualified for the loan or the policy. Choose an aspect of this topic and create a report or poster.

 Teamwork

In groups, brainstorm a list of everything you could do to reduce the cost of your renter's or homeowner's insurance premium. Compare your list with other groups and compile one overall list for the class.

chapter 6 assessment

Chapter Summary

6.1 Risks at Home

A. Homeowner's insurance policies protect you against home and personal property loss. Renter's insurance protects against personal property loss but does not cover the structure.

B. Following safety practices at home can reduce your risk of a loss.

6.2 Basic Policy Types

A. Homeowner's and renter's insurance compensate policyholders for damage to personal possessions and loss of use of their dwelling and often cover personal liability as well. Homeowner's insurance covers the dwelling and detached structures.

B. Policy types follow a standardized numbering system. Coverages differ among policy types and among insurers.

6.3 Coverage and Claims

A. Before buying a homeowner's insurance policy, do your homework to determine your needs. The price of coverage varies based on a number of different factors.

B. Certain steps must be followed when filing a claim and negotiating a settlement.

Vocabulary Builder

Choose the term that best fits the definition. Write the letter of the answer in the space provided. Some terms may not be used.

a. actual cash value
b. homeowner's insurance
c. inflation guard clause
d. loss of use
e. natural risks
f. perils
g. personal liability
h. renter's insurance
i. replacement cost
j. schedule
k. settlement recourse
l. umbrella policy

_____ 1. A special type of liability insurance that provides extra protection which can be added to your coverage if the same insurer handles both your homeowner's and auto insurance

_____ 2. Cost to replace or repair damage to your home or property after depreciation

_____ 3. Current cost of replacing or rebuilding without deducting for depreciation

_____ 4. Protects policyholders from claims made against them by others because of injury, death, or damage to others' property

_____ 5. Protects individuals who reside in a home, mobile home, condominium, or apartment owned by another person against theft, property damage, or loss of personal property

_____ 6. A built-in increase in policy coverage each year based on changes in building costs in your area

_____ 7. Earthquakes, storms, and floods

_____ 8. Sources of danger that result in loss

_____ 9. Contract between the insured and the insurer to protect home and belongings if damaged or destroyed

_____10. Coverage for when your home or rental property becomes uninhabitable

Review Concepts

11. How do you determine how much renter's or homeowner's insurance you need?

12. Why should you try to reduce risk in your home even though you buy enough insurance?

13. Why would you purchase an endorsement in addition to the standard homeowner's insurance?

14. Why should you think about how much your deductible should be when purchasing renter's or homeowner's insurance?

15. Discuss three ways to reduce your homeowner's insurance premium other than increasing your deductible.

16. What is an inflation guard clause?

17. What is the difference between personal liability coverage and umbrella liability insurance?

18. List five factors that will affect the cost of your homeowner's premium.

_____

_____

_____

_____

19. Describe what recourse you have if you are unhappy with an insurance settlement.

_____

_____

Apply What You Learned

20. List five ways to reduce risk in your home.

_____

_____

_____

21. Some people believe it is their moral responsibility to carry as much liability insurance as they can afford, in case their actions should somehow hurt someone else. Other people argue that people who carry liability coverage are more likely to be sued. What do you think?

_____

_____

_____

22. A severe hailstorm breaks windows in your home and ruins the television sitting by the window. Will costs to replace your television be covered in a typical homeowner's insurance policy? Explain your answer.

_____

_____

23. Why do you think homeowners buy a basic, or HO-1 policy, when an HO-3, or special policy, is more comprehensive and does not cost that much more?

_____

_____

_____

24. Choose one of the common perils discussed in this chapter. Provide examples and explain why you believe this is listed as a "common" peril.

_____

_____

_____

25. Your pet parrot likes to sit on your friend Brandi's shoulder and play with her ear studs. One day, Brandi is wearing her diamond stud and discovers later that the setting has been crushed and the stone removed. Should your insurer cover this? If you had difficulty settling this claim, what would you do?

Make Academic Connections

26. **GRAPHIC DESIGN**   By hand or using computer software, draw a picture of a home and surrounding areas. Diagram typical perils covered by homeowner's insurance, for example, a lightning bolt to the roof indicating lightning damage.

27. **BUSINESS MATH**   Jenny and Rita pay $432 a year for their home insurance. Their deductible is $500. They could raise their deductible to $1,000 and decrease their premium by 13 percent each year. Over the next eight years, how much would they save on their premium?

28. **GEOGRAPHY**   Research three different regions in the United States (Southwest, Southeast, Northeast, Midwest) for differences in the homeowners' risks associated with those areas. Write a two-page report on your findings.

29. **GEOLOGY**   Typically, landslides are excluded from insurance coverage. However, landslides are a very real issue in some parts of the country where the soil covering hillsides tends to slip when it is built upon, when the grade of a slope is changed, or when the "toe" of the grade is changed. Visit the U.S. Geological Survey website for landslides and assess landslide risk in your area (http://www.usgs.gov). Make a poster that will educate local landowners about their hillsides.

30. **MARKETING**   Create an imaginary ad campaign aimed at your peers to teach them how to reduce risk in their homes. Discuss how you would reach your target audience. What kinds of ads would you create and where would you place them? Would you stage a media event? Mock up, record, or videotape a sample ad and describe in writing where it would fit in the overall marketing campaign.

31. **CREATIVE WRITING**   Using well-known "Top Ten" lists as inspiration, write a comic top ten best list that will promote home safety or wise consumer behavior in buying insurance.

Life Insurance

PHOTODISC/GETTY IMAGES

climbing the ladder

From Life Insurance Sales Account Executive to Actuary

Emily has worked in the insurance industry for eight years. She has most recently worked as a life insurance sales account executive for the last three of those eight years. She came into her current position with appropriate certification and licensure required by the state.

Although a bachelor's degree was preferred, Emily was employed based on her experience and communication and technology skills. It was also helpful and duly noted during the interview process that she was working toward a bachelor's degree in business administration with a minor in statistics.

Although work as a life insurance sales account executive is demanding, Emily is continuing her education on a part-time basis and is only two semesters away from finishing her degree. It will provide her with other career opportunities in the insurance industry.

Emily currently sells life insurance to clients, analyzes information, and determines appropriate life insurance classifications. Her career goal is to be an actuary for an insurance company. As an actuary, her duties would include assembling and analyzing data to estimate probability—specifically, the probability of death.

Her current position involves more data entry, more marketing via the telephone, more travel, and less mathematical/statistical analysis than she prefers. She enjoys having a variety of duties that challenge her to use a variety of skills. However, to become an actuary, a bachelor's degree is required along with certification, which requires passing a series of rigorous examinations. She is studying for the examinations using CDs and books provided by the certification organization.

Upon passing the certification exams and completing her degree, Emily looks forward to less travel in her job and more analysis duties to make better use of her math and business skills. Colleagues who currently work as actuaries have shared information about their responsibilities, which include developing long-term and annuity policies, explaining complex information to company executives, and assessing risk. These duties will provide Emily with the variety she desires in an insurance career.

Upper Rungs to Consider

Although Emily has been successful in her current position, she seeks more challenging career opportunities as an actuary. The stringent examinations and the high level of mathematical and statistical knowledge required will involve hard work and effort on Emily's part. She looks forward to conquering the challenges over the next year.

Preparing for the Climb

It is important to first set attainable goals and take the essential steps to reach such goals. Your goals may be personal, educational, or professional, which all lead toward your ultimate career goal. Reaching your goals is rewarding and satisfying. Are there choices you can make or responsibilities or projects you could undertake in your current situation to help move you closer to your goals for the future?

7.1

goals

+ Explain the purpose of life insurance.

+ Discuss how life insurance works.

terms

+ beneficiary

+ death benefit

+ insurable interest

+ life pool

+ underwriting

+ mortality tables

Principles of Life Insurance

Insurance Scene

Suzanne and Jackson are newlyweds. They are both 25 years old, have recently graduated from college, and just bought their first home. As they start their careers, Jackson's benefits package at work includes $40,000 worth of life insurance. He can buy additional life insurance if he wishes. What factors should Suzanne and Jackson consider before deciding to buy additional life insurance?

THE FIRST BUT FINAL CLAIM •

You buy health insurance *in case* you get sick. You buy auto insurance *in case* you have an accident. You buy homeowner's or renter's insurance *in case* your possessions in your home/rental property are damaged or someone gets hurt on your property. But you don't buy life insurance *in case* you die. You buy it because you *will* die. Only one claim is ever filed on a life insurance policy, and it is filed by the beneficiary after your death. A **beneficiary** is the person or legal entity, such as a charity, designated to receive the death benefit. The **death benefit** is the sum of money paid to your beneficiary or beneficiaries by the insurance company from which you bought the policy.

Life insurance also differs from health, auto, and home insurance in other ways. You don't buy it to protect yourself, because the event that triggers the payment is your death. Instead, you buy life insurance to protect people who depend on you and who would suffer a financial loss when you die.

When you buy a life insurance policy, you are said to *own* the policy. The owner of the policy designates the beneficiary or beneficiaries and makes other decisions about the policy. Usually, but not always, the person who owns the policy pays the premiums. Who owns a life insurance policy is an important legal distinction. You can buy a policy and later transfer ownership of it to anyone you choose, but you then relinquish all control over it. People usually transfer ownership for tax purposes.

Insurable Interest   Certain people other than you can purchase a policy insuring your life. Because they own the policy, they can name themselves beneficiaries of that policy. (Countless murder mysteries have been based on this fact!) Only people who have a legitimate insurable interest in you are permitted to do this. An **insurable interest** represents someone or something of value that, if lost, would cause financial harm to the insured. Those having an insurable interest often include immediate family members, a business partner or employer, or under some circumstances, an institution or a creditor. A stranger cannot buy a policy on your life.

Protecting Those You Leave Behind

Most often, people buy life insurance to protect their children, a surviving spouse or partner, a disabled relative, or elderly parents. Purchasing life insurance will help ensure dependent family members will be able to afford to maintain the lifestyle or receive the necessary care they had before the insured person died. Frequently, the insured wants dependent children to complete the education he or she would have funded in life. People also buy life insurance to assist business partners in the event of their death, or to make a final gift to a nonprofit cause that is important to them.

There are a number of other specific reasons to buy life insurance.

- To provide immediate cash to pay for a funeral, any other costs arising from the death, or pressing debts

- To provide funds that are tax-free for the beneficiary

- To pay off a mortgage or other personal or business loans

- To provide housekeeping and child care services in the event of the death of a stay-at-home spouse, or to enable a stay-at-home spouse to enter the workforce

- To provide sufficient funds to enable a surviving parent to stay home or reduce work hours for purposes of child care

- To provide dependents with an emergency fund

PHOTODISC/GETTY IMAGES

flat world...

Federal Regulation of Insurers

The China Insurance Regulatory Commission (CIRC) supervises and manages the insurance market in China from a national level. The United States government has no comparable federal agency to regulate American insurance companies. Instead, insurance regulation takes place at the state level. This means that there are 51 different agencies (50 states and the District of Columbia), all with different standards, regulations, and levels of budgeting, looking out for the interests of the insurance industry and the interests of insurance consumers. Although consumer groups have wanted the insurance industry to be regulated at the federal level, the industry has resisted. Recently, the movement to establish federal oversight of the insurance industry has been gaining momentum. Because banks and other financial institutions are now permitted to sell life insurance, even some members of the insurance industry are in favor of federal regulation.

Think Critically
What advantages can you think of for continued state regulation of insurance companies? What advantages can you think of for federal regulation of insurance companies?

Who Needs Life Insurance? Monthly bills for a family can add up quickly with a car payment, a mortgage payment, credit card bills, basic medical expenses, and tuition in addition to food, clothing, and utilities. Young families benefit most from life insurance, should it be needed. Usually couples just starting their families have not yet accumulated many assets. The death of either spouse would be a financial hardship, and a well-chosen life insurance policy would enable the surviving spouse to stay at home or work part time to spend more time with the children.

With tuition and living expenses at state universities topping $20,000 a year, a policy that provides for children's educational expenses is invaluable. Couples in which a longtime stay-at-home spouse has little experience in the workplace are also prime candidates for life insurance coverage. Single people who have family histories of chronic disease might want to purchase insurance while they are young and healthy enough to qualify for lower premiums.

Who Doesn't Need Life Insurance? Despite the claims of some salespeople, life insurance is not considered a particularly wise investment vehicle for many people. People with no dependents or associates who would be harmed financially by their demise should feel free to spend or invest their money in more productive ways than in a life insurance policy. Groups of people who do not need life insurance include the following:

- Single people with no dependents, whose assets will cover their debts and funeral expenses

- Working couples with no dependents or large debts

- Anyone who has sufficient financial resources to cover projected lifetime expenses with interest and investment income

Insurance Needs Change Over Time Whether or not you need life insurance, remember, your needs change as your life changes, sometimes suddenly, sometimes slowly. Marriage, divorce, birth, an accident or disabling illness, death, and other major life events may increase or decrease the necessity for life insurance, as may the simple passage of time. Review your insurance needs annually or every six months, and whenever a major event occurs within your immediate family.

 **checkpoint**

Describe two situations in which life insurance is needed and two in which it is not needed.

_____

_____

_____

HOW LIFE INSURANCE WORKS • • • • • • • • • • • • • • • •

As with other forms of insurance, a life insurance policy is a legally binding contract between the insurance company (insurer) and the insured. In exchange for payment of premiums, the insurer agrees to pay a specified death benefit to the beneficiary/ beneficiaries named in the policy. Depending on what kind of policy the insured buys, the premium amount may be set in advance or may vary with the rise and fall of financial markets.

COMSTOCK IMAGES/JUPITER IMAGES

The premiums collected from policyholders are placed in an insurance pool, in this case called a **life pool**. Death benefits are paid from this pool. The insurance company invests the money from the pool but is required to keep enough readily available reserves on hand to pay out a large number of claims.

What is your life worth? How do your family, friends, classmates, or coworkers depend on you? Write two to four paragraphs explaining your answer. Share your answers with others in class.

How Insurers Reduce Risk   As with other forms of insurance, life insurance companies want to enroll mostly low-risk people because the insurer hopes to collect more money in premiums than it pays out in claims—the law of numbers. With a lifelong life insurance policy, the gamble you and the insurer take does not involve *whether* you will collect on the policy, but *when* your beneficiaries will collect. If you die early in the term of your life insurance policy, the insurer pays out more in death benefits than you have paid in premiums, and it loses money. But if, as both you and your insurer hope, you live a long life, the insurer will make more money from the premiums you have paid over the years than it will pay out in death benefits. A term insurance policy, on the other hand, insures your life only for a certain number of years. If you do not die during the term the policy is written for, the insurer makes even more money.

Underwriting Life Insurance

Life insurance companies are extremely interested in the present health, medical history, and family medical history of potential policyholders. These factors are possible indicators of your life span. The insurers are equally interested in your lifestyle and occupation. The process of assessing applicants to determine whether they are good risks for the company is called **underwriting**. The underwriter's job is to minimize the risk the company takes by finding and rejecting, or charging higher premiums to, applicants who seem more likely to die sooner. For example, if you smoke,

PHOTODISC/GETTY IMAGES

have a family history of heart disease, work in a sawmill, and go mountain climbing on the weekends when you're not racing motorcycles, you may be rejected for a policy. You would almost certainly pay higher premiums than a nonsmoker who exercises regularly and whose parents are both in their nineties.

Gather Information
When you apply for life insurance, you will be expected to answer questions about your health, medical history, and lifestyle. Depending on your age, the insurer, and the size of the policy you wish to buy, the insurer may also require a

physical exam by a physician or medical assistant of its choosing. This may be a very simple exam, unless you are trying to insure yourself for a large amount of money. In that case, you can expect a more extensive exam, including a variety of tests.

Mortality Tables   The information gathered from the exam and the questions you have answered on the application are reviewed by a company underwriter. During the underwriting process, the underwriter consults **mortality tables**, which are sophisticated statistical averages of how long a person of your age, gender, ethnic background, and so on, can be expected to live. The underwriter considers your health, family medical history, occupation, and other factors according to standardized formulas used by the company. Depending on the results, you are either rejected or accepted. If you are accepted, you are put into a predetermined premium class based on your risk factors.

Premium Class   Most insurers categorize policyholders into two or three different levels of premiums based on health and physical risk. The cost differences between the premium levels can be substantial. Policyholders who use tobacco or are overweight are *never* placed in the top health category of lowest risk, no matter how strong their other health criteria may be. You can save yourself a substantial amount of money in premiums by not using tobacco in any form and by keeping your weight at a healthy level.

Buying Life Insurance: Basic Considerations

Once you have decided to purchase life insurance, carefully consider the amount of coverage you need. Ideally, you want to purchase enough life insurance to pay your debts and provide your dependents with everything they need until, for example, your children have completed their education. Unfortunately, such coverage levels may be very expensive. Although it is important to have enough life insurance coverage to prevent a financial catastrophe in case of a breadwinner's death, if you are having trouble making ends meet, it doesn't make sense to pay large life insurance premiums with money that might be better allocated toward your family's immediate health and well-being. It is essential to prioritize your needs.

Life insurance is relatively expensive, considering you probably will not need it in the near future, and some kinds of life insurance are much more expensive than others. However, it is possible to combine different policies and obtain adequate coverage that will prevent financial disaster, even if it will not provide an Ivy League education for your children. The best life insurance policy is the one that fits your objectives and budget.

How Much Is Enough?

It is important to decide how big a death benefit you would like your beneficiary or beneficiaries to receive. Before purchasing life insurance, carefully consider your family's requirements, such as the following:

- Number, ages, and needs of dependents

- Balance on your mortgage, rent, loans, and other debts

- Your health and health insurance needs

- Tuition and other school-related debt

- Food, clothing, utilities, and other expenses

- Factors that may change over time

It may be most accurate to estimate expenses on a yearly basis, multiplying each year's total by 4 percent to allow for inflation and adding and subtracting expenses as you think they will arise or no longer be necessary. Then, add all the year's totals. From the total expenses, subtract all the income you can rely on: death benefits from an employer or from Social Security, a spouse's earnings, and earnings on savings and investments. The difference is what you need to cover with life insurance.

Rough Estimates   There are a number of formulas for estimating a family's need. One formula states you need approximately six to eight times your annual income. For a person earning $40,000 a year, that translates to a lump sum payment of $240,000 to $320,000.

Another quick formula involves multiplying your gross annual income by 5, and then adding funeral and other final expenses; any outstanding debts such as a home mortgage, car loans, and personal debt; and large anticipated expenses such as college tuition. For example, suppose you earned $40,000 a year, had $80,000 left to pay on your mortgage, owed $10,000 on the car, had $5,000 in remaining debt, anticipated sending two children to the state university for $20,000 a year, and figured $10,000 in funeral expenses. Your total need would be $465,000.

Income: $40,000 × 5	$200,000
Mortgage	80,000
Car loan	10,000
Debt	5,000
College: 2 children × $20,000 × 4 years	160,000
Final expenses	10,000
Total desired death benefit	$465,000

The Internet to the Rescue   There are numerous websites featuring life insurance calculators based on complicated formulas. After answering questions, you can then enter different sets of numbers to compare results in a "what if" scenario. An experienced insurance agent can also do the calculations for you.

Online Training and Certification

Insurance agents are required to be certified in the different areas of insurance. They must take continuing education courses to retain their certification. The variety of types of insurance, the increased number of agents, and the wide geographic location of agents have led to an increased need for continuing education classes anytime, anywhere. Continuing education courses offered online are becoming extremely popular.

Think Critically   What are the advantages of insurance agents taking online courses? What are the disadvantages of insurance agents taking online courses?

Group Life Insurance

Some employers offer life insurance as part of their benefits package, often at no cost to you. Free life insurance is a good deal for you, so take advantage of it. Even if you do not need it, you can always find a worthy person or cause to designate as your beneficiary. Because such insurance is a group life insurance policy, though, you need to be aware of potential drawbacks. Most policies your employer buys for you will not be large, almost certainly not large enough to provide adequate protection for a family. If that is the case, you will need to buy additional life insurance to provide appropriate levels of coverage for your beneficiaries.

Pros and Cons of Group Life Insurance   If your employer offers you the opportunity to buy group life insurance, investigate the cost and coverage carefully and compare it with premiums for comparable individual policies you could purchase. You may want to turn down the opportunity to purchase group coverage. Because the insurer must cover everyone enrolled in your employer's group, regardless of medical history and lifestyle, the insurer must charge higher premiums than you might pay for comparable individual coverage. If you are healthy, have a good medical history, and can qualify for the least expensive class of insurance premiums, you may be better off buying an individual policy elsewhere. If you are in less-than-perfect health, smoke, or have a strong family history of heart disease, diabetes, cancer, or other life-shortening diseases, group life insurance may represent a golden opportunity to purchase life insurance coverage you could not obtain for the group price, or at all.

Individual Life Insurance

Life insurance policies are complicated products sold by competitive businesses. Before buying life insurance of any kind, it is essential to do your research to determine the product you want and a company you can trust. Even the simplest short-term policy may mean a five-year relationship with the insurer. In theory, if you bought a policy at age 25 that "cashed in" when you reached age 100, you could have a 75-year relationship with the insurer. After paying premiums for 30 or 40 years, it would be extremely unpleasant to find out your insurer had gone bankrupt. As always, check an insurer's ratings before you consider doing business with the company.

Many policies are sold by different companies over the Internet. Some of these companies are quite reputable, and the pricing can be very competitive. You do not receive the same kind of advice over the Internet as you do from an experienced insurance agent. This may not matter if you are a savvy consumer who has researched the product and company carefully. Whether you buy insurance online or through a local agent is a decision only you can make.

The Issue of Price   Premiums vary widely, so be sure to comparison shop. This is not easy because insurance policies go by many different names, and features are bundled differently from company to company, even within some companies. You need to have a clear idea of what coverage you want and then check each policy for those features.

Be careful not to fall into the trap of automatically buying the cheapest insurance you can find. It does cost more to operate a reputable company than to run one that does not honor its commitments or properly train its agents. On the other hand, disreputable companies that do not honor commitments or train agents sometimes charge top dollar for policies. Get price quotes only from top-rated companies, and do your research carefully.

Briefly discuss two factors you should consider before buying life insurance.

_____

_____

_____

assessment 7.1

Think Critically

1. Why would you purchase life insurance?

_____

_____

_____

2. Who would likely buy life insurance, a childless single person or a parent?

_____

_____

3. List factors to consider to determine the amount of life insurance needed.

_____

_____

_____

Make Academic Connections

4. **GEOGRAPHY** In a small group, pick two states in different regions of the United States and two foreign countries, one developed and one developing country. Research the mortality rates for women, men, and children in those areas. Present your findings through an electronic presentation or a poster.

5. **RESEARCH** Find an online life insurance calculator. Enter estimated amounts for each category to calculate your life insurance needs. Send your instructor an e-mail discussing what kinds of information you had to supply and what you learned about your life insurance needs.

6. **PERSONAL FINANCE** Visit insurance websites or call or visit insurance companies. Research the premiums charged to tobacco users and non-users. Investigate the average price of a pack of cigarettes and calculate how much a one-pack-a-day smoker spends in a year. Using spreadsheet software, calculate how much money a smoker would spend in cigarettes and higher life insurance premiums over ten years.

 **Teamwork**

In a small group, create a fictional family and discuss what they would need to consider when buying life insurance to ensure they would have enough coverage to provide for their dependents if a breadwinner died.

7.2 Basic Policy Types

Insurance Scene

Wallace and Wynonna are excited about being parents. They have been married five years and have just purchased a $200,000 home with monthly payments of $1,200. Monthly payments on their two cars total $1,000. Wallace has $80,000 in life insurance through his company. Wynonna plans to be a stay-at-home mom. Do you think they should buy additional life insurance? If so, what type and how much?

JUST TWO TYPES, WITH VARIATIONS

Although it may be difficult to believe when you look at the hundreds of different life insurance products on the market, there really are just two basic kinds: term insurance and permanent insurance.

Term Insurance

Term insurance is the simplest, and typically most inexpensive, form of life insurance. Therefore, many consumer experts recommend people buy term insurance, either alone or in combination with permanent life insurance. **Term insurance** is a life insurance policy limited to a specific length of time, or term. Therefore, if you die during the term, the death benefits are paid to your beneficiaries; otherwise, the benefits are not paid. The most common terms are 1, 5, 10, 15, or 20 years, although 25- and 30-year terms are sold. Term insurance is set up so your premiums buy only insurance coverage, with no, or rarely any, cash value in the policy, as there is in many permanent policies. The lack of cash value is reflected in the dramatically lower premiums you pay for term coverage than you pay for comparable permanent coverage.

If you cannot afford permanent insurance, you can still protect your dependents by buying term insurance. You can purchase the same amount of death benefit for a fraction of the cost of permanent insurance. Many families buy a small permanent policy for the long term and then also purchase a sizable term policy to cover their needs until the children finish school or leave home. Presumably then, in 25 years or so, they will have fewer insurance needs and will need only the permanent policy to cover their reduced needs. There are three kinds of term insurance: level term, decreasing term, and increasing term.

Level Term Insurance   This type of policy pays the same, or a "level," death benefit throughout the term. For example, a 15-year term policy for $50,000 will pay $50,000 in death benefits whether you die in the first, last, or any year of the term. The premiums you pay typically remain level throughout the entire term, although sometimes different premium payment plans are available. This is the most straightforward kind of life insurance policy you can buy.

Decreasing Term Insurance   This type of policy provides for the death benefit to decrease over the length of the term, while the premiums remain the same. For example, a 10-year decreasing term policy may pay $20,000 if you were to die in the first year, $18,000 in the second year, and so on, until by the end of the term the death benefit would be zero and the policy would expire. Because the death benefit decreases, this insurance is less expensive than level term insurance. However, because the death benefit decreases, some consumer experts believe decreasing term insurance is not a good purchase for consumers.

Decreasing term insurance is often sold for the purpose of mortgage insurance, because, as with the insurance payout amount, the principal in a mortgage decreases over time as well. If you die, your mortgage can be paid with the death benefit. There is a particular type of decreasing term insurance called **mortgage decreasing term**, which is tied directly to the policyholder's mortgage interest rate and term. Consumer experts point out that the mortgage decreasing term death benefit can only be used to pay off the mortgage, whereas a standard decreasing term insurance policy can be used for any purpose, as can a level term insurance policy. Many banks and other mortgage

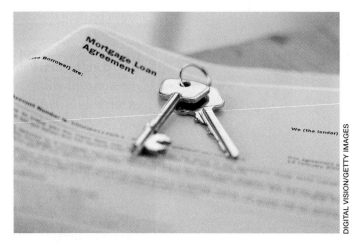

holders offer mortgage decreasing term coverage to homeowners, usually at inflated rates. To purchase this coverage, go to an insurance company independent from the institution that holds your mortgage.

Increasing Term Insurance   In an increasing term insurance policy, the death benefit, and premiums, increase over the length of the term because as the insured grows older, there is an increased risk of death. Increasing term insurance is not often sold on its own but is attached as a rider to another policy. A **rider**, in insurance terms, is an amendment or addition to a policy, similar to an endorsement in auto insurance.

Term Policy Options

When a term policy has expired, that is it—you paid your premiums and you were covered throughout the term of the policy. But you are still living and might still need insurance. What do you do? Your insurer wants to keep your business, so the industry has created two options to persuade term insurance policyholders to continue their coverage.

- **Renewability Option**   As noted in the name, this is an option. You don't have to exercise the renewability option, but after your term has expired, you may choose to renew the policy for another term without having to prove you're still insurable. For example, imagine at age 20 you bought a 20-year term policy, and at age 40, when the policy expires, you now have a ten-year-old dependent. Meanwhile you've developed some health problems. You need life insurance but are less insurable now because you have a higher risk of dying, making it more likely that the insurer will have to pay your death benefit. If the policy you bought at age 20 had a renewability option, you can automatically renew your insurance without a medical exam, although, as you are now older and at greater risk, you will pay a higher premium.

- **Convertibility Option**   The convertibility option permits you to convert from term insurance to whole life, a permanent policy, with the same company without having to prove your insurability. If your working spouse suddenly became disabled, for example, you would probably want to convert from term to whole life because he or she will now always be dependent upon you financially.

Insurance Math *Connection*

Isabel currently has $150,000 of life insurance, but she is not sure this is enough. Use the following information to calculate how much additional life insurance Isabel should purchase.

Final expenses	$11,000
Debt	$245,000
Living expenses per year	$48,000
Income per year	$45,000
Years of need	20
Savings	$40,000

Solution

Living expenses − Income = Income short per year
$48,000 − $45,000 = $3,000

Income needed: 20 years × $3,000	$ 60,000
Debt	245,000
Final expenses	11,000
Total financial need	316,000
Savings	−40,000
Total insurance needed	276,000
Current life insurance	−150,000
Additional life insurance needed	$126,000

What the Experts Say Whether or not you need to renew or convert, it is wise to make sure these two options are part of your insurance policy in case you need them in the future. Some experts also suggest buying term insurance for a longer term than you think you'll need, again, just in case. It is important to remember that term insurance is often referred to as "pure" insurance because the only thing premiums buy is insurance protection. Permanent, or "cash value" insurance, adds a savings component to insurance protection.

COMSTOCK IMAGES/JUPITER IMAGES

Paying Term Insurance Premiums

To accommodate different people's financial needs—and to sell more insurance—many insurance companies offer different premium payment plans. The varied payment plans often allow for lower premiums in the early years of a term with increases later, based on the assumption that a young policyholder's income will increase over the life of the policy. The most common plans offered with term insurance are the following:

- **Level** The premium remains the same throughout the term.

- **Increasing** The premium increases by a specified amount at a specified time into the term.

- **Level/Increasing** After being level for a specified time, the premium increases by a specified amount every year.

- **Indeterminate** Two premium rates, a maximum and minimum, are established. The policyholder pays the minimum rate for a specified time, after which the premium rate rises, but never above the maximum.

 **checkpoint**

List two differences between level term and decreasing term insurance.

_____

_____

_____

PERMANENT LIFE INSURANCE ● ● ● ● ● ● ● ● ● ● ● ● ● ● ● ● ● ●

Permanent insurance policies, as their name implies, cover you for your life-time or until a specified age such as 100, whichever comes first. If you live to the specified age, the insurer will pay you your own death benefit. Some policies "cash in" at a younger age, but the premiums will likely be higher. There are three main types of permanent life insurance.

- Whole life (also called straight life or ordinary life)

- Universal life

- Variable life

There are also many hybrid or blended policies that combine different features of these three life insurance policy types. In all types of permanent insurance, your premiums buy not only insurance coverage but also a savings or investment component. This savings or earnings component is tax-deferred and, depending on the policy and on the policyholder's financial situation, can be a useful savings or investment vehicle for policy owners who understand their needs and buy an insurance policy to fulfill those needs. Permanent insurance, for example, can be a solid income tax shelter for people in high income tax brackets.

Cash Value   Permanent insurance is also referred to as *cash value insurance* due to the cash reserves accumulated in the policy. It costs less to insure

you when you first buy the policy than when you are older. In effect, you over-pay in the early years of a policy and underpay in the later years. The overpayment that accumulates in your policy is called the **cash value**. As with some retirement plans, you can take a loan out against your cash value and repay yourself later.

If you wish, you can cash in your policy at any time for whatever cash value has accumulated; however, you then give up the insurance coverage the policy afforded you. There are a number of reasons people choose to do this.

- Your health is declining, you do not have dependents any more, and you need money for medical reasons.

- You decide to use the funds from your insurance to accumulate savings.

- You need the money to pay off a loan or handle an emergency.

Be careful in your decision to withdraw the cash value and forfeit the life insurance coverage.

Are There Dividends?   Some policies are referred to as **participating policies**. Such policies may pay *dividends* to policyholders calculated on the amount of your policy. Insurance dividends are not like stock dividends. In fact, the policyholders fund the dividends because companies selling participating policies charge higher premiums. Dividends may be applied to future premium payments or paid directly to the policyholder.

You can use the dividends in any of four ways: (1) to receive cash, (2) to reduce your premiums, (3) to accumulate interest so that it increases the death benefit, or (4) to buy what are called "paid up additions" to increase the policy's cash value. Remember, though, that *dividends are never guaranteed.* If a company has a bad year investment-wise, it may elect not to distribute dividends.

Buyer Beware   Many permanent life insurance policies are extremely complicated products that are aggressively marketed. Be sure to read any fine print and know what is guaranteed and what is not guaranteed by your insurance policy.

STOCKBYTE/GETTY IMAGES

Whole Life Insurance

Whole life insurance is the most clear-cut of all the different kinds of permanent insurance. Typically, you pay the same premiums for a certain number of years in exchange for a predetermined death benefit.

The annual premiums for whole life are higher than those for term life. Over a lifetime, the total premiums paid for a whole life policy may be cheaper than those paid for a comparable death benefit on term life. This is due to the fact that whole life premiums are *fixed*, meaning they remain constant for the duration of the policy, which is an entire lifetime. Term insurance becomes more expensive each time the term is renewed. Therefore, when the same number of years have passed as for a whole life policy, the total amount of the term premiums may well be higher.

The Bottom Line   If you don't plan on keeping a life insurance policy more than 20 years, you will probably want to buy term rather than whole life. Term insurance is cheaper in the short run, and you'll be able to buy a larger amount of coverage. However, if your plans include keeping the insurance more than 20 years, whole life is advantageous over the long run.

Advantages of Whole Life   Whole life policies are absolutely predictable. Whole life insurance is zero risk for the insured. The insurance company is the party that takes the risk on its investments. For this reason, the return to the policyholder on the savings component is not high, but it is guaranteed. The common wisdom on whole life insurance is that it is the insurance of choice for people who don't like to think or worry too much about insurance.

Disadvantages of Whole Life   Whole life policies are relatively inflexible. It may not be possible to change your mind about the amount of a death benefit, or to defer paying premiums if you lose your job, or to pay off the policy if you receive a large inheritance. More and more, however, companies are offering whole life options to increase flexibility, while leaving the nature of the policy untouched.

Variations of Whole Life   Some whole life policies actually insure two persons, usually a married couple or business partners. These types of whole life have names such as "Joint Whole Life" or "Last Survivor Whole Life." Typically premiums are lower than the cost of two comparable separate policies, especially for last survivor policies. However, investigate these policies carefully to be sure you understand the tax implications of a last survivor policy because estate taxes will be due.

Paying Whole Life Premiums   As with term insurance, many insurance companies offer different whole life premium payment plans to accommodate different people's financial needs. The most common plans offered with whole life insurance are the following.

- **Continuous**   Policyholders pay level premiums throughout the life of the insured.

- **Limited payment**   Policyholders pay higher premiums for a shorter time period.

- **Single premium**   An extreme form of limited payment in which the policyholder pays off the policy premiums in one large lump sum.

- **Modified**   The opposite of limited payment, in which the policyholder pays smaller premiums for a specified time and larger payments afterward.

- **Graded**   Similar to modified, in which the transition to higher premiums takes place in several steps.

Universal Life

Universal life is a type of permanent insurance created to take advantage of high interest rates and yield higher earnings on the cash value of a policy. If interest rates are high, your earnings on the cash value of the account will increase above the minimum rate the company guarantees you.

Unlike whole life, in which most of the values in the policy are fixed, universal life insurance is flexible. Within limits, you can adjust the premiums you pay and the death benefit, either up or down. If funds are tight and you want to lower your premiums, you can. If you have extra disposable income that you want to apply to your account, you can increase your premiums and increase the cash value and death benefit.

Advantages of Universal Life   The flexibility of this type of policy is particularly attractive. You can increase or decrease your coverage almost at will. In times of high interest rates, universal life can be a very good investment. You can move large sums (up to a legal maximum) into your policy and allow the earnings to grow in a tax-sheltered environment.

Disadvantages of Universal Life   The risks of the investment market are passed on to the policyholder. Nothing in a universal life policy is guaranteed except for the minimum rate of return specified in the policy.

NETBookmark

There are many types of life insurance policies, clauses, and premium payment plans. Therefore, buying life insurance may be confusing. Access www.cengage.com/school/pfinance/insurance and click on the link for Chapter 7. Take the life insurance quiz. Write two to three paragraphs to explain what you learned after taking the quiz, or how the quiz re-emphasized what you already knew. Share your report with the class.

www.cengage.com/school/pfinance/insurance

When the interest rate drops far enough, company costs that were paid for by high earnings will be passed on to the policyholder. In this case, you face the unpleasant choice of paying higher premiums to cover the company costs or canceling the policy.

Variable Life

Variable life is considered both life insurance and a security, meaning it is an investment product similar to shares of stock, bonds, and money market accounts. Variable life is subject to regulation by the Securities and Exchange Commission, which also regulates stockbrokers. Variable life insurance can be sold only by agents who have passed the Financial Industry Regulatory Authority exam.

Variable life insurance is similar to whole life insurance because both insurance policies provide for a minimum death benefit. However, an important difference is that the death benefit and cash value depend on how well a variable policy account performs in the stock market. The policyholder either directs how the funds are to be invested or purchases the policy from a company that agrees to manage the funds for an additional fee.

Advantages of Variable Life Policyholders who are knowledgeable about the stock market can potentially earn a handsome yield. These earnings are tax-sheltered because they are classified as life insurance.

Disadvantages of Variable Life   As with universal life, the risk of the investment is passed on to the policyholder. The only entity guaranteed is a specified minimum death benefit. The policyholder could possibly lose most of his or her principal.

The Bottom Line

Most people's insurance needs can be met with term insurance, whole life, or a combination of the two. Individuals should not purchase universal life unless they can afford to risk the money they invest in a policy. People should also not purchase variable life unless they are knowledgeable about the stock market.

 checkpoint

Describe two types of permanent life insurance.

_____

_____

_____

assessment 7.2

Think Critically

1. List three benefits of term insurance.

_____

_____

2. Discuss why or why not to buy mortgage decreasing term insurance.

_____

_____

3. Why would you want your term life policy to be convertible or renewable?

_____

_____

Make Academic Connections

4. **MARKETING**   If you were a marketing manager for an insurance company, how would you sell life insurance? Pick a type of life insurance, complete research at the media center or over the Internet, and write a memo to the company vice president outlining the "talking points" you would include in a campaign.

5. **ETHICS**   Many people might find an ethical dilemma in selling insurance that also has a risky investment component. How can an agent make sure potential buyers understand the risk? Should people who cannot afford to lose money on an investment somehow be prevented from buying these kinds of life insurance policies? Research the issue and write an essay about how you would deal with this issue if you were an insurance agent.

6. **CONSUMERISM**   Some critics of the insurance industry believe insurance companies deliberately structure insurance policies so that it is difficult to compare costs with those of other policies. Industry defenders claim the variety of products is in response to consumer need. Research this issue. Write a consumer article for your school paper, or prepare a class presentation, summarizing what you've learned.

 **Teamwork**

In small groups, discuss the potential risks involved in universal and variable life insurance. Do you find the potential earnings attractive despite the risks? Write a short personal response to your group discussion.

7.3 Applying for a Policy

goals

+ Describe different types of life insurance clauses.

+ Explain how to apply for a policy and how to file a death claim.

terms

+ primary beneficiary

+ contingent/secondary beneficiary

+ double indemnity

Insurance Scene

Guyen Aleria has chosen to pay her life insurance premium on a monthly basis. Her payments are due on the 15th of every month. On July 10, she took an extended vacation and forgot to pay her insurance premium before she left. While on vacation, she had a heart attack and died August 1. What clause must be included in Guyen's life insurance policy so that it will pay death benefits? What would happen if this clause were not in the contract?

LIFE INSURANCE POLICY PROVISIONS • • • • • • • • • • • • • • •

The thought of reading an insurance policy is not exciting to most people. Policies are filled with legal language in small print and, for most people, are difficult to read and even more difficult to comprehend. Nevertheless, it is essential you understand everything in your life insurance policy. Taking the time and effort to carefully read your policy and ask questions of the insurance agent can make the difference between getting exactly the coverage you thought you were paying for and leaving your family or other beneficiaries only partially protected.

PHOTODISC/GETTY IMAGES

Life insurance policies differ from company to company and from state to state. There really is no "standard" life insurance policy. It is up to you, the consumer, to be sure everything you want is included in your policy. The following provisions are typically included in a life insurance policy.

• Entire Contract Clause or Insuring Agreement

• Ownership Rights and Assignment

• Death Benefit

- Beneficiary Clause

- Settlement Options

- Incontestability Clause

- Misstatement of Age Clause

- Grace Period Clause

- Reinstatement Clause

- Alteration of Policy

- Suicide Clause

Entire Contract Clause or Insuring Agreement   This basic clause, which is in all life insurance contracts, states that the application you completed together with the policy represent a contract between you and the insurance company—the insurer. This is based on the assumption that the information provided on the application is truthful. If the insurer believes you misrepresented yourself on the application, the contract may be deemed void.

Ownership Rights and Assignment   Like property, a life insurance policy is one of your assets. You, as the insured, are the owner and are entitled to certain rights. You have the right to

- designate beneficiaries and change the designation

- determine settlement options, which is how the death benefits are distributed to the beneficiaries, and change the determination

- receive dividends of a participating policy

- cash in or borrow against the policy as specified

- transfer ownership rights

Death Benefit   This provision specifies how the death benefit is handled before it is paid out. For example, does the insurer pay interest on the amount of the death benefit between the date of death and the date the settlement check is written? Does the insurer refund to the beneficiary the "unearned" portion of the latest premium, or does the insurer consider the latest premium fully earned no matter when the insured died? To provide more clarity, if Ed pays his annual premium of $1,000 in January and dies in June, some insurers would refund Ed's widow $500 on the premise that Ed's death instantly brought the policy to maturity; therefore, half of the year's premium had not been earned. Other insurers would consider any premium fully earned once paid.

Beneficiary Clause   This provision gives you the opportunity to name the beneficiary (or beneficiaries) who will receive the death benefits. You can name your estate, family members, friends, charities, universities, and other people or organizations. If you choose to name more than one beneficiary, you must also designate how much of the death benefits each beneficiary will receive. Think

carefully about whom you wish the money to go to and how you wish it to be divided. Be specific. A **primary beneficiary** receives the death benefits first. In case of his or her death, a **contingent or secondary beneficiary** would receive the remaining death benefits if he or she survived you and the primary beneficiary. Policy owners have the right to change a beneficiary at any time by contacting the insurance agent and completing the necessary forms.

Settlement Options   This policy provision determines how the death benefit is paid to the beneficiaries. The death benefits may be paid in a lump sum, in installments, as an annuity, through a money market checking account in the beneficiary's name, or some other means. The way the death benefit is paid may be specified by the settlement options as a decision to be made by the beneficiary.

Incontestability Clause   In this clause, the insurance company agrees that after a specified period of time, typically two years, it will not contest the contract for any reason. The incontestability clause is critical in protecting the beneficiary against any misstatements made, either inadvertently or fraudulently, by the insured. Without this clause, an insurance company theoretically could deny a death claim years later, when the insured was no longer available to argue the case.

Misstatement of Age Clause   This clause correlates to the incontestability clause. If the insured misstates his or her age, the insurance company has the right to adjust the death benefit to the amount the beneficiary would have been paid had the premiums based on the insured's correct age been paid throughout the duration of the policy. This clause is in effect whether the insured misstated his or her age as either older or younger than the actual age.

Grace Period Clause   This clause is required by most states. It provides for a grace period, typically 31 days, to pay your premium without your policy lapsing if you neglect to pay your premium by its specific due date. You may, however, have to pay a late fee. If you were to die within the grace period without having paid your premium, the insurance company is obligated to pay your beneficiaries the death benefit.

Reinstatement Clause   If a policyholder neglects to pay premiums beyond the grace period and the policy lapses, it is possible to have the policy reinstated under the terms of this clause. However, certain conditions would first have to be met, such as payment of outstanding premiums and evidence of continued insurability.

Alteration Clause   This clause states that no modification of the policy can be accepted unless the modification is in writing and signed by one of the officers of the insurance company. It serves as a warning to policyholders that the spoken word or even the signature of an agent is not valid in this instance.

Suicide Clause   This clause is designed to protect insurers from people contemplating taking their own lives so that their dependents would receive a death benefit. The policy is considered void if the insured commits suicide before a specified time has passed, typically one or two years, after the policy was purchased. If the specified time has passed and the insured commits suicide, the insurance company may pay the beneficiaries the premiums paid into the policy over the years, but the company has no legal obligation to pay the death benefits.

Special Options

No matter how many clauses there are in a life insurance policy, you can also purchase special provisions and options in the form of riders to your policy. Riders will, however, increase the premium. The expense varies in proportion to how it increases the insurer's risk.

- **Accidental Death**   Also called **double indemnity**, this rider doubles the death benefit if the insured dies in an accident rather than of natural causes.

- **Guaranteed Insurability**   This rider is sometimes added to a whole life or universal life policy. It gives the insured the right to buy a new policy from the insurance company, or to increase the death benefit on a present policy, without having to undergo a medical exam.

 checkpoint

Describe two different types of life insurance policy clauses.

APPLYING FOR LIFE INSURANCE • • • • • • • • • • • • • • • • • •

After you have decided what type of insurance will meet your needs, you must also decide from what company you want to purchase the insurance.

Once these decisions have been made, it is time to apply for insurance. The application process is accomplished by completing and signing the insurance company's application form. If you purchase insurance online, you will complete the form online. If you buy insurance through an agent, he or she will generally ask you questions, complete the form for you, and ask you to sign as the insured. If you buy insurance or are provided insurance through your employer, you will probably complete the forms yourself with the assistance of human resources personnel.

The actual application form for life insurance is relatively simple. Generally an application has two parts. The first part consists of basic information such as your name, address, birth date, and other generic facts you would provide on any insurance application. The second part contains information the underwriters will examine to determine your insurability. You will be expected to answer questions such as the following:

- Have you ever been unable to obtain life insurance before?

- Have you been told surgery is necessary for a current condition?

- Have you engaged, in the last 3 to 5 years, or do you plan to engage, in the next 6 months to 1 year, in any dangerous sport or adventure? (There will be a list of activities such as rock climbing, skydiving, and racing to which you must respond yes or no).

- Have you used tobacco in any form in the last year?

Tell the Truth   You are expected to answer each question on the application or asked by the agent honestly. The insurance company has the right to, and probably will, investigate your answers through the Medical Information Bureau (MIB), which is a medical information clearinghouse for insurance companies. You must sign a contract stating the information you provided is completely true. Do not take this responsibility lightly. Failure to sign the contract or lying on the contract will create a void contract, depriving your beneficiaries of some or all of the death benefits you thought you were purchasing for them.

Before you sign, read the form carefully and completely, especially if an agent has completed it for you. Make sure there are no blanks. You, not the agent, must take responsibility for the application's accuracy.

Will There Be a Medical Exam?   Generally, if you are under the age of 40, the insurer will not go to the expense of paying for a medical exam. However, there may be exceptions if you are applying for a large amount of insurance or if you have a medical condition.

Pay When You Apply   You may have the option of paying your first premium, or part of your first premium, when you apply for coverage. You may also wait until your application is accepted. Most consumer experts encourage you to pay when you apply so that you are covered instantly upon acceptance of your application. There is a small chance, but still a chance, you could die without coverage between the time your application is accepted and you mail your first premium, so why take the chance? If you are not accepted, the company will refund your payment.

Most companies have a "free look" provision in which you have a period of time, often ten days, to decide if you don't like the policy or any components of the policy and to ask that it be amended, or canceled and your premium refunded without penalty. When you apply for your coverage, you should be able to get a sample policy, similar to the one you are purchasing, to take home and review at your leisure. This will make reviewing your own policy much quicker when it arrives.

Are You Uninsurable?

If an insurance company rejects your application saying you are too high of a risk to insure, you do have options. Some insurance companies specialize in insuring people with specific medical conditions, such as heart disease, diabetes, or extreme obesity. However, the premiums will be higher than a regular insurance policy. The only option to reduce the premium is to reduce the death benefit.

Graded Death Benefit Policy　One way insurance companies are able to provide benefits is through a *graded death benefit policy*. The death benefit is calculated on the amount of time you live. You pay into the insurance policy, and then, if you die within the first year, your dependents receive the premiums paid in, plus typically 10 percent interest. If you live two years, they receive 25 percent; three years, 50 percent; and so on. You may have to live five years beyond the time you buy the policy for your beneficiaries to receive 100 percent of the death benefit.

Group Insurance　If you are uninsurable individually, you can seek group life insurance through an employer, a union, or a professional organization. Group plans must accept everyone belonging to the group. The premiums may even be lower than what you would have to pay to a company specializing in the otherwise uninsurable.

Filing a Death Benefit Claim

The first step in filing a claim is simple. You should give the name and phone number of your life insurance company, as well as your policy number, to any appropriate members of your family and friends. Also, prepare a list of all bank accounts, investments, and insurance policies and give them the information. Keep a copy of this information at home where people know to find it, and put a copy in your safe deposit box as well. Have everyone in your family do the same thing.

Life insurance benefits are not paid out automatically. The beneficiary must file a claim or no money will be received. When the insured dies, the beneficiary should contact the insurer. Typically beneficiaries need money for funeral expenses, but if you don't need the money immediately, you can wait until after the funeral.

When you call the insurer, give the insured's name, policy number, and date of death. The company will send the relevant forms for you, or possibly a lawyer assisting with the will, to complete. Along with the completed forms, the company will need an attached, certified copy of the death certificate. You may also need to complete a W-9 form so the insurance company can notify the IRS of the policyholder's death.

After you file a death claim, the insurance company confirms the beneficiaries and processes the claim. The company has a specified period, for example 60 days, to pay or begin paying the death benefit, or to notify the beneficiaries of any problems with the claim.

 checkpoint

Who files a claim for a life insurance policy?

assessment 7.3

Think Critically

1. Describe four of your rights as a life insurance policy owner.

_____

_____

2. Why do you have to sign the insurance contract stating your application information is truthful?

_____

_____

3. Describe how beneficiaries claim death benefits.

_____

_____

Make Academic Connections

4. **RESEARCH** Using the Internet, media center, newspaper, or other source, find a feature article about life insurance. List four important points in the article. List terms used in the article with which you are not familiar. Compare your list of terms with another student. Discuss similarities and differences in your two lists and work together to define the unfamiliar terms.

5. **CREATIVE THINKING** Develop a new life insurance clause. This might be a clause that you see as being useful in the future. Write a description of the clause plus a one-page document explaining how the clause works for both parties in an insurance contract and why this new clause is necessary.

6. **LITERATURE** Books, movies, and/or TV shows indicate ethical issues such as lying on an insurance application, committing suicide to provide beneficiaries with death benefits, and so on. Use a story or movie as inspiration to write an essay about the ethical implications of insurers offering clauses specific to these kinds of situations.

 **Teamwork**

With a partner, make a list of everything you should consider when naming beneficiaries. Based on your list, work separately to choose primary and secondary beneficiaries. Explain your choices in writing.

chapter 7 assessment

Chapter Summary

7.1 Principles of Life Insurance

A. Life insurance provides income to dependents/beneficiaries when you die.

B. Life insurance is both similar to, and different from, other kinds of insurance. It is a legal contract in which you pay premiums to an insurer who agrees to pay a death benefit to your beneficiaries when you die.

7.2 Basic Policy Types

A. Term insurance is the simplest and typically most inexpensive form of insurance. The entire premium goes toward insurance protection.

B. Permanent life insurance is also called cash value insurance because the premiums provide a savings component as well as insurance protection. There are three basic kinds of permanent insurance—whole life, universal life, and variable life.

7.3 Applying for a Policy

A. There are a number of standard clauses in a life insurance policy. It is important to understand all clauses, especially those in your policy.

B. Applying for insurance involves answering specific questions about your health, medical history, and lifestyle. You may be asked to undergo a physical to prove insurability. If you are deemed uninsurable, you may want to consider a graded death benefit policy or group insurance.

Vocabulary Builder

a. beneficiary
b. cash value
c. contingent/ secondary beneficiary
d. death benefit
e. double indemnity
f. insurable interest
g. life pool
h. mortality tables
i. mortgage decreasing term
j. participating policy
k. permanent insurance
l. primary beneficiary
m. rider
n. term insurance
o. underwriting

Choose the term that best fits the definition. Write the letter of the answer in the space provided. Some terms may not be used.

_____ 1. Life insurance that provides protection for a specific period of time

_____ 2. An addition or amendment to an insurance policy

_____ 3. Lifelong life insurance

_____ 4. The overpayment that accumulates in a permanent life policy

_____ 5. Represents someone or something of value that, if lost, would cause financial harm to the insured

_____ 6. Insurance policy that pays off your home if you die

_____ 7. Cash amount from a life insurance policy given to designated beneficiaries

_____ 8. The first person or entity designated to receive the death benefit of a life insurance policy

_____ 9. Rider that doubles the death benefit if the insured dies in an accident

_____10. A policy that may distribute dividends to policyholders

Review Concepts

11. What is the main reason for buying life insurance?

_____

_____

12. What is a rider and why would you purchase one?

_____

_____

13. What is the main difference between term and whole life insurance?

_____

_____

14. Describe two advantages of term life insurance.

_____

_____

15. What is a grace period?

_____

_____

16. List three factors to consider when determining how much life insurance to purchase.

_____

_____

_____

17. Why is whole life insurance considered permanent?

_____

18. Why do you think suicide clauses have been incorporated into life insurance policies?

_____

_____

19. List three questions you may be asked on an application for life insurance.

_____

_____

_____

20. What is the main difference between universal and variable life insurance?

_____

_____

_____

Apply What You Learned

21. Do you think a five-year term insurance policy that is renewable and convertible would require a higher premium than a five-year term insurance policy without these options? Explain your answer.

22. Why are medical exams important when insuring a person over age 40?

23. Why should you make sure there is an incontestability clause in a life insurance policy?

24. Why would you buy variable life insurance?

25. Why would a single person buy life insurance?

26. Why would you list a primary and secondary beneficiary?

27. Discuss why you might want to exercise an option allowing you to vary your insurance premiums.

Make Academic Connections

28. **CREATIVE WRITING** Imagine what might happen if anyone could buy a life insurance policy on anyone else. Write a description of a movie you would use to persuade a movie producer to film your screenplay based on this idea. In the description, briefly sketch out the plot, characters, setting, and tone of the movie. Include any details you think will "sell" the idea to the producer.

29. **MARKET ANALYSIS** You are working for a new insurance company and have been assigned the task of surveying the local community for their life insurance needs and health status. In a small group, brainstorm a list of questions you would ask to complete the market analysis. Write the questionnaire and distribute it to other groups for constructive criticism.

30. **TECHNOLOGY** CPR may not be what you think it is. A CPR is a Computer-Based Patient Record. This is a way to electronically store and maintain an individual's lifetime health status and health care records. It includes such items as medical history, past and present medications, lab results, X-rays, surgical data, and so on. Make a list of pros and cons for this type of recordkeeping. Using the list, write an essay discussing whether you think CPR is a good or bad idea, and what could be done to safeguard privacy. If you prefer, create an oral presentation, or write a futuristic story about CPR technology.

31. **RESEARCH** Contact local life insurance agents or search for rider information on the Internet. Upon a complete investigation, write a description of three commonly purchased riders. Be prepared to discuss the rider, its impact on both the insured and the insurer, and why the insured would purchase such a rider.

32. **PERSONAL HEALTH** With a partner, divide a piece of paper into two columns. In the left column, list the lifestyle changes people could make to improve their health and become more insurable. In the right column, list the diseases or medical conditions that might cause people to pay higher insurance premiums or even be denied coverage. Discuss which lifestyle changes in the left column are directly related to the medical conditions in the right column. Compare your results with the class. If you see any lifestyle changes you could implement yourself, choose one and do it.

33. **CONSUMER ECONOMICS** Review your family's life insurance coverage and think about what you've learned in this chapter. Do you think your family's coverage is sufficient? If not, what can you and your family do to improve the coverage? Without invading your family's privacy, write a brief report on what you've learned about the reality of life insurance protection.

Insurance

8 Disability and Long-Term Care

PHOTODISC/GETTY IMAGES

climbing the ladder

From Insurance Claims Clerk to Auditor

DaSheena has worked for the North Star Insurance Company as a claims clerk for three years. She has a degree in art history but became interested in insurance due to issues she had at her last job.

She was previously employed as a tour guide at the Glandour Museum of Art and was injured on the job. She had disability insurance through that position, but not a substantial amount and not an amount large enough to provide for her family while she was out of work. She had to work closely with the company's human resources representative and the insurance claims clerk to settle her claim.

Through this experience, her interest in insurance grew, and she obtained a position at a local insurance company. She now works as an insurance claims clerk. Her duties include reviewing insurance claim forms, contacting the insured to obtain missing information, calculating the amount of the claim, and transmitting claims for payment or further investigation. DaSheena particularly enjoys any type of work that is investigative and more broad-based than working with a single client.

Therefore, she is looking into the possibility of becoming an insurance auditor. Auditors examine and analyze business records to determine financial status and prepare reports noting strengths and deficient areas. Through this type of position, DeSheena would consult with company officials about particular regulations and financial matters.

She would be able to utilize her communication and critical thinking skills and would be required to use problem-solving skills. She realizes, however, she will probably need additional education. She would need to enhance her bachelor's degree in art history by taking more accounting and finance courses. However, her experience in the insurance industry will serve her well.

DaSheena is willing to take more classes and even earn a master's degree to get a job as an auditor. One coworker suggested DaSheena talk to several auditors and ask the following questions about their jobs.

- What type of degree do you have?
- What skills are the most important in performing your job successfully?
- How much time do you spend sitting at a desk?
- What is a typical day like in your position?
- How often do you work with groups?
- How often do you work alone?

The answers to these questions should help DaSheena determine if being an auditor is the right job for her. DaSheena wants to be sure she is headed in the right direction.

Upper Rungs to Consider

DaSheena enjoys many aspects of her current position as an insurance claim clerk, but she wants to progress in the field of insurance and move on to other jobs. She is ready for a change. She will continue to analyze the work environment for auditors, educational opportunities, and job openings in the area.

Preparing for the Climb

Different careers have different requirements. What career are you thinking about? What questions would you like to ask about the career? Who could you ask?

PHOTODISC

8.1

goals

+ Explain the principles of disability insurance.

+ Describe ways to reduce the risk and cost of disability insurance.

terms

+ disability insurance

+ elimination period

Disability Insurance

Insurance Scene

Ron Hall is an apprentice electrician. He works for a company specializing in outdoor, high-voltage power systems; therefore, he spends a lot of time on ladders, on scaffolds, and in bucket trucks. He had one potentially serious incident stepping off a scaffold, and once he forgot to stabilize the truck before starting up in the bucket. So far he has not been injured. Ron jokes about his absentmindedness. He says his union insurance plan includes 90 days of full disability benefits and that's long enough for a broken leg to heal. He's young and strong, has no dependents, and has siblings and cousins who could nurse him through a disabling injury. What does Ron not understand about potential disability? What would you say to him about reducing risk? What would you advise him to do about financial risk?

WHEN YOU CAN'T MEET YOUR OWN NEEDS • • • • • • • • •

Most people would choose to live a long, healthy, independent life and enjoy a vigorous old age. No one would choose to suffer a disabling illness or accident that would render him or her unable to work, temporarily or permanently. Nor would anyone choose to become frail in his or her final years so that assistance would be needed for basic tasks such as bathing, dressing, and eating.

Unfortunately, you do not have control over all life events. You cannot ensure you are not in the intersection when another driver runs a red light. You cannot be sure you are not served a contaminated piece of food. You cannot go back and remodel your genetic heritage. Even if you take excellent care of your health, you cannot guarantee your heart, lungs, kidneys, or mental function will not fail as you age, making you dependent upon others for your well-being. You can, however, buy insurance to protect you from financial disaster in case you become disabled.

Disability Insurance

Disability insurance is designed to replace all or part of your income if you cannot work or, because of disability, can earn only a reduced income.

Surprisingly, more Americans are underinsured for disability than for any other basic form of insurance. In part this is because people believe other kinds of insurance they already carry will protect them in case of long-term disability, but this is not true.

- Health insurance pays medical expenses, but does not replace lost income. Your ongoing living expenses must be paid, even if you're in the hospital for an extended period of time.

- Workers' compensation pays a portion of your wages, but only if you become disabled because of your employment. For example, workers' compensation will not cover a disability you suffer in a non-work-related auto accident or from a non-work-related illness.

- Social Security pays benefits only if you are totally disabled and cannot work. For example, if you were a financial analyst who suffered a brain injury and could no longer carry out the analytical tasks your job required but could work in the company shipping department at one-fifth your former salary, Social Security would probably not consider you disabled.

The "It Can't Happen to Me" Syndrome

Some people do not buy enough insurance, or the right kinds of insurance, because they do not want to consider the possibility of painful events. Subconsciously, they may even believe if they don't think about something, it won't happen. They believe they are invincible.

Many people with permanent disabilities like to refer to the rest of the population as "temporarily able-bodied." This is because people can, and do, become disabled any time during their lives, no matter how healthy they are and how carefully they live. You are not immune to traffic accidents, chemical exposure, infection, or genetics that may cause a radical life change.

Disability Does Happen   You have a higher chance of being disabled for longer than three months than you do of dying prematurely. The statistics provided in 2007 by Insurance.com are just a sample of your chances of becoming disabled.

- A 30-year-old male has a 1 in 5 chance and a female has a 1 in 3 chance of sustaining a long-term disability before retirement.

- Approximately 50 percent of those suffering a disability lasting longer than six months remain disabled after five years.

- 1 in 7 employees will be disabled for five years or more before retirement.

Many Americans live paycheck to paycheck. If they become disabled, would they be able to continue to pay their bills? Over half of all personal bankruptcies and foreclosures on homes are due to becoming disabled. ▪

These statistics show the need to protect yourself with disability insurance. Did you know more people lose their homes because of disability than because of fire or death? Disability insurance can help provide financial stability through the rough times.

Rough times may include being hurt in a bad accident requiring hospitalization and rehabilitation. You could undergo radical medical treatment such as a bone marrow transplant for cancer. You could develop severe depression or another mental illness that makes you unable to function in the workplace. You could discover you have multiple sclerosis, muscular dystrophy, Parkinson's, or another debilitating disease. You might recover, in whole or in part, from some of these disabling events. Then again, you might not.

Lose Income, Add Expenses   The need for disability insurance is even more pressing when you consider there may be added expenses if you are disabled. These expenses may include medical fees not covered by your health insurance or assistance with housekeeping or personal care. Your household income might be further reduced if a spouse or other family member must cut back on employment. This may happen for many reasons, including the need to take on more of the normal household duties or to care for you.

✔ **checkpoint**

Briefly describe the purpose of disability insurance.

_____

_____

REDUCING YOUR RISK OF DISABILITY • • • • • • • • • • • • •

While it is impossible to protect yourself against some health events, you can reduce your overall chances of becoming disabled if you are thoughtful, careful, and willing to live a healthy lifestyle.

Take Care of Your Health

The saying, "If I'd known I was going to live this long, I'd have taken better care of myself," is so true. Individuals who avoid tobacco, eat a varied and balanced diet high in plant foods and low in animal fat, keep their weight under control, and exercise regularly can prevent or minimize many health problems now and in the future. These individuals will recover faster from accidents and illnesses, and they will avoid complications that plague people who are not in the best of health.

A diet high in saturated fats and an inactive lifestyle can contribute to heart disease, high blood pressure, diabetes, and other potentially life-threatening conditions. Remember, though, these conditions might not merely shorten your life. They could also cause chronic poor health throughout adulthood or set you up for a frail and dependent old age. Modern medicine may keep you from dying from these conditions, but the life-saving medications themselves sometimes have problematical side effects. Such side effects detract greatly from your quality of life. It is essential to take care of yourself with diet and exercise.

What You Do Now Does Matter   Establish a healthful lifestyle when you are young. Think of it as an insurance premium you pay in time and effort instead of dollars.

Research your family medical history to learn about any disabling illnesses and conditions to which you might be prone. You can reduce your chances of contracting them if you take care of yourself. Consider your ethnic heritage and take appropriate action. For example, fair-skinned women and men are at a higher risk than darker-skinned people of developing osteoporosis, a weakening of the bones in middle and old age that can lead to disabling hip and spine fractures. For this reason, fair-skinned people should be careful to get sufficient calcium and Vitamin D in their diets and do weight-bearing exercises to develop and maintain stronger, denser bones. People of Amerindian, Hispanic, and African heritage are at a higher risk than other groups for diabetes and its many complications and should be sure to get regular exercise and maintain a healthy weight.

Be Careful with High-Risk Activities   Few activities are without risk. You can hurt your back reading in an easy chair if you sit improperly. But some activities are riskier than others. It's up to you whether the satisfaction is worth the risk. You can, and should, reduce risk by always wearing recommended safety equipment and following proper safety practices. Often, when someone is killed or disabled, it's because he or she either wasn't properly trained or wasn't taking the right precautions for the particular situation. For example, you may love feeling the wind blow through your hair as you motorcycle bareheaded down the highway, but remember that people who are brain-dead don't feel anything. Dying is not a good way to avoid disability. Do yourself and your loved ones a favor and wear a helmet and other safety equipment.

DIGITAL VISION/GETTY IMAGES

Take Care of Your Financial Health

If you become disabled, you can lessen the financial impact by taking good care of your financial health, such as by reducing the cost of insurance when possible. For example, if you have an emergency fund to cover all your living expenses for six months, you might not need to collect disability benefits immediately. Thus, you could purchase an insurance policy that has a longer **elimination period**, which is a clause in your insurance policy that specifies how soon after the disability the policy will begin to pay benefits. A longer elimination period, for example 90 days instead of 30, is similar to having a higher deductible in other kinds of insurance. A longer elimination period substantially reduces the premiums on disability insurance.

Live Below Your Means

Many Americans carry a sizable amount of credit card debt as well as a mortgage and car payments. When their flow of income is interrupted by a layoff or a medical or other emergency, many quickly experience serious credit and cash flow difficulties. If you live relatively debt-free and have substantial savings, you may be able to ride out a financial crisis or have more time to consider your options before taking action. Knowing how to live modestly, for example, understanding how to eat well and entertain yourself without spending a lot of money, is an excellent life skill to develop.

The Two-Career Family Many married couples decide both spouses should work, not just for the joy of working or for the sake of the additional income but as a kind of insurance against a layoff, death, disability, or other financial crisis. One spouse's income is still coming in and health benefits will still be provided during the time the other spouse cannot work.

List three ways you can reduce the risk of becoming disabled.

_____

_____

assessment 8.1

Think Critically

1. Describe three financial strategies to help you reduce the cost of, or dependence on, disability insurance.

2. Explain why so many Americans are underinsured for disability.

3. Many people refuse to make lifestyle changes to decrease their chances of becoming disabled. List three reasons why.

Make Academic Connections

4. **RESEARCH**   Advances in medical technology enable people not only to survive disabling accidents and diseases but to lead long and productive lives despite their disabilities. Research one of these technologies and prepare a report, presentation, or taped radio feature about it.

5. **COMMUNICATION**   Through an advocacy agency, locate and interview three employed people who have become disabled as adults. How did their work life change, and how do they cope? Summarize your interviews and present your information to the class in whatever format you feel is best.

6. **PUBLIC HEALTH**   Research the leading causes of disability among teenagers and write a report, make a poster, or write and record a public service announcement publicizing what you learn.

7. **PERSONAL FINANCE**   Do you know how to live below your means? Make a list of a typical week's activities and expenditures. See how many entries you can substitute with a less expensive activity or purchase.

 Teamwork

In small groups, discuss your dream career and how different disabilities you might develop would affect your performance in that career.

8.2 Disability Policies

goals

+ Define disability.

+ Explain various disability insurance benefits.

+ Describe how to buy disability coverage.

terms

+ total disability

+ own-occupation protection

+ residual benefits

+ cost of living adjustment

+ waiver of premium

Insurance Scene

LaTashia, age 32, a highly skilled and well-paid machinist, is thinking about buying an individual disability insurance policy. Her job benefits include disability benefits for one year, but her skills are not easily transferable to other positions paying at the same level. If LaTashia's hand-eye coordination were somehow impaired, she would need to go back to school to supplement her degree and skills. LaTashia and her husband, a school teacher, live in a city with high real estate costs, and they would like to buy a house as well as start a family within the next five years. If you were LaTashia, what kinds of coverage would you look for in a disability policy?

UNDERSTANDING DISABILITY INSURANCE

Like other forms of insurance, a disability insurance policy is a legally binding contract between the insured and the insurer. You agree to pay premiums to the insurer, while in return, the insurer will pay specified benefits when and if an event that triggers the insurance payout occurs. As with all forms of insurance, disability insurance has its own terminology. Consumers must understand this terminology in order to make intelligent purchasing decisions.

Defining Disability

Exactly what does it mean to be "disabled"? A disability policy's definition is critical. It could mean the difference between collecting benefits you've paid for and planned on or having to start back at square one.

Total Disability Some policies define "total disability" more strictly than others. Some insurers define **total disability** as not being able to perform any of the main functions of the job you held when you became disabled or of any similar job appropriate to your education, training, and experience. Other insurers define it as not being able to perform *any* job, much the way Social Security defines it. If you are totally disabled as defined by your policy, the insurer will pay full benefits, up to the amount of coverage you purchased, for as long a benefit period as you purchased.

Own-Occupation Protection   Own-occupation protection is extra coverage you can buy if you have a highly specialized and highly paid job. For a hefty addition to your premium, you can buy a specific definition of "total disability" as your "own occupation." For example, if you were a brain surgeon and your muscle control became impaired, you could no longer perform surgery of any kind. You would still be able to be a diagnostician, a consultant, a researcher, or a medical professor, but at a substantial drop in income. If you had purchased own-occupation protection, the insurer would pay benefits to make up your drop in income or even pay your full former income, depending on how much coverage you had purchased.

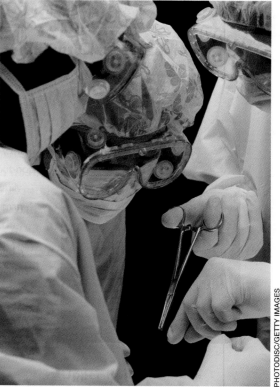

Residual Disability   This coverage is standard in some policies and can be added as a rider on others. Residual coverage is important because it protects you when you are able to work part time but not full time. For example, residual disability would pay you benefits if you are diagnosed with multiple sclerosis and have to cut back your hours because of your condition, or if you are receiving weekly chemotherapy and it takes one whole day for the treatment and another to recover. With **residual benefits**, if you have an income loss of at least 20 percent, the insurer will pay a percentage of your full benefits to compensate you for the income you lose. Be careful, though, that the insurer does not require that you first be totally disabled before residual disability will be paid.

You need to be sure you have residual coverage. If you had only total disability coverage, for example, but could work one day a week, you would by definition not be totally disabled and might not receive any benefits at all. Because you were working only one day a week, you would lose 80 percent of your income, but without residual disability coverage in your policy, you would not be eligible for any benefits at all. Be sure to add residual coverage to your policy if it is not standard with your insurer.

Presumptive Disability   Under this provision you are "presumed" disabled under certain specified conditions, even if you can still perform some or all of your job functions. Because you are presumed disabled, you are entitled to full benefits. Typical conditions include loss of sight or hearing or the loss of use of a limb.

checkpoint

Why is it important to specifically define "disabled"?

ALL ABOUT BENEFITS •

Most policies pay a specified percentage of your income, defined as stable, earned income, at the time you become disabled. Typically this is no more than 80 percent of your income. You cannot buy more disability insurance than you make in income. Also, the total of all income replacement benefits paid to you by different kinds of insurance cannot exceed the maximum benefit you could receive from your disability insurer. For example, if you were badly injured in an auto accident in which another driver was at fault and you were awarded lost wages, those payments would be subtracted from the total benefits that would be paid by your disability insurer. You might have short-term disability coverage as a benefit through your employer that would pay 30 or 90 days' wages. Those payments, too, would be taken into consideration when your long-term benefits are paid.

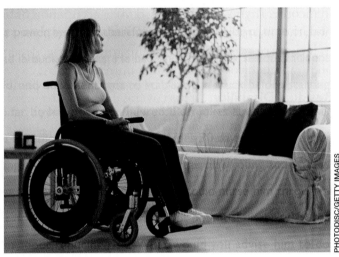

PHOTODISC/GETTY IMAGES

You can buy less than maximum coverage. For example, if you have a working spouse or substantial investment income, you might decide to cover only 50 percent of your income and thus lower your premiums.

Benefit Period   Most policies offer benefits for one, two, five, or sometimes ten years. The idea is to buy yourself enough time to recover as much as you can and then, if necessary, retrain for another occupation, even if it pays less than your old one. It is also possible, although extremely expensive, to buy coverage up to age 65 or even for life. Most experts recommend buying no fewer than five years of coverage, because a severe accident or illness could completely disable you for two or three years, and then you would need time to retool your career.

Cost of Living Adjustment   Called COLA for short, the cost of living adjustment is a rider you can purchase to prevent your benefits from losing value due to inflation. It is a fairly expensive rider, but it is important to have if you are purchasing coverage up to age 65. It may not be so important, even for five years of coverage, unless inflation rates are high at the time. Of course, when you buy disability insurance, you have no idea whether inflation will be high at the time you might be receiving benefits. In your annual insurance review, consider the state of the economy and buy the rider if you think you might need it.

Renewability Options

Even if you think you will not need to renew a policy, it's always a good idea to have the option to renew. Disability insurance is like term insurance: stop paying premiums and the policy lapses. Remember, tremendous life changes can occur suddenly, and you may need to renew after all. Here are the renewability options you are most likely to encounter.

Guaranteed Renewability This option guarantees you can renew coverage up to age 65 but it does not guarantee the rate will remain the same. The rate may increase when you renew.

Noncancelable Renewability This option guarantees you can renew coverage up to age 65 and also guarantees the rate will not increase. Because it locks in the rate, it costs more than guaranteed renewability.

Conditional Renewability This option places certain restrictions on renewability, such as requiring the insured to be employed at the time the policy is renewed. Also, the insurer can increase the premiums or cancel the policy.

Future Purchase Option When you qualify for disability insurance, the future purchase option guarantees that you can buy increased coverage no matter what the state of your health. If you make a career change into a specialized field, for example, you might decide you would rather have ten years of disability coverage than five. Or, at age 50, you might decide it would not be worth the effort to retrain yourself for a new career and, thus, increase your coverage to age 65. It is relatively easy to be medically disqualified for disability insurance, so the future purchase option maintains your insurability.

DIGITAL VISION/GETTY IMAGES

Waiver of Premium Most policies have a **waiver of premium** provision, so you don't have to keep paying premiums after you are disabled for a specified period, such as 90 days. Be sure this provision is present in any policy you buy.

Coverage to Avoid

As with any insurance, there are policies that leave you unprotected in critical areas, or that cost much more than they should for the amount of protection they offer.

Accident-Only Insurance   Many healthy, young people try to economize by buying accident-only disability insurance, reasoning that if they are disabled, it will most likely be due to an accident. How could young, healthy people possibly get sick enough to become disabled?

Accident-only insurance is relatively inexpensive, as well it should be, because it does not provide very wide coverage. It is not a smart buy. Young, healthy people get sick. Even superb health will not prevent a close personal encounter with a disease-carrying tick or mosquito or a piece of contaminated shellfish. It will not protect you from meningitis, mononucleosis, or even the mumps, which can cause severe complications in adults. Dozens of types of cancer can develop in healthy, young adults. Heart disease and back pain are the top two disabilities. Many disabling diseases are no more unlikely than an accident. Don't waste your money on accident-only coverage.

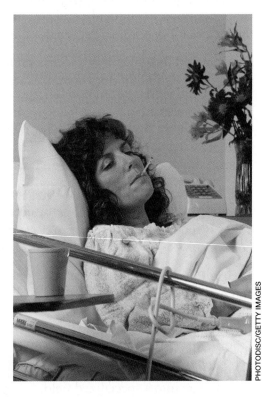

PHOTODISC/GETTY IMAGES

Nonmedical Disability   Disability by its definition has to do with your physical body. However, even mental illness is a physical disorder because it originates in the brain. Most disability insurers therefore ask questions about your health when you apply for coverage. Beware if they don't. By not asking medical questions, the insurer may be grouping you with people who are in poor health and are, therefore, at higher risk. Consequently, you will pay more for the coverage than you should, providing you are in good health. If your health is not good, though, a nonmedical disability policy may be right for you.

Other insurers that do not ask medical questions may not charge high premiums, but their policies contain exclusions for pre-existing conditions that may be well hidden in fine print and legal terminology, so that in the end you might not be covered when you most need it.

 checkpoint

List two provisions you should make sure are in a disability policy.

_____

_____

BUYING DISABILITY INSURANCE

Before you buy a disability policy, review your employee benefits package, if you have one. Many employers' packages offer paid short-term disability coverage for anywhere from 30 days to a year. Do you belong to a union or professional association that would pay disability benefits? Even minimal coverage of 30 days is time you can add to the elimination period of any policy you buy, and the longer the elimination period, the smaller the premium you'll pay.

How Much Coverage Do You Need?

Review your expenses. How much does it cost your household to live for a month, including rent or mortgage payment, grocery costs, utilities, and other monthly fees and payments? Review your bank statement for a quick total of the checks you write each month. Add 20 percent to that total just in case.

Separately, add up the household income you can rely on if you are not receiving your wages. Is there investment income? Are there two working adults? Some experts counsel caution about relying solely on one spouse's income because unemployment and/or disabilities can occur. Subtract reliable household income from your expenses and you have a rough idea of the disability benefits you need to be paid.

Group or Individual Disability?

Group disability coverage is not always the most economical because higher-risk and lower-risk people are grouped together in the plan. If you are in good health, you may find lower premiums buying individual disability coverage. You may also be able to tailor individually purchased coverage to meet your needs better than you can with a group plan. However, if you have health problems, the group plan may allow you to buy coverage you would have difficulty getting on your own.

If you have short-term disability provided as part of your employer benefit package or health plan, take advantage of it. Even if it is not top-quality coverage, it's something to build on and will save you money. You can plug any gaps in the coverage with a policy you purchase on your own.

 checkpoint

When is group disability a better option than individual disability coverage?

assessment 8.2

Think Critically

1. When might you want to purchase own-occupation protection?

_____

_____

2. Describe three provisions you should have in a disability insurance policy.

_____

_____

_____

_____

3. Discuss when you might, and when you might not, need a cost of living adjustment rider on a disability insurance policy.

_____

_____

_____

Make Academic Connections

4. **COMMUNICATION**   Obtain a disability insurance application form. Review all the questions. Explain why you believe the questions are asked. Summarize your findings and present them to the class.

5. **GOVERNMENT**   Research the kinds of Social Security benefits available to people whose disabilities meet the eligibility requirements. Condense and organize the information you consider most important and create a one-page overview of what you feel people need to know.

6. **CONSUMERISM**   Research disability insurance costs in your state. Compare the costs of at least three policies that have similar duration of benefits, elimination periods, benefits provided, and inflation protection. See if your state department of insurance website is helpful to you. Write a brief report describing your research.

 **Teamwork**

In small groups, discuss the ethics of insurers who do not offer residual disability benefits as a standard clause in a disability insurance policy.

Long-Term Care Insurance

Insurance Scene

Sandi is 30 years old. Her mother, age 58, recently survived a stroke, but it left her paralyzed on her left side, requiring her to be placed in a health care facility for physical and nutritional therapy. Sandi's mom will stay in this facility for three to four months. Sandi's father is spending retirement savings on his wife's health care because their regular health insurance only pays for the first 30 days of long-term care. Sandi's mother did not have long-term care insurance. Sandi is considering whether she should buy long-term care insurance. She also wonders if her 65-year-old father should buy it. If you were Sandi or Sandi's father, would you buy long-term care insurance? Why or why not?

goals

+ Explain the principles of long-term care insurance.
+ Describe alternatives to long-term care insurance.
+ Describe the impact of long-term care on financial planning.

terms

+ long-term care insurance
+ primary caregiver
+ home health aide

LONG-TERM CARE INSURANCE

Long-term care (LTC) insurance is designed to cover substantial expenses involved in the extended care of individuals who have difficulty with basic functions such as eating, bathing, or dressing. This type of care is offered in nursing homes, assisted living facilities, or at home by visiting health care workers. Most long-term care is given to the elderly, but younger individuals who may have been injured in an accident or suffer from a debilitating illness may also seek benefits from LTC insurance. Alzheimer's disease, Parkinson's disease, emphysema, arthritis, cancer, heart disease, stroke, diabetes, dementia, and depression are only a few of the reasons people may need long-term care.

Societal Changes Less than a century ago the elderly in the United States were survivors. They lived through outbreaks of diseases, such as whooping cough, diphtheria, and polio. Polio is just one example of a disease children are now immunized against. In the past, the elderly avoided or managed to fight off bacterial infections that today are treated with antibiotics. And, because families were larger and lived nearer to each other, elderly people lived with their children or other family members.

tech talk

These elderly people were strong and tended to remain active until they contracted pneumonia or the flu, suffered a stroke, or died of cancer. There was little medication for a weakened heart or high blood pressure, and no oxygen for impaired lungs. People who didn't die suddenly with a heart attack or stroke took to their beds and often died in a matter of weeks. Therefore, there was little need for long-term care.

Changing Demographics   As longevity increases, the elderly population rises, and many aspects of our society are affected. Health care is especially affected, and long-term care is more important each year. According to U.S. census information, as the baby boom generation (those born between 1946 and 1964) ages, the elderly population will more than double. This will occur between 2010 and 2030 as the baby boom generation reaches the age of 65.

Additional information from the U.S. Census Bureau indicates a continuous rise in the population aged 65 and over. In the year 2000, approximately 35 million Americans fell into the 65-and-over category. However, the increase in the 65-and-over category is predicted to continue as shown in the table below.

Year	Millions Over Age 65
2010	40
2020	55
2030	72
2040	80
2050	87

What Is the Probability of Long-Term Care?   The U.S. Department of Health and Human Services estimates approximately 9 million current Americans over 65 years of age will need long-term care. As the number of people over the age of 65 increases, so will the number who need long-term care. It is estimated that approximately 12 million people will need long-term care by 2020. It is also important to note that not everyone who needs long-term care is elderly. Forty percent of the people currently receiving long-term care are ages 18 to 64 years of age.

Age obviously increases the risk of needing long-term care. Approximately 70 percent of those over age 65 will require some type of long-term care, and over 40 percent will spend extended time in a nursing home. There is no magic formula to calculate how much time or what type of care any individual might need; however, typically someone age 65 today will need long-term care for approximately three years. Although approximately one-third of today's 65-year-olds may never need long-term care, approximately 20 percent of them will need it for five years.

Not every individual who needs long-term care goes into a nursing home and stays there. Many people enter nursing homes for a few weeks or months to recover from a fall, a stroke, or other medical event before returning home. Services may be provided in a rehabilitation center or a community or home facility.

Cost of Long-Term Care According to a 2006 MetLife survey, the average cost of a year in a nursing home ranges from $67,000 to over $100,000. The cost depends on the cost of living in the area where the facility is located. It has been estimated the average nursing home patient runs out of money typically within six months of staying in a nursing home. Once the patient depletes his or her money, Medicaid benefits begin. Today, due to the high costs of living in a nursing home, many individuals are choosing to stay at home by utilizing in-home care or have found community-based facilities to support their needs at a lower cost.

Who Pays for Long-Term Care? As with regular health care, long-term care can be paid out of pocket, paid by private insurers, or paid by government programs for those who cannot afford to pay for long-term care. The Medicaid program pays for long-term care for low-income Americans. In fact, many middle-income people are eligible for Medicaid if they "spend down" their assets, meaning that they use up their savings and sell other assets to pay for their long-term care. For this reason, Medicaid pays for about half of all the long-term care provided in the United States.

People who do not want to rely on Medicaid or who do not want to spend down their assets buy LTC insurance. These consumers buy LTC insurance to pay for care they might need, enabling them to keep their assets to enjoy and/or pass on to their beneficiaries.

Long-Term Care Insurance Isn't for Everyone   People who have a low or limited income and have few assets may not be able to afford LTC insurance because coverage can be quite expensive. The Medicaid program was created to help people in this situation. It is part of our society's social safety net. At the other end of the economic scale, the very wealthy typically do not need LTC insurance because they can pay the cost of the care out of pocket. It is middle-income people who have some assets who need to assess their financial, physical, and family situation and decide whether to buy LTC insurance, what kind, and how much.

Benefits of Long-Term Care Insurance

LTC insurance augments your regular health insurance—Medicare and Medigap for senior citizens—which pays for physician visits, hospitalization, diagnostic tests, and other covered expenses. It also pays for care you need outside a hospital setting. For example, if you develop a chronic illness or disability and are unable to care for yourself, you might move to an assisted-living community or a nursing home, where LTC insurance would help cover your costs.

Many long-term care recipients remain at home, especially if another family member lives with them. The other family member, if he or she is able to, becomes the **primary caregiver**, or the person who attends to all of the recipient's medical needs. Various health care workers would visit as needed to supplement the care given by the primary caregiver, other members of the family, and friends. A **home health aide** might help the recipient bathe and dress, change the bed, and perform other housekeeping tasks, as well as socialize and support the individual. Physical, occupational, respiratory, or speech therapists might visit to help the recipient with rehabilitation exercises and activities to improve or maintain the individual's strengths and abilities. A registered nurse or licensed practical nurse would visit periodically to monitor the recipient's specific impairment and overall health.

More Than Mere Care   LTC insurance can help provide services that enhance the quality of the recipient's life and that of his or her family caretakers. An LTC insurance policy might pay for services such as the following:

- *Adult day care* in a supervised facility to which clients are transported each day to socialize, exercise, engage in different activities, and receive some health care

- *Respite care* at home, in a nursing home, or medical facility, giving the primary caregiver time off from taking continual care of the client

- *Hospice care* for terminally ill patients at home or in a hospice unit, offering counseling and relief for the family as well as comfort and care for the patient

Protecting Family Assets   In addition to ensuring that they can afford long-term care, most people who buy LTC insurance wish to protect their family's lifestyle and assets from the high cost of long-term care.

✔ checkpoint

Briefly describe the purpose of long-term care insurance.

_____

_____

ALTERNATIVES TO LONG-TERM CARE INSURANCE • • • • • •

PHOTODISC/GETTY IMAGES

Many individuals think they will have to spend years in a nursing home when in reality most people may only need long-term care for housekeeping, cooking, and personal care services. For security, as well as social reasons, daily contact with family, neighbors, and friends is essential to quality of life. Unfortunately, many elderly people do not have this type of social contact. Someone who suffers a stroke or a bad fall can lie helpless at home for hours or days if he or she is not in regular contact with others. Also, since an older person's health can deteriorate quickly, people worry about getting into a desirable facility with a long waiting list.

Alternative Living Arrangements

There are a number of ways to avoid or at least delay the need for formal long-term care. There are also alternatives to traditional options for long-term care. These alternatives are being explored by many social service agencies and communities.

Continuing Care   One popular arrangement is retirement communities. These provide a variety of services and facilities to accommodate people's changing needs as they age. Residents typically have a choice of independent living apartments or townhomes, assisted care units, or nursing home facilities. A full array of housekeeping and personal care services is available, as well as a range of recreational activities. A great advantage of these retirement communities is the security of knowing various forms of care can be obtained easily and on-site. Residents will not have to search for visiting health aides or a nursing home. These communities are a good solution for couples with differing care needs. Buying into such a community, however, can be expensive.

Ethics in Action

Consumer advocates predict that the probability of needing long-term care is about 25 percent. Some insurance agents and lawyers claim the probability is 50 percent. Elliot is an insurance agent who specializes in long-term care insurance. He frequently makes sales calls to people over 70 years of age who have recently been hospitalized. He exaggerates the probability of needing long-term care. He emphasizes they will be forced to use all of their savings and become a terrible burden on their families if they do not purchase long-term care insurance, although the premiums may be unaffordable.

Think Critically

Do you feel Elliot's actions are unethical? What would you say to him? Do consumers have a legal remedy for actions such as this?

Shared Housing   Some agencies pair elderly people living alone with younger, typically middle-aged, people in need of housing. The tenant lives free or at a reduced rent in the home of the older person in exchange for light housekeeping, shopping, or other services. Many times they also provide companionship and security as well. However, not everyone is a good candidate for this type of living arrangement. Sponsoring agencies screen applicants carefully in order to pair compatible individuals, oversee the agreement and rule-setting, and resolve any disputes.

Another shared housing arrangement growing in popularity is the small group or communal home for the elderly. The residents share the rent, utilities, and other expenses. Some of these homes may be subsidized by the state. The residents share some housekeeping and other household duties, depending upon the home and the level of fitness among the inhabitants. Each resident has his or her own bedroom and shares common areas. The residents vote on various rules of the house. A caseworker may oversee arrangements, solve problems, and resolve disputes the residents cannot handle themselves.

Mixed Generation Communities   These types of communities involve groups of people living in the same community who abide by covenants, conditions, and restrictions. For example, in a condominium development, single people, families, and elderly people might all live in separate households but meet regularly, share some community duties and activities, and help each other out as needed. The idea is to deliberately re-create old-fashioned, extended-family and small-community relationships by bringing together a diversity of ages and occupations to interact with and learn from each other.

Accessory Housing   Accessory housing typically refers to a separate living unit that is adjacent to a main home. For example, a small apartment, manufactured home, or detached cottage can be placed near an ordinary home for the use of a relative or close family friend. This preserves the independence of the relative while providing privacy, security, and easy sharing of meals, activities, and socializing.

Remodeling Your Home   While not strictly alternative living, remodeling a home to be more accessible to a person with limited mobility could enable the elderly to remain at home longer and reduce the cost of long-term care. While such renovations can be expensive to make all at once, periodic remodeling with accessibility in mind minimizes building costs and might make huge savings possible on long-term care costs.

Typical accessibility features to consider when remodeling include a bedroom, bath, and laundry facilities on the main level, uniform floor levels, thresholds flush with the floor, doorways wide enough for a wheelchair, and grab bars in the bathroom. Single-lever water faucets, side-opening oven doors, motion sensors on lights, and dozens of similar accommodations are available to increase accessibility.

 **checkpoint**

List three ways to reduce the need for long-term care.

_____

_____

FINANCIAL PLANNING AND LONG-TERM CARE • • • • • • • • •

Planning for retirement is difficult enough without thinking about long-term care, but the fact is, you face a significant risk of requiring some sort of long-term care before you die. You need to be prepared for this possibility, the same way you prepare for the possibility of severe illness, an auto accident, or a fire or other loss of your belongings. People must make financial provisions to protect themselves. Typically, they do this by buying insurance.

An LTC insurance policy would be a useful element in financial planning. However, many individuals are uncertain about buying LTC insurance for a number of reasons. They believe the following:

• LTC insurance is too expensive and unaffordable

• They won't live long enough to need it

• Their family will care for them at home

• It's a waste to pay so much in premiums when they might never collect benefits

• If the worst should happen, Medicaid will pay for care

Who Should Buy Long-Term Care Insurance?

Insurance Industry Guidelines	*Consumer Group Suggestions*
1. You are 40–84 years of age.	1. If you can afford long-term care insurance, buy it by age 65, because the premiums rise sharply after that age.
2. Your average household assets are at least $75,000 per person.	
3. Your annual income averages at least $30,000 per person.	2. If you are worried that your health may make you uninsurable, buy long-term care insurance earlier.
4. The long-term care insurance premium is no more than 5% of your income, and this will not hinder your lifestyle.	3. Paying for the premiums should not cause you to lower your standard of living. If it would, you can't afford it.
5. You could still afford the premiums if they increased up to 30% in the future.	

To Buy or Not to Buy?

The decision to purchase LTC insurance should not be taken lightly. However, the consensus, even among consumer advocates, the most vocal critics of LTC insurance, is that middle-class people cannot continue to fall back on Medicaid for long-term care expenses. Therefore, LTC insurance can be useful protection against potentially devastating long-term care expenses.

Obtaining Affordable Coverage

The premium for LTC insurance is directly related to your age at the time you buy the policy, the amount of the daily benefit, the length of the elimination period, and the duration of the benefits period. A policy that pays $200 per day for up to ten years will cost more than a policy that pays $100 per day for up to three years. Options also increase the cost of premiums. You should purchase some options, such as compounded inflation protection, if you want your coverage to be effective.

Advantages of Youth   LTC insurance is medically underwritten. Thus, it is easier and cheaper to buy if you are healthy because you are a lower risk for the insurer. It is even easier and cheaper to buy if you're young. A 65-year-old may pay as much as three times more than a 50-year-old for the same benefits, and an 80-year-old may pay ten times more. Industry experts recommend buying a policy when you're in your 40s, certainly by age 50, to lock in a low premium rate. By buying an LTC policy when you're young, you minimize the possibility of being rejected for health reasons or being placed in a less desirable premium class for health problems that might develop later.

Affording Coverage Later   Non-industry experts say the real issue with buying LTC insurance isn't whether you can afford the coverage at the time you buy it, but whether you can afford it later. Although you lock into a premium rate when you buy most policies, the insurer can and almost certainly will raise premiums for everyone to cover the increasing costs of health care. After 20, 30, or 40 years, the increased premiums may no longer be a manageable expense, especially after you retire. Also, any coverages you might add later when you have a better idea of what your long-term care needs might be will substantially increase the premium.

Alternative Financial Arrangements

Even those who need the services of a nursing home or extensive home care might be able to have this care paid for without having to buy LTC insurance.

PHOTODISC/GETTY IMAGES

Veterans Health Administration Veterans of the U.S. armed services meeting certain criteria can enter a Veterans Health Administration (VHA) facility or have care paid for in a private facility. First priority is given to veterans with a service-related disability or illness. The VHA may also provide some payments for personal care at home or in a non-VHA facility.

Home Equity Many older people who have paid off their homes own a tremendous asset. If needed, they could sell their home, invest the proceeds, and pay some expenses from that income.

Reverse Mortgages It might also be possible to obtain a *reverse mortgage* on a home. In such an arrangement, the homeowner sells the equity in the home back to the bank, and the bank makes a monthly payment to the homeowner. The homeowner may remain in the home, paying utilities, upkeep, and property taxes, or use the payment to fund care. The bank receives back its money, with interest, when the house is sold or when the homeowner dies. There are different ways to structure such an arrangement, and it is not an option for everyone, but it works very well for some people.

Life Insurance It is possible to buy a "living benefits" or "accelerated death benefit" rider on some life insurance policies. This type of rider permits you to use the cash value of the policy, or part of the death benefit, to pay for long-term care. You can also take out a loan against the policy. This will, however, reduce or even eliminate the death benefit.

Viatical Settlements Many people who discover they are terminally ill sell their life insurance policy to a third party and use the lump-sum payment to pay for care. For example, if you owned a life insurance policy paying $150,000 and discovered you had a fast-moving inoperable cancer, you might sell your policy for $100,000 or another reduced amount. After you died, the company that bought your policy would receive the $150,000 death benefit. Viatical settlements are not legal in all states and are risky, so this is not always an option. In addition, the person you originally designated as your beneficiary would not receive any benefits upon your death.

The Medicaid Program   Medicaid pays for long-term care for people who cannot otherwise afford it. Even people who work hard and live frugally all their lives can easily deplete retirement savings if they require expensive care. If their families cannot afford to pay for their care, it is good to know a government subsidy may provide some financial support.

The fact is Medicaid does reimburse providers at a lower rate than some private insurers do, and the providers know Medicaid recipients will not be able to pay out of pocket. Some providers will not accept Medicaid patients up front; therefore, if you can afford LTC insurance, you may have more health care options than you would under Medicaid.

On the other hand, it is illegal to discriminate against Medicaid recipients. So, if you are paying out of pocket in a nursing home and decide to spend down your assets and shift into the Medicaid program, the nursing home is not permitted to force you to leave unless it warned you when you entered that it would do so. It is also not permitted to offer you a lower quality of care.

Health providers know that, although Medicaid may reimburse them at a lower rate, it *will* reimburse them. A poor-quality LTC policy might not be as consistent. Some private policies may contain exclusions or benefit limits that are unknown to the buyer. Just because you buy LTC insurance does not mean you are guaranteed good coverage. It is quite possible to buy overpriced insurance that provides poor coverage. "You get what you pay for" does not necessarily hold true for insurance. Do your research.

Buyer Beware   As with all insurance, it is essential that you be knowledgeable when buying. LTC insurance is an evolving product that is often not entirely understood, either by the insurance industry or by the public that buys it. Therefore, the risk of making a bad purchase is considerable. Many people who purchase LTC insurance stop paying the premiums because they are too great a financial burden. Be careful of agents who try to use scare tactics or other unethical behaviors to sell a costly LTC policy.

✔ **checkpoint**

What factors affect the affordability of LTC insurance?

assessment 8.3

Think Critically

1. Describe three financial strategies to help reduce the need for LTC insurance.

_____

_____

2. Explain how changing U.S. demographics increase the need for LTC insurance.

_____

_____

3. List three kinds of supplemental services that might be covered under LTC insurance.

_____

_____

Make Academic Connections

4. **RESEARCH** Non-nursing home facilities and services such as assisted living and home health care are increasing. Research your community or state. Is this a growing business in your area? Write a brief report.

5. **PUBLIC POLICY** In developed nations such as the United States, birth rates have dropped while the elderly population has increased. Research the social implications of this trend and make a presentation.

6. **CONSUMERISM** The National Association of Insurance Commissioners (NAIC) has published a booklet titled *A Shopper's Guide to Long-Term Care Insurance*. Borrow a copy from your local library or a senior care agency or find it online. List five recommendations and describe them in detail. Be prepared to discuss your findings in class.

7. **INTERVIEWING** Locate an alternative living arrangement facility in your community. Get permission to interview at least three residents about the pros and cons of the arrangement. Create a multimedia presentation summarizing the interviews.

 ## Teamwork

In small groups, discuss the pros/cons of buying LTC insurance. Select a spokesperson from the group to summarize the top three pros and cons that developed through your discussion and share with the class.

8.4 Long-Term Care Policies

goals

+ Describe the different levels of services covered in a long-term care policy.

+ Explain how long-term care benefits are paid.

+ Discuss considerations when applying for long-term care insurance.

terms

+ physical impairment

+ cognitive impairment

+ custodial care

+ indemnity policies

+ daily maximums

+ integrated policy

Insurance Scene

Cassandra, age 40, is worried about being secure in old age. Her parents died young, but most of her other relatives have lived into their 90s. She remembers visiting relatives in nursing homes where they received minimal care because that was all they could afford. These are not happy memories. Cassandra's automobile insurance company recently began offering long-term care insurance. The agent quoted Cassandra an extremely affordable rate on a basic policy and promised to lock in that rate forever. What should Cassandra do before agreeing to buy the policy? If you were Cassandra, would you buy this policy or any long-term care insurance policy at this time?

UNDERSTANDING LONG-TERM CARE INSURANCE • • • • • •

Long-term care (LTC) insurance is a legally binding contract between you and the insurer. You pay premiums to the insurer, and in return, the insurer pays specified benefits if and when you need long-term care.

There are a variety of different LTC policies. These policies can be difficult to understand due to the combinations of ways different benefits, options, and features are bundled. This also makes it difficult for consumers to compare the different policies. However, the consumer affairs publications of your state insurance department will provide information to help you separate and compare benefits and costs.

Know What You Want   Some LTC policies pay for different services. A policy that covers a variety of services costs more than a simpler policy. You might not be able to afford the premiums for a deluxe policy. Some experts suggest the most economical way to cover long-term care needs is to buy a "no-frills" policy designed to protect against the catastrophic expense of an extended stay in a nursing home and find ways other than LTC insurance to cover less expensive services, such as adult day care. It is essential when considering LTC insurance that your future needs are met and you understand your policy thoroughly.

Read the Policy   The rapid increase in the cost of health care and fears of an aging population have fueled tremendous growth in sales of LTC insurance. Much of the growth may be attributed to group policies. However, don't rely solely on what the human resources representative or agent says. LTC policies are extremely complicated, and simple answers are often not completely accurate. When you need benefits paid, what the brochure, agent, or other representative relayed to you may be completely irrelevant. The only factor that determines what benefits will be paid is what is specified in the policy.

Carefully read the policy and make sure you understand all components. If you don't understand, some consumer advocates suggest hiring an attorney experienced in insurance coverage to help you interpret the language. The cost of a few hours of legal time is minuscule compared to the costs of long-term care.

Allocating Coverage When you buy LTC insurance, the coverage can be allocated in different ways, depending on the flexibility of the policy. Nursing home care costs differ drastically from full-time home health care. Depending on how you allocate your benefits, you may exhaust them more slowly or more quickly. However, when purchasing LTC insurance you can't see into the future. What you need to do if you decide you want to buy LTC insurance is to make educated guesses based on your health, your income and assets, and the cost of health care at the time you buy your policy. Remember, the more coverages and options a policy contains, the more it will cost.

Triggering Long-Term Care Benefits

Policies vary, but to activate long-term care benefits, a patient must exhibit significant physical or mental impairment. **Physical impairment** is typically defined as not being able to perform without assistance two, or sometimes three, of the six basic activities of daily living (ADL): eating, bathing, dressing, toileting, continence, and transferring (the ability to move from bed to standing, from a chair to standing, from a bed to chair, and the reverse of these activities). The determination of the type of long-term care, such as home care or nursing home care, depends on an individual's ability to perform ADLs.

Insurance Math *Connection*

Calculate the monthly and annual long-term care premiums for a 50-, 60-, and 70-year-old based on a $30 monthly premium for a 40-year-old. At age 50, the monthly premium will increase 50% from the 40-year-old's premium. At age 60, the monthly premium will increase 140% from the 40-year-old's premium. At age 70, the monthly premium will increase 180% from the 40-year-old's premium.

Solution

Age	Monthly premium	Annual premium
40	$30	$12 \times \$30 = \$360$
50	$\$30 \times 0.5 = \$15, \$30 + \$15 = \$45$	$12 \times \$45 = \$540$
60	$\$30 \times 1.4 = \$42, \$30 + \$42 = \$72$	$12 \times \$72 = \$864$
70	$\$30 \times 1.8 = \$54, \$30 + \$54 = \$84$	$12 \times \$84 = \$1,008$

flat world...

Japan and other countries, like the United States, continue to age. It is projected that approximately 32 percent of Japanese citizens and 20 percent of U.S. citizens will be 65 years of age and over by 2030. Nursing homes continue to see more patients who exhaust their savings and rely on the government to fund their long-term care. This is a heavy burden on the government health care budget.

Think Critically Quickly, research changing demographics in three other countries. Do all of the countries have a problem with increasing populations of the aged? Why or why not? Is there a decrease in birth rates in the country? Can you characterize countries that may have the need to deal with long-term care?

Cognitive impairment (also referred to as a mental impairment) is defined as a loss of mental capacity that requires you to have substantial supervision to maintain your safety and the safety of others. The loss of mental capacity may be due to Alzheimer's, dementia, an accident, or other causes. Many individuals with a cognitive impairment are unable to function without prompting by someone else. The impairment must be certified by a licensed health care practitioner or by a physician.

Levels of Care

There are three basic levels of long-term care: skilled care, intermediate care, and custodial care. In effect, the levels of care are determined by how much employees who deliver each type of care must be paid. It is essential that you understand whether your policy covers all three levels of care and the situations in which it pays or does not pay for care.

For example, if you wanted to buy a relatively inexpensive policy to protect you from the expense of a long stay in a nursing home, you might buy a policy emphasizing skilled care. You would need to be careful, though, that the policy would pay the daily benefit toward the nursing home's daily cost. If the policy paid only fees for skilled care, it might not pay a significant amount toward the nursing home fee, because even in a nursing home, much of the care is custodial.

Skilled Care The skilled level of care is given by physicians, registered nurses, and certified therapists under the supervision of a physician. It is typically delivered in a hospital, nursing home, or other medical facility such as a hospice; however, it can be delivered at home. Necessary skilled care delivered in a hospital would be provided, for example, if you break a hip or suffer a stroke or heart attack. It would be paid for by Medicare or other regular health insurance, not LTC insurance. Medicare will typically pay for up to 20 days in a skilled care nursing home when you move there from a hospital. LTC insurance will pay most of the entire cost of the nursing home. After that, Medicare will only pay a small percentage of the skilled care fees for another 80 days.

Intermediate Care   Intermediate level of care is provided by trained medical workers. For example, licensed practical nurses or licensed vocational nurses who work under the supervision of a registered nurse and within a physician-ordered care regimen can provide care to an individual. Intermediate care can be delivered in a medical facility, nursing facility, or at home. After having your broken hip pinned in the hospital, for example, you might be sent to a nursing home for recovery and therapy, where in addition to skilled care, you would receive intermediate care and custodial care.

Custodial Care   Also called *personal care*, **custodial care** consists of assistance with ADL, such as bathing, eating, and dressing. Approximately 90 percent of long-term care is considered custodial care. Custodial care can be given in any facility or in your own home. No medical skills are necessary for custodial care. Some insurers, however, do not pay for custodial care. Depending on your needs, you may want to make sure custodial care is covered.

Other Services   Adult day care, respite care, hospice care, and similar services can enable you to be cared for at home and reduce or eliminate time spent in an assisted care facility or nursing home. If you want these services covered by LTC insurance, do not simply assume that any policy you buy will cover these services. Always double check and ensure coverage.

Licensed or Certified Providers

An LTC policy that specifies the insurer pays fees of only licensed or certified health care or other providers might be an overly restrictive policy. For example, many states do not license or certify adult day care providers. Therefore, a policy that paid only licensed providers would never pay for that kind of care. In addition, if the policy specifies a provider should be licensed or certified but does not specify what licensing or certification is acceptable to the insurer, that clause might be designed to restrict coverage.

STOCKBYTE/GETTY IMAGES

 **checkpoint**

List and describe the three levels of long-term care.

Write a one-page essay about which level of long-term care you feel is most important and why. Discuss what this level of care includes and what kinds of people are most likely to need it.

PAYING BENEFITS •

Most LTC insurance policies pay the nursing care facility, home health care agency, or elder care agency a fixed amount for each day you receive care at a benefit level you choose when you purchase the policy. These policies may be referred to as **indemnity policies,** *per diem* policies, or *expense-incurred* policies. They specify daily coverage amounts for various kinds of care. These daily fixed amounts, called **daily maximums,** range from approximately

$50 to $500 per day for a nursing care facility, less for in-home care and for services such as adult day care. If the daily cost of care exceeds the specified amount, the insured pays the rest out of pocket. For example, if your policy's daily maximum is $150 but your nursing home's daily cost increases to $165, you are responsible for paying the extra $15 out of pocket.

Insurers may offer an **integrated policy,** also called a *pooled policy* or *pooled benefits policy*. This policy specifies a total dollar amount that may be spent on specified types of long-term care. The total dollar amount, though, is subdivided into a daily, weekly, or monthly dollar limit. For example, you may have purchased a $200,000 total dollar limit for nursing home, assisted living, or home care with a limit of $100 per day. If you receive home care for $75 a day, $75 is deducted from your pool of benefits each day. If you enter a nursing home at $150 a day, the insurer pays the nursing home $100 and deducts $100 from your benefits pool. You are responsible for paying the other $50 out of pocket.

Inflation Protection   Health care costs rise high and rise fast. Costs will double in 10 or 12 years. Without inflation protection, a policy's specified benefits will pay only a fraction of the cost at the time you collect the benefits.

Some states require insurers to offer inflation protection, although policyholders are not required to buy such coverage. Many policies offer inflation protection that automatically increases benefits by 5 percent a year. Some companies calculate this increase at simple interest. Others use compounded interest, which is better. It will, of course, be much more expensive, and it may increase the cost of your premium by 50 percent. However, currently it is the most effective way to address the problem of spiraling costs.

Duration of Benefits   When you purchase LTC insurance, you buy a specified length of time during which you will receive maximum benefits. This typically ranges from one year to five years. It is possible to buy lifetime benefits, but it is expensive. Remember, for those who require nursing home care, the average length of stay is two and a half years. Very few people spend more than five to six years in a nursing home.

Policy Provisions

There are a number of provisions and options to look for and investigate in an LTC policy.

Free Look After applying and qualifying for an LTC policy, you typically have a 30-day "free look" period. During this time, you can change your mind about purchasing the policy, cancel the policy, and have your premium returned without a penalty.

Waiver of Premium LTC insurance is term insurance; therefore, if you stop paying premiums, the policy is canceled. However, the waiver of premium provision enables you to stop paying premiums after you become disabled for a specified period, for example 90 days, without the policy being canceled. After that time, you are probably already collecting LTC benefits or are waiting for a long elimination period to end before you begin collecting. The elimination period is the time period that must pass before you are eligible to start receiving long-term care benefits. Once you begin collecting benefits, you no longer pay premiums.

Accidental Lapse Protection In some states, insurers are required to protect policyholders from the possibility they may forget to pay premiums because of cognitive impairment. Insurers must reinstate a policy canceled for late payment if a physician certifies the policyholder is mentally disabled.

Renewability Clause Most LTC policies are guaranteed renewable. These policies even permit the insured to "lock in" a certain premium rate. For example, if you buy a guaranteed renewable policy at age 50, you will never pay a higher rate than new policyholders who buy at age 50. Insurers use this as a sales point: buy a policy now while you're young and pay lower premiums through the life of the policy.

Unfortunately, when you renew the policy, the premium may increase if it increases for all the policyholders belonging to a certain class. And although your premiums do not automatically increase just because you age, any add-ons you may purchase will not be priced at the low premium rate at which you purchased the policy. The premiums will be priced at a rate corresponding to the age you are when you buy the add-ons. Premiums increase dramatically with age, so the increase can be substantial.

Nonforfeiture Benefit This option permits you to recover a percentage of paid premiums if for any reason you stop making payments on the policy. For example, if you discovered you were terminally ill and your current health care needs were covered by your health insurance, you would certainly stop paying premiums on the LTC insurance you bought for your old age. If you previously purchased a nonforfeiture benefit on your LTC policy, you would receive some of the money you paid. This option is expensive, increasing the premium anywhere from 10 to 100 percent. Many consumer experts feel it is a questionable purchase.

Limitations and Exclusions

Similar to the disability insurance elimination period, LTC insurance has an elimination period before benefits can be paid. Specifying a longer elimination period will save you substantial amounts of money on your premium. Note that no insurance policy exists without limitations and exclusions. Some common limitations and exclusions are listed below.

Calculating the Elimination Period   Different insurers count days differently. The best policies count days cumulatively. Imagine you have a 30-day elimination period on your policy. You spend ten days in a nursing home with pneumonia and then return home. A few months later, you need home health care, and the insurer starts counting with day 11. Other insurers might go back to day 1 every time benefits begin or are interrupted.

Pre-Existing Conditions   Like other medical insurance, LTC insurance does not cover pre-existing conditions you were treated for around the time you purchased the policy. A specified period of time, usually three or six months, must elapse before the policy will cover the cost of care needed for that condition.

Family Care   Family members may provide most of your simple custodial care. However, insurers typically will not pay your family or friends to care for you because the possibility for fraud is too great.

Other Insurance Coverage   LTC will not pay any expenses covered by Medicare or other health insurance you may carry.

Prior Stay Restrictions   Some LTC policies do not cover care unless you have received other, specified care first. For example, the policy may not cover nursing home care unless you are moved from a hospital, or the policy will not cover home health care unless you have first been in the hospital. Avoid buying this type of policy.

Alcoholism or Drug Addiction   If you are disabled because of alcohol or drug abuse, LTC policies will not cover your disability. However, if you are disabled by a bad reaction to a drug prescribed for you, you might be covered. Other restrictions include injuries and disabilities caused by war, self-inflicted injuries, and care given outside the United States and Canada.

Describe three options you should consider when buying a long-term care insurance policy.

_____

_____

APPLYING FOR LONG-TERM CARE INSURANCE ● ● ● ● ● ● ● ●

When applying for LTC insurance, there are many factors to consider. You must decide upon the amount of coverage needed and complete an application to determine your insurability. You should also consider the limitations of LTC insurance.

How Much Coverage

Determining how much long-term care coverage to buy is easier for older than younger buyers. If you purchase LTC insurance at age 65, you will probably need it sooner than someone who buys at 45, and you have a better idea of how much nursing home care will cost 15 years from now than 35 years from now.

Daily Benefits   Before you buy an LTC policy, determine the average daily cost of nursing home care in your area, or in the area in which you intend to retire. Use that average as a baseline to determine your daily benefit. Buying compounded inflation protection is an important consideration.

Duration of Benefits   Almost half of all nursing home stays last three months or less, but more than a third last a year or more. Protect yourself against catastrophic costs. Because lifetime benefit periods cost a fortune in premiums, and relatively few stays are longer than five years, some consumer advocates suggest buying a benefit period of four years.

Flexibility, Flexibility, Flexibility   Be sure your policy covers a variety of care settings. Do not assume you will need less expensive care at home. Remember, many people often cannot be cared for at home unless there is an able-bodied person present to be primary caregiver. If no one is available to fill this role, you may be forced to move into some sort of assisted living unit.

When You Apply

As always, when you apply for insurance, be completely honest in your answers. Typically, if you buy the LTC policy from an agent, he or she will ask you the questions and fill out the application form. However, before you sign the form, carefully read the answers to make sure they are correct. By signing the form, you, not the agent, take responsibility for the accuracy of the information. And it is you, not the agent, who will suffer the consequences if the information is incorrect and the company cancels the policy or refuses to pay benefits.

COMSTOCK IMAGES/JUPITER IMAGES

If you don't remember the answer to a health question, for example the year you were treated for a particular condition, give as much information as you can remember and state that you do not recall all the details. Do not guess and do not say you don't know. There is a legal distinction between saying "I do not recall" and saying "I do not know." An insurer could use the latter statement against you to say that you were concealing information about your health.

Are You Uninsurable?

The underwriting standards for LTC insurance are rather strict. If you are rejected for coverage, what should you do? Request that the insurer send you a complete explanation of why you were denied coverage.

PHOTODISC/GETTY IMAGES

Your doctor may be able to write a letter describing your physical condition that would make the insurance company reconsider your application. You could also apply to a different long-term care insurance company whose underwriting standards might differ. You might be accepted, possibly at a higher premium.

What Long-Term Care Insurance Won't Do

Even if you buy the most deluxe LTC policy available, it won't solve all the long-term care problems with which you might have to deal.

- LTC insurance does not guarantee you will receive better care.

- LTC insurance will not enable you to move to the top of a care facility waiting list. Many long-term care facilities do not have enough beds for those who desire their care. Having LTC insurance doesn't guarantee admission to the facility you want.

- LTC insurance will not make your decisions about long-term care easier. You must still compare nursing care facilities and in-home care providers to make sure you are getting the best care you can afford.

 checkpoint

How can you decide how much long-term care coverage to buy?

_____

_____

_____

assessment 8.4

Think Critically

1. List criteria that would make a person eligible for long-term care benefits.

_____

_____

2. Why are there exclusions in an LTC insurance policy?

_____

_____

3. Discuss whether you should purchase inflation protection on an LTC insurance policy.

_____

_____

Make Academic Connections

4. **CONSUMERISM**   Research long-term care insurance costs in your state. Compare the costs of at least three policies that have similar duration of benefits, elimination periods, benefits provided, and inflation protection. Use your state department of insurance website as a resource. Write a brief report describing your research. Was it easy? Was it confusing? Do you feel you obtained accurate information? Do you think most people could perform this research and get reliable answers to their insurance questions?

5. **GOVERNMENT**   Two government programs, Medicare and Medicaid, provide health care for older Americans. Investigate each program's rules about when and how much they pay for long-term care. Remember, these programs are administered separately by each state, and rules/rates vary among states. Write a one-page summary of your findings and discuss it in class.

6. **COMMUNICATION**   Obtain a long-term care insurance application form. Review all questions. Explain why you believe the questions are asked. Do you think they are fair? Do you think there are other questions that should be asked, or should some questions be left out? Explain. Summarize your findings and present them in class.

 Teamwork

In small groups, discuss what you would consider quality of life to be like after the age of 80. Would you want your life to resemble the one you have always lived or would you make changes?

chapter 8 assessment

Chapter Summary

8.1 Disability Insurance
A. There is a substantial chance of becoming disabled during your working years. Disability insurance replaces a percentage of lost income.
B. Leading a safe and healthy lifestyle and closely monitoring your financial health can reduce risks related to being disabled.

8.2 Disability Policies
A. Disability insurance policies have a number of features and options.
B. Disability insurance policies vary in quality and price. Certain options are essential to the quality of a policy.
C. Guidelines have been developed to help you determine how much disability coverage you need and ways to reduce the cost of the premiums.

8.3 Long-Term Care Insurance
A. There is a substantial chance you will require costly long-term care sometime. Long-term care insurance pays a portion of long-term care expense.
B. Alternative living arrangements can reduce your need for long-term care.
C. Long-term care is an important part of financial planning. If you decide to buy long-term care insurance, there are guidelines to follow.

8.4 Long-Term Care Policies
A. LTC insurance policies have a number of desirable features and options.
B. LTC policies vary widely in quality. Certain options are essential to the quality of a policy. Avoid overly restrictive clauses.
C. When applying for long-term care insurance, carefully consider the amount of coverage you need and fill out the application accurately.

Vocabulary Builder

a. cognitive impairment
b. cost of living adjustment
c. custodial care
d. daily maximum
e. disability insurance
f. elimination period
g. home health aide
h. indemnity policy
i. integrated policy
j. long-term care insurance
k. own-occupation protection
l. physical impairment
m. primary caregiver
n. residual benefits
o. total disability
p. waiver of premium

Choose the term that best fits the definition. Write the letter of the answer in the space provided. Some terms may not be used.

_____ 1. Policy that pays the nursing care facility or home care agency a fixed amount for each day that you receive care

_____ 2. Time that elapses before disability or long-term care benefits begin to be paid

_____ 3. Enables you to stop paying premiums after you become disabled

_____ 4. Condition where there is a loss of mental capacity, also called mental impairment

_____ 5. Policy that replaces all or part of your income if you cannot work

_____ 6. Policy that provides for a total dollar amount that may be spent on long-term care

_____ 7. Care that includes bathing and feeding and requires little medical knowledge

_____ 8. Helps the recipient bathe and dress, changes the bed, and performs other housekeeping tasks

Review Concepts

9. Describe three provisions found in a good disability insurance policy.

10. Discuss the difference between total disability coverage and residual disability coverage.

11. What should you do if you are rejected for disability or LTC insurance?

12. Describe three alternatives to purchasing LTC insurance.

13. How does purchasing LTC insurance help your beneficiaries?

14. When does it make sense to purchase own-occupation disability coverage?

15. Describe when you should purchase disability insurance through an employer (if offered) or as an individual.

16. List five criteria for a person considering buying LTC insurance.

17. Why would an individual not buy LTC insurance?

_____

_____

_____

18. Describe two different ways LTC insurance premiums might increase over the years.

_____

_____

Apply What You Learned

19. List two conditions that would be considered a cognitive impairment.

_____

_____

20. Why is long-term care a major concern of families in the United States?

_____

_____

_____

21. Explain why more people do not purchase disability insurance.

_____

_____

_____

22. How would LTC insurance be affected if more employers began to offer group LTC insurance plans?

_____

_____

_____

23. Explain why disability insurance is medically underwritten.

_____

_____

_____

24. Discuss what you consider to be the two most important kinds of long-term care that should be covered in an LTC insurance policy.

_____

_____

_____

25. Explain how the inflation protection feature works in an insurance policy.

_____

_____

_____

Make Academic Connections

26. **MEDICINE**   It has been estimated that 4 million Americans have Alzheimer's disease. A person with Alzheimer's disease generally lives between 8 and 20 years from the time symptoms begin. Using the Internet, media center, or other resources, research the number of cases of Alzheimer's disease in your state or area of the United States. Write a two-page report explaining your findings and how you think this affects long-term care in your area.

27. **PROBLEM SOLVING**   Work a word puzzle. LTCI stands for Long-Term Care Insurance. Using spreadsheet software, use rows 1-4 for L, T, C, and I. In cells B-Z, type as many words as you can think of that begin with L, T, C, and I that represent aspects of long-term care insurance. For example, L could stand for longevity, C could stand for continuous, T could stand for time, and so on.

28. **ACCESSIBILITY**   Companion animals are trained to assist people with mobility limitations and other disabilities. Dogs are the most commonly used animals, but other animals have also been trained to perform different tasks to aid their human companions. Research this topic and write a report or make a presentation.

29. **SOCIAL PLANNING**   Many experts believe the Medicaid system as it is known will collapse under the expense of long-term care. Research Medicaid and the growing burden of long-term care for the elderly. Explore the alternatives that are being proposed. Which means of funding long-term care sound most reasonable to you? Write a persuasive presentation to bring people around to your way of thinking.

30. **MARKETING**   Disability and long-term care planning is important. Create a marketing program to alert young people like yourself to the need to save and invest to ensure that costs related to disability and long-term care will be covered. Describe where and how you would place ads, public service announcements, billboards, and commercials. Write, describe, and, if necessary, draw a mock-up of a sample message or ad.

31. **MENTAL HEALTH**   The issue of parity, or equal coverage, for mental disorders is an insurance issue of increasing urgency. Some states have mandated insurers to provide equal coverage for both mental and physical disorders. Is your state a parity state? How does mental health parity affect disability and long-term care insurance? Research this issue and write a report or create a presentation describing what you have found.

9

Be a Wise Consumer

PHOTODISC/GETTY IMAGES

climbing the ladder

From Legal Assistant to Consumer Advocate Representative

Jacob has always been interested in law and legal issues. He earned his paralegal associate's degree from Barnwell Community College and has aspirations of becoming a lawyer once he saves more money and can go to school full time. Jacob currently works as a legal assistant for the Department of Insurance in his state.

Jacob works closely with other employees in the department. When a consumer has a complaint and legal issues arise, Jacob researches data, such as legal articles, codes, and statutes, to investigate legal decisions made in the past. Past decisions are often used as precedents for current legal issues. He has learned how to appropriately organize and communicate his findings.

Jacob is also responsible for monitoring cases that go to court. If a case does go to court, he logs the outcome in the electronic database he is responsible for updating. The database contains pertinent information about the customer, the complaint, steps leading to an outcome, and the outcome (judgment) itself. With this database, he is able to datamine information from past cases to help build a case for current issues.

His strong technology and organizational skills, along with his paralegal associate degree, have helped him succeed in his position. However, this position does not allow him to directly interact with customers, nor does it allow him to delve deeper into the laws associated with the cases. Knowing this is only a temporary position until he can earn his law degree, he has decided to move into another area in which he may get more experience and interaction with people.

Therefore, Jacob is applying for a position as a consumer advocate representative for the Consumer Advocacy Association (CAA) in his state. In this position, he will be more involved in consumer advocacy through a variety of departments such as insurance fraud and identity theft.

As a consumer advocate representative, he will be assigned to a specific area in which he will work directly with consumers who report deceptive business practices. He will help investigate complaints and develop tips for consumers so they can avoid becoming a victim of fraudulent activities or other crimes. He will also travel throughout the state giving presentations and dispersing information to help protect consumers.

Upper Rungs to Consider

One main reason Jacob wants to work for the advocacy group is that he will learn about legal issues and laws dealing with crimes. This knowledge will be beneficial when he continues his education in the area of law. Jacob considers himself a lifelong learner, and this is one opportunity to enhance his knowledge.

Preparing for the Climb

It is essential to be a lifelong learner. You can learn as you further your education, get involved with a student organization, work a part- or full-time job, or provide service to the community. Are there responsibilities or projects you could undertake in your current setting that would give you experience for a job you would like to have in the future?

PHOTODISC

9.1

Insurer's Responsibilities

goals

+ Describe insurance company responsibilities.

+ Describe agent responsibilities.

terms

+ readability

+ predatory pricing

+ Better Business Bureau (BBB)

+ captive agent

+ churning

+ misrepresentation

+ independent agent

Insurance Scene

Lana is a private investigator whose business revolves around insurance crime. She lives in Minnesota, and she wants to move to a warmer state with a lively insurance crime scene. She thinks a state with a less strictly regulated insurance industry and comparatively low enforcement budget would attract people who commit insurance crime. If you were Lana, how would you research which states fit her criteria? What factors would you investigate? Can you research whether her theory about the relationship between regulation, enforcement budget, and the amount of crime is correct?

LAWS ABOUT INSURANCE •

Insurance companies exist to make money for their shareholders by selling insurance policies to their customers. Insurance laws regulate activities of the companies. The insurance industry is regulated on the state rather than the federal level. Consequently, this means there are 50 different sets of laws governing insurance in the United States. Every insurer doing business in a particular state must abide by the insurance laws of that state.

The main reason for regulation of most industries is to protect consumers. Secondarily, industries are regulated to maintain competitiveness. Insurance regulations are designed to keep track of the financial condition of the insurer, standard provisions in contracts, licensing of companies and agents, and premium rates.

Financial Condition of the Insurer   Insurance regulations mandate that insurers have sufficient funds to pay claims. Also, insurers are not allowed to make certain risky investments that might cause them so much financial harm they would not be able to pay claims. Insurers are audited regularly to make sure they are in compliance.

Standard Provisions in Contracts   Insurance regulations ensure that all policies of a given type sold in a state are somewhat uniform. This helps make coverage and price comparisons easier and also ensures policies provide, or at least offer, a minimum standard of coverage. For example, in the state of Ohio, long-term care policies must offer policyholders age 75 or older an inflation protection option. This coverage is not mandated, but policyholders must be offered the option to purchase inflation protection if they want it.

A state may establish a standard format each policy must follow, or it may require **readability**, meaning the language in a policy should be relatively easy to understand. Before offering a particular policy for sale in a state, an insurer must submit the policy for approval to those who regulate insurance in the state.

Licensing of Companies and Agents   States issue, renew, suspend, and revoke licenses of insurance companies and of individual insurance agents. Licensing criteria ensure that agents, agencies, and companies meet certain minimum criteria of training and competency. Also, the power to suspend or revoke a license gives the state a means to easily rid itself of unscrupulous companies or agents without having to prosecute the companies or individuals for crimes.

Premium Rates   Each state reviews insurers' rate structures to ensure they are not excessive or discriminatory. Different rates can be charged for different groups of policyholders posing different degrees of risk for the insurer. Insurers are not permitted to charge some policyholders higher premiums in order to underwrite premiums for others.

Also, premium rates must be high enough for the insurer to cover costs and show a profit. This discourages large or cash-heavy companies from practicing "predatory pricing." **Predatory pricing** is the practice of lowering prices temporarily to undercut smaller or less financially healthy competitors. The company sustains losses until the smaller or weaker companies are driven out of business, at which time it takes over that share of the market.

The Letter of the Law

It is important as consumers and citizens to remember that state and federal laws offer only partial protection. A regulation cannot protect you unless it is enforced. And it cannot be enforced unless the authorities know the law is being broken.

You must be knowledgeable about any insurance policy you buy. If you believe the policy provides certain coverage, but the insurer denies your claim and continues to deny it even after you dispute the claim, you need to contact your state department of insurance and make a complaint. Sometimes just contacting the state makes the company reconsider its actions. The state can take an offending company to court.

"communicate"

Pretend you are searching for an insurance agent to meet your needs. Compose a list of questions you would ask agents in the interview process. Write him or her a letter or an e-mail asking those questions and inviting a response.

State Oversight Varies   Because insurance is regulated by the states, the strictness of regulation varies. Some states devote more money to their departments of insurance than others. Some also devote more money to investigation and enforcement than others. Consequently, some states are easier for unscrupulous companies or agents to "set up shop."

Why Do Some Insurers Break the Law?   Often, breaking the law is just a mistake on the part of somebody who does not understand the regulations. Laws and legal documents are complicated and are often worded in such a way that they are difficult to understand.

Laws are also subject to interpretation. Much of the ongoing work of our legal system is based on the need to interpret and reinterpret laws as they are put into practice in a constantly changing society. An insurer may choose, for example, to interpret an insurance regulation in such a way that it does not pay certain kinds of claims. If the state disagrees, it may bring the insurer to court to force payment of the denied claims. If the insurer's attorneys persuade the judge that its interpretation is correct, it will be permitted to not pay those claims. If the state attorneys win, the insurer will be required to pay the claims it denied and may be fined as well. However, it costs the state money to prosecute cases, and the state will not prosecute every case, even when it seems obvious that the insurer is deliberately misinterpreting and breaking the law.

Corporate Ethics   Be aware that a corporation's first loyalty is to its shareholders. This often means that a corporation seeks to maximize profits in order to pay the highest possible dividends to its shareholders. The corporation may also decide to maximize profits for its shareholders at the expense of its policy owners, for example, by denying certain kinds of claims it once paid without question. This brings the shareholders' interests into conflict with the interests of the corporation's customers.

One way insurance consumers easily avoided this conflict in the past was to buy insurance from mutual stock companies in which the policy owners are in effect the shareholders. This is no longer always a reliable solution because many mutual companies have converted to private shareholding companies, and changes in the industry have made the differences between the two kinds of companies less meaningful.

Corporate Responsibility Ends Here   Insurance companies must comply with the law. However, the law is open to interpretation. Over and above their legal responsibilities, though, many companies pride themselves on selling quality products at reasonable prices. These companies might even pay claims or benefits when, strictly speaking, they are not required to do so. Companies may feel it is important to their reputation to honor the spirit, and not merely the letter, of their policies.

As a consumer, remember, your financial well-being is not an insurance company's concern. The company's business is to sell you what it believes to be a good product. Its main concern is whether you can pay the premiums to keep the policy in effect. If you cannot afford the premiums, the insurer will cancel or reduce the benefits of the policy as specified in the contract.

Protecting Yourself

It is essential to understand any policy you buy and make sure it matches your insurance goals. You should also know about the company from which you buy insurance.

Whenever you are in the market for insurance, check with your state department of insurance. Review if the companies are licensed to operate in your state. Sometimes these lists of companies are conveniently accessed from the state department of insurance website. Your state insurance website may also list how much business an insurer does in the state and how many complaints have been lodged with the state against the insurer. It may contain a table of insurers licensed in the state and list the basic premiums they charge.

Check Them Out   Investigate insurers through the Better Business Bureau to see if complaints have been made against them. You can do this online or by calling or writing. The **Better Business Bureau (BBB)** is a greatly respected alliance of U.S. and Canadian businesses that promotes consumer education and ethical business practices. The BBB website includes a searchable database of complaints against businesses that is available to anyone. Also, check the ratings of companies online to determine an insurer's financial stability. Generally, but not always, top-rated insurers are less likely to deny reasonable claims for coverage than less highly rated companies.

Describe the four main categories of insurance regulations.

_____

_____

_____

_____

AGENT RESPONSIBILITIES •••••••••••••••••••••••

Just as an insurance company needs to comply with state regulations, so does an insurance agent. A **captive agent,** who sells only the products of one insurance company, must also comply with company policies.

Certain practices are obviously criminal and strictly prohibited. An agent must not steal a policyholder's premiums. An agent must not misrepresent information given by an applicant for insurance. An agent must not forge a customer's signature on an application. An agent must not engage in **churning** or *twisting* client policies, which means persuading a customer to replace a perfectly good policy with a new one so the agent can earn a new commission. An agent must not discriminate against a policyholder or an applicant for a policy because of ethnic background, country of origin, gender, marital status, or physical or mental disability.

Be Aware   These practices are against the law, but it does not mean they don't happen. There are law-abiding employees in every industry, but there may also be unethical people. Generally, these agents aim at taking advantage of customers who may not understand they are being victimized: people who are elderly, young, uneducated, naive, ill, disabled, newly emigrated, or somehow frightened or desperate. Insurance agents who are dishonest, just like any con artist, can size up people and select likely victims who will either not realize they are being scammed or are unlikely to report it if they are scammed.

Gray Areas   Problems with agent behavior are more likely to occur in areas that are less clearly defined. Misrepresentation, for example, is a relatively common problem in the insurance industry, especially with complex products such as cash value life insurance or long-term care insurance. With **misrepresentation,** an agent makes claims that are not true about an insurance product. For example, stating that a long-term care policy covers at-home care when it does not is misrepresentation. A dishonest or poorly trained agent may also misrepresent a competitor's product in order to make his or her own product look better.

Sometimes, agents misrepresent a policy out of sheer ignorance, in the confusion of making a sales pitch, or as a result of poor communication skills rather than actual dishonesty. Whether or not agents are dishonest, the effect is the same. The potential buyer is misinformed about the product and may believe he or she has coverage that does not, in fact, exist.

Agents Are Not All Alike   Licensing and certification are intended to ensure a degree of competency among insurance agents. Many certification programs require prospective agents to pass an exam. However, simply passing an exam does not ensure an agent is competent. You don't want to buy insurance from an incompetent agent any more than you want to take your car to an incompetent mechanic or be operated on by an incompetent surgeon.

When you buy insurance, look for an experienced agent. Ask family and friends for referrals. Ask how long the agent has been in business. Usually a truly incompetent agent will not last in the business more than a few years.

Credentials Count   Insurance agents are required to continually update and upgrade their insurance knowledge. Look for meaningful credentials and memberships in professional organizations. These vary by insurance specialty, but some significant certifications include the following:

- AAI: Accredited Advisor in Insurance

- CIC: Certified Insurance Counselor

- CLU: Chartered Life Underwriter

- CPCU: Chartered Property Casualty Underwriter

- INS: Certificate in General Insurance

Characteristics of a Good Agent   It should go without saying that good agents thoroughly understand the products they sell and the financial impact on you. An agent should also understand comparable products sold by other companies. An agent should also be able to understand your needs and be able to explain how his/her products will meet your needs.

Agent Ethics   An agent's ethical role is different from that of the company because he or she has a personal relationship with you and should understand your needs. A good agent not only conforms to the law but also places the needs of the client above his or her own interests. An agent should not try to influence you to buy a whole life insurance policy, for example, when term insurance would serve your needs as well for less money, even though commissions are much higher for whole life than for term insurance.

Agent Compensation   Good agents will either volunteer how they are paid or will not hesitate to tell you if you ask. Some products pay much higher commissions than others. Also, new business pays an agent better than servicing existing policies.

PHOTODISC/GETTY IMAGES

The Agent's Point of View   Remember, most insurance agents believe insurance is a good thing and more insurance is better. They're selling peace of mind as well as insurance coverage. Think about buying a new car. You may not need the leather interior and other expensive options, but you will certainly enjoy them, right? Most insurance agents feel the same way about insurance.

Also, remember that while highly ethical agents place your needs above their own, they are actually working for the insurance company, not for you. This is a difficult role, and agents can interpret the ethical demands and conflicts in a number of different ways.

What About a Broker?   Because of this conflict of interest in a captive agent's business, some experts recommend buying insurance from an insurance broker, or **independent agent**, who sells the products of several insurance companies instead of just one, to ensure you get a policy to meet your specific needs. Finding a broker is more important for people with many assets and complicated insurance needs.

Do You Even Need an Agent?   With insurance widely available over the Internet, do you even need an agent? The answer is, it depends. There are good insurance prices available through brokers who do business over the Internet, but the quality of Internet insurance websites varies widely. Online sites may not always give you the best value because they may not perform an extensive investigation of insurance policies available. Some insurance is complicated, and adequate information may not be gathered. Therefore, you may not get the lowest price, or the prices may be misleading.

Before you buy insurance over the Internet, visit and review different websites and don't hesitate to ask questions. Your state insurance department may have links to respectable online agencies. You might also want to restrict yourself to buying relatively simple coverage, such as auto insurance or term life, over the Internet.

Shop Around   Some experts recommend that every couple of years or so you should do some comparison pricing on property and casualty policies comparable to those you hold. If you find better prices on similar coverage, call your agent. He or she may be able to meet the price or demonstrate why your premiums are higher than the new policy you've found.

 **checkpoint**

Describe the difference between a captive agent and an independent agent.

assessment 9.1

Think Critically

1. List three reasons why standard provisions regulations protect consumers.

2. Describe five illegal practices in which an unethical agent may participate.

3. Describe three types of agent certifications.

Make Academic Connections

4. **BUSINESS HISTORY** Most industries are regulated on the federal level. Why is insurance different? Research the history of insurance regulation in the United States and write a report explaining why and how the insurance industry escaped federal control. If you prefer, create a presentation supporting your ideas about how insurance should be regulated.

5. **ETHICS** Many ethicists believe "corporate mentality" enables people to make questionable decisions that the same people would never make as individuals; for example, marketing a product they know is dangerous under some circumstances. Research this topic and write suggestions for promoting more ethical decision making at the corporate level.

6. **CONSUMERISM** State insurance department websites vary in content, functionality, and user-friendliness. Visit five state insurance department websites, including your own state, and evaluate them. Write an e-mail to your state insurance commissioner offering suggestions to improve the website, or praising specific components of it.

 Teamwork

In small groups, discuss the advantages and disadvantages of state regulation of the insurance industry. Do you think there should be more federal regulation of insurance? Why or why not?

9.2

Your Rights and Responsibilities

goals

+ Describe your responsibilities under the insurance contract.
+ Describe your rights under the insurance contract.

terms

+ small claims court
+ binding arbitration
+ preapproval

Insurance Scene

Satajit is a tropical medicine specialist in Illinois. He treats malaria, dengue fever, occasional cases of typhoid, and other exotic diseases that hapless travelers contract during vacations. He also orders vaccinations and other preventive medications for travelers before they leave the United States. One day his insurance manager tells him that nearly half the claims submitted for care he provides are denied. Satajit's theory is that these diseases and medicines probably aren't covered in the insurers' training. Therefore, the easiest and fastest thing for the claims processors to do is deny the claims, assuming that the doctor's office will resubmit them if it really wants them to be paid. What do you think Satajit could do to encourage the processors to pay the claims?

MEET YOUR RESPONSIBILITIES

Just as insurance companies and agents must abide by the laws of the state in which they do business, you must do so as well. When you apply for insurance, you become involved in a legal contract. When you sign the application, you give your word that all the information you have provided on the application is true to the best of your knowledge. This is similar to being sworn in at a court of law before offering testimony. It's serious business. Don't underestimate the legal importance of signing your name to a legal document.

Don't undermine the truth by fudging the facts. If you know you drive your car 9,000 miles a year on average, don't say you drive less than 7,000 to get a lower premium. Technically, such a statement is insurance fraud, though on a small scale.

Don't Volunteer Unnecessary Information When you apply for health insurance and are asked if you have ever been treated for a heart condition, you do not need to mention the time the doctor ran an EKG and found your heartbeat to be perfectly normal. You were not treated for a condition.

You were merely tested and found to be okay. Simply tell the truth and answer the questions asked.

Don't Submit Fraudulent Claims

Honesty is equally important when you submit a claim as when applying for a policy. But some individuals find it difficult to be strictly honest.

Some people find opportunities to commit minor insurance fraud to be irresistible. If you have been driving with a cracked windshield because your deductible wouldn't cover replacing it and you are later in an accident, you might be tempted to have the careless driver's

insurance pay for the windshield replacement. This is unethical. You should tell the claims adjuster about the prior damage so it is not attributed to the accident. If damage to the car is severe, the windshield may have to be replaced anyway, and the insurance claim will cover it. If damage is confined to the bumper, your car's stay at the body shop is an ideal time to replace the windshield at your own expense. In either case, your conscience is clear.

Liability Coverage

Because cars are such dangerous possessions, most states mandate that licensed drivers purchase liability coverage. Drivers are asked to show proof of coverage when involved in an accident, stopped by the police, or when they renew their driver's license. Drivers who do not carry the mandated liability coverage are subject to citation, fines, and possible suspension of their license.

There is also an ethical responsibility involved in buying liability coverage. Other people can be seriously injured, maimed, or even killed as a result of your actions behind the wheel. Although you have no intent to harm anyone, the fact is you can disrupt someone else's life or the lives of his or her family forever. While you cannot restore a limb, or a life, by carrying liability coverage, you can lessen some of the financial impact of an accident that is your fault. And so, ethically, you should carry as much liability coverage as you can reasonably afford. If you cannot afford more than the minimum, you are not ethically bound to buy more, but if you can afford extra coverage you should buy it. Fortunately, liability coverage is relatively inexpensive. Many people increase their liability coverage affordably by raising their deductible and transferring those savings to liability coverage.

Homeowner Liability Coverage   Although usually not mandated, liability coverage for your home or apartment also protects people who might be injured as a consequence of your actions. If you don't salt your driveway and a visitor breaks his hip after slipping on ice, or if your friend's toddler mistakes used motor oil for chocolate syrup, liability coverage will pay medical bills, as well as any legal fees you might incur.

Paying Your Premiums on Time

Another obvious responsibility you agree to when you purchase insurance is to pay your premiums according to the specified schedule. Unlike creditors whose payments can be delayed for months, if you exceed the grace period specified in an insurance policy, it will be canceled or you may have to pay a penalty.

Auto insurance for young drivers is extremely expensive, so to "help" policyholders make the payments, many insurers will allow or even encourage you to make smaller monthly payments instead of large semiannual payments. You do, however, pay for this privilege because the insurer will assess an additional fee. You may not notice the additional fee because it probably is not itemized, but you can be sure it is included. Charging additional fees is not unreasonable because additional work is required in order for the insurer to offer this service. If you can budget for larger payments, pay quarterly or semiannually.

Your Responsibility to Your Dependents

There is yet another insurance ethical issue and that is the degree to which you protect your dependents by buying insurance. This is a highly individual and private matter and no one can tell you what to do. You need to look at your philosophy, your finances, your family situation, and your life goals. Is it irresponsible not to carry health insurance if you can afford it? What about life insurance, disability insurance, and property insurance? It is one thing to decide that you as an individual will accept the financial losses of any of life's catastrophes that may be handed to you, but is it fair to ask the same of your family?

Insurance Math *Connection*

An insurance company charges an annual premium of $1,800.00, a monthly premium of $156.25, a quarterly premium of $462.50, or a semiannual premium of $915.00. Calculate the annual premium using each payment plan. Which is the least expensive way to pay premiums?

Solution

Payment Period	Frequency	× Premium	= Annual premium
Monthly	12	$156.25 =	$1,875.00
Quarterly	4	$462.50 =	$1,850.00
Semiannually	2	$915.00 =	$1,830.00
Annually	1	$1,800.00 =	$1,800.00

Paying the premium in a lump sum once a year costs the least.

Your Responsibility to Those on Whom You Might Become Dependent

If you were to become seriously ill or injured, you may become a dependent yourself. Could your spouse or partner support you without any of your income? Would you expect your parents, siblings, or friends to take care of you in their home? Do you owe it to those individuals to make sure health and disability insurance would cover at least some of the bills?

 checkpoint

Why do you think auto insurance liability coverage is mandated while homeowner liability coverage is not mandated?

ASSERT YOUR RIGHTS

Your rights are specified in your insurance policy. You have bought and paid for the coverage in that policy. Nevertheless, it is up to you to make sure you receive what is due to you. You cannot lie in your hospital bed or sit among the charred ruins of your home and wait for your benefits to arrive as if by magic. How would the insurer know you've suffered a loss? You must file a claim. You may even have to fight to get the claim paid. And whether the insurer rushes payment to you or it takes time to receive

flat world...

International Students and Health Care

Many international students go to school in the United States. Colleges and universities have particular medical and insurance requirements for all students, and international students are no exception. It is not uncommon for colleges and universities to require international students to provide immunization records and carry health insurance. Some colleges and universities provide specific details about the coverage requirements. For example, a university's policy could state that international students must obtain a health insurance policy covering all of the following requirements: (1) medical benefits of at least $50,000 per accident or illness; (2) a deductible not to exceed $500 per accident or illness; (3) repatriation of remains in the amount of $8,000; and (4) medical evacuation to the home country of at least $10,000. Additional requirements note that the health insurance company must "have a Best or Standard & Poor's rating of at least an A–."

Think Critically   Why do you think these regulations exist? Whom do these regulations protect? Would you add or remove any regulations?

payment, you should have laid the groundwork for receiving your benefits at the time you bought the policy.

Be Prepared

When you buy an insurance policy, you've taken the second step toward protecting yourself. The first step was the research you did before you bought the policy. But you're not done preparing yet.

- **Know Your Policy** If you haven't already read your policy, read it now. Know what coverage you have, what benefits you are entitled to, and how to file a claim. With your health insurance, for example, you must know what providers are covered. If you need stitches because you cut your finger slicing onions, unless the wound is life-threatening, you cannot go to just any emergency room or urgent-care facility and expect the visit will be fully paid for unless your coverage is unrestricted. Know ahead of time which health care facilities your policy will pay for so you don't have to review it while you're injured.

- **Keep the Necessary Forms on Hand** Carry auto accident report forms in your glove compartment. Keep your policies, claim forms, and related materials in an easily accessible drawer, closet, or other safe location in your home.

- **Rehearse What You'll Do in an Emergency** Mentally prepare yourself by running through different scenarios in your mind. If you come

upon an accident scene, what will you do? If a tornado blows part of your roof off, what will you do? If you've rehearsed a situation several times before it happens, chances are you'll remember what you should do and will be able to get through the situation safely even while under stress. Also, mental preparation for one situation will help train your mind for another.

- **Document Your Assets** If you file a homeowner's or other property claim, you will have to document what you lost. This is much easier if you documented what you owned before it was damaged or stolen. It is also helpful in reporting property more accurately. It is important to list, create a database, or videotape your belongings for documentation. Make sure you keep the documentation in a safe place, such as a safe deposit box.

- **Notify the Insurer**   If you are involved in a car accident or if other property loss occurs, call your insurer. Even if you are involved in a car accident in which another driver is cited and whose insurance will pay for your repairs, call your insurer to let them know what has occurred. Your insurer can tell you the reputation of the other insurer, offer suggestions for dealing with that company, and be prepared to step in if you need help in settling the claim.

- **Call the Adjuster**   Set a time and place for the claims adjuster to look at your car or other damaged property. When you first make contact with the adjuster, get all office and cell phone numbers, including an office number where you can always reach a live person to leave a message in addition to voicemail. Adjusters spend much of their time investigating claims in the field and are not always behind their desk.

- **Document Your Loss**   As soon as it is appropriate, sit down with the documentation you prepared ahead of time and determine what items are damaged, destroyed, or stolen.

- **Document All Contacts Relating to Your Claim**   Keep a notebook with your insurance documents. Whenever you speak with a representative of your insurer, note the date, time, the name of the contact, and the content of the conversation. Whenever you speak with anyone about your claim, whether the manager of the auto body shop or a physician's scheduling assistant, document the contact. It may seem like too much work, and you may not need all that information, but if you have trouble getting your claim paid, every second you spent jotting down names and numbers and notes will help you build your case.

Ethics in Action

Sarah Jane, 32, has just had a recurrence of the rare blood cancer she was treated for three years ago. She underwent extensive chemotherapy at that time, and the treatment was relatively successful. This time the doctors at the research hospital who are treating her want to be sure they kill specific kinds of cancer cells in her body. They plan to do a bone marrow transplant in addition to chemotherapy with two different drugs known to be effective against this cancer. Sarah Jane has a 20 percent chance of dying from the treatment but a 50 percent chance of a cure if she survives. She has two small children and is willing to try anything. The doctors are waiving their fees, but the transplant, the chemotherapy, and the lengthy stay in a hospital isolation unit will cost over $400,000. Sarah Jane works at home, her husband drives a bus, and there's no money to spare. Her insurer has agreed to pay for the chemotherapy but denied the transplant on the grounds that it is experimental treatment. Sarah Jane's doctors appealed that denial, saying that bone marrow transplants are standard therapy for blood cancers. Sarah awaits her insurer's second decision. Her chances of survival decline the longer she waits.

Think Critically

What ethical issues are involved in this case? What do you think are the insurer's real concerns? If you were the insurer, what would you decide? How will the insurer's decision affect others in the future?

If a Claim Is Denied or Insufficiently Paid

Despite your best efforts, your claim may be denied. You have the right to find out why it was denied, appeal to the insurer, and/or appeal to the designated state agency if necessary. Property claims and health claims are handled differently. Therefore, make sure you know the proper steps to follow to work toward an appropriate appeal.

Property Claims

Property claims are usually processed quickly because you cannot begin repairs or replacement until the claim has been approved. Do not accept payment from an insurer unless the shop or contractor you have selected has agreed to make repairs for the agreed-upon price. If the claims adjuster has offered a settlement that is insufficient, ask the adjuster to explain how he or she arrived at this settlement figure. If you're not satisfied with the explanation, say so and explain why. The adjuster may realize he or she made a mistake or didn't have enough information and agree to adjust the settlement. If the adjuster won't adjust the settlement and you're convinced you're right, go to the adjuster's supervisor. Try to document your case with your own materials or with materials from the shop or contractor.

Finding More Damage   It's quite common in a car or house repair to uncover underlying damage as repairs take place. These damages could not have been seen before the damaged sections were dismantled. Don't panic. Insurers have dealt with this before. Give the adjuster the new information immediately. The work to repair the damage may be stopped until the adjuster can investigate the new damage discovered.

If the Claim Is Still Denied   Every insurance policy should describe how to appeal a claims decision within the company. An insurance agent may also describe specifics to help you understand the process more clearly. If you still aren't satisfied with how the appeal is being handled, contact your state insurance department and file a complaint against the insurer. Sometimes this act alone encourages the insurer to pay the claim, especially if the state insurance department reports complaints on its website. Complaints posted against an insurer allow thousands of potential clients to view this information. In addition to accepting a complaint, the state insurance department may review or arbitrate the dispute or move to enforce any regulations if the insurer is in violation. You can also file complaints with the Better Business Bureau.

Small Claims Court   If your claim against an insurer falls under the proper criteria, you can take the insurer to small claims court. **Small claims court** is a special court designed for rapid and simple handling of claims, usually of less than $2,000. You don't need a lawyer, the filing fee is minimal, and you will receive a decision quickly. The downside is that small claims court rarely takes the step of enforcement, so a hardened company may simply ignore a judgment against it.

Binding Arbitration   The insurer may agree to participate in **binding arbitration**, in which a neutral third party recommends a solution to a problem that both parties must accept. If the insurer agrees to arbitration, this process typically takes longer and is more costly than small claims court. If your dispute with the company is less than several thousand dollars, binding arbitration is probably not worth the time. If the disputed amount is large enough, however, you may want to retain an attorney and sue.

Health Claims

Due to the large volume of claims handled by health insurers, a large percentage of claims is initially denied or insufficiently reimbursed. In part, this may be due to problems with electronic filing procedures. These procedures vary from insurer to insurer and may be difficult for providers to execute. Claims can be rejected by the computer simply because a patient's middle initial is wrong

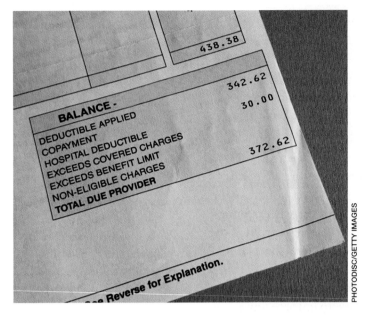

BALANCE -

DEDUCTIBLE APPLIED
COPAYMENT   30.00
HOSPITAL DEDUCTIBLE
EXCEEDS COVERED CHARGES
EXCEEDS BENEFIT LIMIT
NON-ELIGIBLE CHARGES
TOTAL DUE PROVIDER   372.62

438.38

342.62

...e Reverse for Explanation.

or too many or too few zeros are keyed in a specific area in the form.

Other rejections are basic human error. For example, the claims processor might automatically reject a claim for chiropractic care because the patient is a member of an HMO and few HMOs pay for chiropractic procedures, although in fact this particular HMO does cover chiropractic care. In simple rejections such as these, a single phone call to the customer service representative of the insurer is generally sufficient to correct the error, although the provider will probably have to resubmit the claim.

When in Doubt, Deny the Claim Other denials of coverage may result from unfamiliar treatments, procedures, or vaccinations. A highway worker, for example, bitten by a wild animal that escaped and could not be tested for rabies would need to receive the full series of rabies shots, consisting of one dose of rabies immunoglobulin and five shots of rabies vaccine given over the course of three or four weeks. Because few claims processors are familiar with the medical protocol for possible rabies exposure, claims covering rabies vaccinations are frequently denied or are only partially paid. A phone call to the insurer's medical staff will typically resolve a problem such as this.

Lengthy or expensive treatments such as cancer chemotherapy or treatments for difficult conditions such as psoriasis may require telephone calls or letters from the attending physician and documentation certifying the treatment is not considered experimental before claims are paid. Many insurers, particularly managed care organizations, require providers to get preapproval before some treatments or any non-emergency surgery take place. **Preapproval**, also called *certification* or *advance authorization*, provides the insurer with the opportunity to determine if a procedure is medically necessary. If preapproved, the claims should be paid.

Persistence Pays Many health care claims initially denied will eventually be paid. Don't give up. If you know you are covered under your policy, keep in contact with the insurer and provide documentation. Some people tire of making phone calls and simply give up and pay out of pocket. Be persistent.

If you are insured through your employer, union, professional organization, or other group, enlist the help of your benefits coordinator. This is especially true if your group is large because the insurer will be sensitive to the possibility that the group may change insurers if it does not provide the contracted coverage. If necessary, ask the insurer for an internal review of the claim. If it is still denied, go to your state department of insurance and

file a complaint. You can also file a complaint with the Better Business Bureau and health care consumer groups in your area.

The Bottom Line Most legitimate health claims are eventually paid. If an insurer continues to resist settling the claim, it is trying to set a precedent, for example, to identify a treatment that it will not cover for whatever reason. This is typically an attempt to "close the gates" against similar claims that will be expensive to cover in the future.

These situations can be frustrating. Most health insurance coverage excludes "experimental" therapies. During the time when experimental treatments begin to be performed outside of research settings, insurers are reluctant to pay. This is understandable because such therapies may cost tens, even hundreds, of thousands of dollars and are not yet proven totally effective or the side effects have not been completely identified. The insurers are often reluctant to pay in these situations.

 checkpoint

Discuss why mental rehearsals are useful when preparing for a crisis.

assessment 9.2

Think Critically

1. Why should you document all relevant contacts related to a claim?

_____

_____

2. Describe four different ways to be prepared to file a claim.

_____

_____

3. Describe three problems you might have in filing a property claim.

_____

_____

_____

Make Academic Connections

4. **CREATIVE WRITING**   Choose a crisis you can imagine facing and write a scenario to help prepare you for a real-life crisis.

5. **PSYCHOLOGY**   A technique for communicating effectively is to express your desires in terms that any individual would understand. This technique works best when you express your desires in such a way that the other party cannot resist granting your request. What if you needed to present a claim to an insurance adjuster investigating a property claim or a health insurance claims processor? Describe the scenario and write your communication dialogue to the insurance adjuster or claims processor.

6. **INSURANCE LAW**   Using the Internet or other sources, research a small claims court case and write a brief report to describe the process.

7. **ENTREPRENEURSHIP**   The difficulty involved in understanding, filling out, and filing health insurance forms has given rise to a new kind of small business: personal insurance claims specialists. Investigate this new business and prepare a presentation.

 **Teamwork**

In small groups, discuss the issue of insurance and responsibility. How does insurance, or the lack of insurance, impact individuals? How does it impact society as a whole?

Developing Consumer Savvy

9.3

goals

+ Explain the fundamental principles behind smart insurance purchases.

+ Describe how to avoid insurance fraud.

terms

+ Medical Information Bureau

+ credit score

+ insurance score

Insurance Scene

Harold was a natural-born risk manager. While other little boys were bungee-jumping from swing sets, Harold would have no part of the activity. While his high school classmates took a rowdy graduation trip to Florida, Harold helped build a boardwalk through a swamp preserve. Before Harold and his college roommate threw their first party, Harold bought renter's insurance and added extra liability coverage. When Harold and his friends got their first real jobs after graduation, his friends all bought sports cars, while Harold bought a disability policy and opened a 401(k). And now, Harold is engaged to Brigit, the woman of his dreams. After they honeymoon in Salzburg, Austria, they plan to buy an old house and renovate it themselves. If you were Harold and Brigit, what would be your next insurance purchase? Why?

OVERCOMING INSURANCE SHORTCOMINGS ● ● ● ● ● ● ● ● ● ●

Most Americans have significant gaps somewhere in their insurance coverage. Long-term disability insurance is absent from many insurance portfolios, as is long-term care and retirement planning.

Many individuals do not read their insurance policies. Therefore, they cannot accurately describe their insurance coverage. Many individuals believe they have purchased insurance coverage that they in fact have not purchased. Luckily, they may have avoided disaster if the need for insurance has not yet materialized.

What's the Lesson Here? Most people worry about what might happen in the future and want insurance to ensure against financial loss. However, few are willing to put sufficient time and effort into understanding products that cost hundreds, or thousands, of dollars every year. Insurance is important to society as a whole. Appropriate coverage can provide the financial means to rebuild one's life when death, disease, or disability occurs. Insurance is simply an important fact of life.

Many Americans allocate their insurance dollars in a way that does not reflect the reality of the way claims are filed and paid. For example, many individuals file claims on a property policy every seven or eight years on average. This means low deductibles are a particularly expensive option compared to the likely return. Yet many people pay high premiums for low deductibles. At the same time, they may not carry sufficient coverage for catastrophic events such as a fire or a disabling auto accident.

General Principles to Follow

When you're reviewing insurance policies prior to purchase, here are some guidelines to keep in mind.

- **First, Protect Against Big Losses**   The most important goal in any kind of insurance is to protect against catastrophic financial loss. You should purchase large amounts of coverage in selected areas, such as liability, where your greatest potential vulnerability lies. Replacement value, rather than actual cash value, of your home and possessions is another important coverage. This is not a coverage where you want to "pinch pennies." Inflation protection on long-term policies such as disability, long-term care, and homeowner's rebuilding coverage is also important.

- **Don't Buy More Insurance Than You Can Afford**   The premium printed on the declarations page of your insurance policy may not seem like much money, but when you add it to all your other household expenses, the total may be overwhelming. If you're struggling financially, you may need to review your insurance plan or home budget carefully. Retain coverage to protect you in case of disaster, and trim financial expenses elsewhere. For example, you may need to replace whole life insurance with term life insurance or increase deductibles wherever possible.

- **Pay Small Losses Out of Pocket**   A high deductible saves you money on your premium in two ways. First, your basic rate will be lower. Second, when you carry a lower deductible, you usually file more claims. But when your number of claims increases, your basic premium rate increases as well. So, unless you have a compelling reason to pay for the privilege of a low deductible, you might as well raise your deductible, put the savings to better use, and pay small losses out of pocket.

PHOTODISC/GETTY IMAGES

- **Don't Buy Too Many Different Policies**   Buy one really good policy for each kind of insurance you need. Supplement policies with another one only when there is an obvious gap in coverage. For example, if your employer-provided health insurance lacks dental coverage, which is important to you, you can buy an individual health plan tailored to cover your dental needs. Typically it is not essential to pay for insurance for dread disease policies, accidental death policies, or similar policies that pay out only under limited circumstances. Instead, invest the money you would spend on this insurance for improved coverage on your main policies, or invest in savings.

- **Don't Buy on Price Alone**   Insurance is complicated. You shouldn't buy insurance the way you buy groceries, reaching for the cheapest brand. It is essential you decide what coverage you need, find policies offering appropriate coverage, compare prices for different coverages, and then purchase the insurance. Investigate carefully.

- **Don't Confuse Insurance Protection with Investment**   Interest-sensitive life insurance policies such as universal life and variable life can be useful investments when the economy is good and the funds are well managed. However, if the market drops, your insurance protection may also drop or disappear. If you want true life insurance protection, buy term insurance. If you want cash-value insurance protection, buy a whole life insurance policy. If you want investments, buy universal or variable life, but only when your life insurance needs have already been met.

- **Three More Life Insurance Rules**   (1) Don't buy it until you need it. Unless you acquire dependents, you may never need life insurance, so why pay the premiums? (2) If you have children, cover your spouse. Even if he or she isn't a breadwinner, the coverage will pay for household services that may have to be contracted for in case of his or her death. (3) Limit buying life insurance policies on children. Buy more coverage for yourself or your spouse instead.

- **Don't Buy Long-Term Care Insurance Too Young**   Of course, premiums are lower when you're young, but you'll pay them for a longer period of time. The premiums are sure to rise for all classes of policy owners. Unless you're truly worried about your health deteriorating so badly you won't be able to find coverage, most consumer advocates advise against the purchase of long-term care insurance before age 50 unless special circumstances exist.

- **Buy Disability Insurance When You Work Full Time**   The financial impact of becoming disabled and not being able to support yourself or your family is devastating. Therefore, if you're supporting yourself or anybody else, you should have long-term disability coverage. The household expenses remain the same whether you are working or disabled, so make sure you can cover your expenses in case of a disabling accident.

Some Bureau Is Watching

Your premium is not determined by the insurer acting in isolation. Almost certainly, your insurer exchanges information about you with any or all of the major credit bureaus and possibly with the Medical Information Bureau as well. Be aware this information exchange is an important privacy issue.

Under the provisions of the Fair Credit Reporting Act, you have the right to check records held by these bureaus. You also have the right to place a letter in your file disputing and correcting any inaccurate information a bureau holds. You have the right to forbid the bureaus to release information about you without your written and notarized consent. You can withdraw any prior consent you might have given. However, you must do all of this in writing. A telephone call will not suffice.

The Medical Information Bureau   Usually referred to as the MIB, the Medical Information Bureau is a clearinghouse for medical information about individual policyholders. Insurers subscribe to the MIB and pay an additional fee when they request information about someone. Because medical information is considered more private than credit information, the MIB's privacy policy is somewhat stricter than those of the credit bureaus. When you apply for a policy with a life, health, or disability insurer that is a member of MIB, you must be notified in writing that the insurer may share your medical information with the MIB. The MIB will share information only with insurers that are MIB members and will not share it without your signature authorizing the exchange. Although you have the right to know what information is contained in your MIB file, the MIB will not disclose it directly to you, but only to your personal physician.

Credit Bureaus   The major credit bureaus in the United States are Equifax, Experian, and TransUnion. These companies keep track of your retail credit standing, including mortgages and other loans. Exactly what information is in your file varies from bureau to bureau, depending on how well a bureau's tracking and reporting system maps your payments and transactions.

PHOTODISC/GETTY IMAGES

tech talk

Detecting Insurance Fraud

Insurance investigators use sophisticated computer technology to detect fraud. "Data mining" software, for example, quickly locates specific kinds of data much the way a miner can follow the vein of gold in a wall of ordinary rock. A data mining program can be instructed to analyze vast networks of databases for particular identifying factors or patterns. For example, an arson investigator working on a suspicious fire can use data mining to search years of fire data for similar events. The investigator would select several factors from the case to frame a search pattern—for example, Monday nights between 11 p.m. and 2 a.m. with kerosene used to accelerate the flames. The investigator could then instruct the program to search the last five years of fire data in two New Jersey counties. Quickly, the software identifies 17 fires matching the search criteria. Four of the burned buildings were insured by the same agent and investigated by the same claims adjuster and insurance agent. Coincidence—or fraud?

Think Critically Explain how other industries could use data mining software. Do you think data mining technology has the potential for abuse?

Insurers pay the credit bureaus for the right to examine a credit report based on the information in your file. They use the report to draw inferences about you, your lifestyle, and the degree of risk you represent. Each factor reveals a different angle of your ability to manage your finances. These factors include:

- Payment history
- Outstanding balances
- How long you've had credit
- New credit
- Type of credit

The Credit Score   A credit report includes a number called the credit score. The **credit score** is a measure of credit risk calculated by weighting different kinds of information in a credit report using a certain formula. In short, the credit score is an analysis at a glance. The higher the number, the better your credit rating and the lower the risk you represent for the insurer. A high credit score should translate into lower insurance premiums. A credit score of 700 and above is excellent, and a score below 500 is a bad credit score.

The Insurance Score   Insurance scores, a more recent phenomenon than the credit score, were developed because credit scores have proved to be extremely accurate in predicting consumer credit behavior. An **insurance score** is a calculation designed to help determine insurance risk based on an individual's credit history and credit rating. However, the purpose of the insurance score is to predict the likelihood of a policy applicant causing a loss to the insurer by filing claims. Thus, information in your credit report is weighted differently in the insurance score analysis than it is for a credit score analysis. Insurance scores are similar to credit scores in that the higher the score, the better. A high insurance score might reduce your premium.

✔ checkpoint

Describe the difference between a credit score and an insurance score.

_____

_____

_____

AVOID INSURANCE FRAUD •

Insurance fraud may be committed by the insurer, the insured, providers, and/or employers. The amount of money lost to insurance fraud each year

DIGITAL VISION/GETTY IMAGES

varies with the method that different organizations use to make the calculation, but by any measure, the amount is huge. The Coalition Against Insurance Fraud calculates the loss at over $85 billion. The cost is passed on to consumers through higher premiums.

These losses are direct costs that raise the price of insurance premiums and increase the prices consumers pay for goods and services. The term *insurance fraud* includes every kind of deceptive or dishonest insurance practice, ranging from exaggerating a homeowner's claim for a baseball through a window to setting up phony offshore corporations. Insurance fraud can be defined as *hard*, meaning the perpetrator designs and executes a fraudulent scam or scheme, or *soft*, meaning that the perpetrator simply takes advantage of an opportunity that presents itself. The FBI itself classifies insurance fraud as *internal*, carried out by an insurance professional, or *external*, carried out by anyone not an insurance professional, such as a physician or nursing home administrator who files fake Medicare reimbursement claims.

A Crime Waiting to Happen If ever there were an industry that seemed designed to invite fraud, insurance would be that industry. Insurance involves the transfer and investment of vast sums of money that policyholders trustingly sign over and never see again for decades, if ever.

The existence of so much money is too much of a temptation for many insurance agents, brokers, and managing agents. Diversion of premiums is the most common form of insurance fraud the FBI investigates.

Where the Fraud Is No segment of the American insurance industry is free from fraud, but some are worse than others. The American health care and reimbursement system, for example, deals with a wealth of money and thus attracts con artists. But because it is also a troubled system full of stresses, physicians and administrators struggling with the rising cost of health care may make bad decisions and submit to fraud.

It is entirely possible to be an unsuspecting instrument of fraud without suffering a financial loss yourself. This can easily happen in the confusion of a busy medical facility. However, there are a number of ways you can discourage fraud in medical insurance and elsewhere. Pay attention to the details and follow these rules.

- Never sign blank claim forms.

- Insist on receiving itemized bills for all services and check the bills carefully for accuracy. Be sure you actually received the service or medical treatment listed. Watch for double-billing or unexplained excess charges. Question discrepancies.

- Be sure "free" services are not really hidden somewhere in the bill.

Staged Accidents and Repair Scams Auto insurance is another segment of the industry where opportunity beckons fraud artists and greedy car owners. There are plenty of cars in America, and they all need repairs at one time or another.

PHOTODISC/GETTY IMAGES

- Beware of cars that suddenly cut in front of you, forcing you to follow too closely. You might be the victim of a staged accident.

- After an auto accident, be wary of strangers who offer you quick cash or urge you to see a specific medical clinic, doctor, or attorney. This may be a fraud ring.

Insurance fraud is the second most common white-collar crime in the United States. ■

• Carry a disposable camera in your glove compartment. If you're in an accident, take pictures of the damage and people in the other car(s) if you can. Get the driver's and passengers' names and telephone numbers.

General Precautions Against Fraud Before buying insurance, always contact your state insurance department to make sure the company is licensed and covered by the state's guaranty fund, which pays claims in case of default. Also, investigate the insurer with the ratings agencies and the Better Business Bureau. There are guidelines you can follow to protect yourself against fraud.

• Don't consider buying insurance sold door to door or over the phone.

• Beware of insurance agents you've never done business with who initiate contact with you.

• Be suspicious if premiums seem too good to be true.

• Be suspicious if your agent pitches a new life insurance policy to you out of the blue with no major life event to trigger the need to change.

• Beware of agents who offer to replace your current cash value life insurance policy with a new, "better" one. Carefully review the premium schedule and benefits of the "better" policy as well as first-year restrictions on benefits, such as pre-existing conditions.

• Whenever you buy a policy, make sure you receive a printed copy of the policy from the insurer's home office within 60 days of paying your first premium. This is proof the agent forwarded your premium to the company's headquarters.

• Keep your insurance identification number secret. Individuals planning insurance fraud can steal insurance identification numbers to use in scams.

✔ checkpoint

Describe the difference between internal fraud and external fraud.

_____

_____

_____

assessment 9.3

Think Critically

1. Name three mistakes people can make when buying life insurance.

2. In your own words, describe the concept of the credit score.

3. Why might an unethical agent try to sell you a new life insurance policy?

Make Academic Connections

4. **PRIVACY ISSUES**   Electronically accessible records make research easy. Unfortunately, this may include research of confidential information. Conduct research related to privacy issues. Explore one aspect in detail and make an informal presentation to the class.

5. **TECHNOLOGY**   "Intelligent" computer technology is being used to analyze and track the online behavior of insurance criminals and other fraud artists. Research this or a similar technology. Summarize and explain your research in a written report or other medium.

6. **CONSUMER EDUCATION**   Research ways to improve your credit and increase your credit score. Research short- and long-term solutions. What lifestyle changes would enable you to improve your credit rating? Design and draw a poster, record a public service radio or video ad, or find some other effective means of reaching consumers with this message.

 Teamwork

In small groups, brainstorm a list of extended warranties and product insurance policies you or your family have purchased. Discuss any instances in which these policies proved useful. As a group, discuss whether it is worthwhile to buy these types of insurance policies.

chapter 9 assessment

Chapter Summary

9.1 Insurer's Responsibilities

A. Insurance companies are regulated by the individual states. In addition, some members of the industry may voluntarily hold themselves to higher ethical standards of business practice than the law demands.

B. Insurance agents are licensed by the individual states and must obey state laws and parent company rules. In addition, some agents may voluntarily hold themselves to high ethical standards of behavior and business practice.

9.2 Your Rights and Responsibilities

A. You must answer the questions on an insurance application truthfully and must comply with the terms of the insurance policy, which is a legally binding contract. You must comply with state laws mandating auto liability insurance. You also have a moral responsibility regarding liability.

B. You are legally entitled to all the benefits specified in the insurance policy. You may have to dispute or appeal denials and unsatisfactory settlements of claims in order to receive those benefits. There are a number of avenues to follow to complete the appeals process.

9.3 Developing Consumer Savvy

A. When purchasing insurance, there are a number of general principles to help you obtain optimal coverage at a competitive price.

B. Insurance fraud costs the U.S. economy many billions of dollars each year. There are a number of precautions to take to prevent being victimized or used by a perpetrator of insurance fraud.

Vocabulary Builder

a. Better Business Bureau
b. binding arbitration
c. captive agent
d. churning
e. credit score
f. independent agent
g. insurance score
h. Medical Information Bureau
i. misrepresentation
j. preapproval
k. predatory pricing
l. readability
m. small claims court

Choose the term that best fits the definition. Write the letter of the answer in the space provided. Some terms may not be used.

_____ 1. Measure of credit risk arrived at by weighting different kinds of information in a credit report using a certain formula

_____ 2. Designed for rapid and simple handling of claims

_____ 3. Sells insurance products from different companies

_____ 4. Alliance promoting consumer education and ethical business practices

_____ 5. Sells insurance products of only one insurance company

_____ 6. Untruthful claims about an insurance product

_____ 7. Using a neutral third party to recommend a solution to a problem that both parties must accept

_____ 8. Clearinghouse for medical information

_____ 9. Advance authorization to treat if medically necessary

_____10. Replacing a policy unnecessarily so the agent can earn a commission

Review Concepts

11. Why do you think it is important for the government to maintain competition among businesses?

12. What role does the public play in the enforcement of laws regulating the insurance industry?

13. Why are standard provisions in insurance contracts an issue of regulatory concern?

14. Why might a legitimate health care claim initially be denied?

15. Why does oversight of the insurance industry vary among states?

16. Describe three ways to investigate an insurance company's record before you do business with it.

17. Why is paying premiums annually or semiannually preferable to paying more frequently?

18. List three ways your agent can help you deal with another insurer that is handling your loss due to an accident that wasn't your fault.

19. Why is it important to document insured property?

20. Describe four general principles to follow when buying insurance.

Apply What You Learned

21. Discuss the difference between answering questions fully and not volunteering unnecessary information.

22. Discuss the ethical considerations involved in purchasing liability coverage.

23. Discuss the impact on family and friends of an uninsured long-term disability.

24. Summarize why it is important to know which health care providers are covered in your health insurance policy.

25. Number these steps in contesting a settlement in the correct order.
    _____ Find an attorney and sue
    _____ Call the adjuster's supervisor
    _____ Tell the adjuster why you disagree
    _____ File a complaint with the state department of insurance
    _____ Ask for an internal review

26. Why do you think people pay for low deductibles when they infrequently file claims?

Make Academic Connections

27. **CONSUMER PROTECTION** Where does corporate responsibility end and consumer responsibility begin? This issue is a matter of fierce debate, and it's not as simple as business interests on one side and consumer interests on the other. Some businesses protect themselves legally by affixing so many warnings and disclaimers to their products that any real safety issues are obscured in all the fine print. Also, consumers quickly learn most of the warnings are of no real use and thus do not bother reading them. To research this issue, visit stores and read warning labels. Categorize the warnings as useful, useless, or mixed, and keep count. Make note of warnings and disclaimers that seem distinctive. When you've read 50 labels, count how many are in each category and write a report and analysis of your findings.

28. **EDUCATION** Research different professional certifications, memberships, and designations of the insurance industry, for example, CPCU, CLU, or CIC. Find as many as you can. List them by segment of the industry and describe what criteria must be met before they are awarded. How many represent an accredited program? How many are sales based? How many are experience based? Can you draw any conclusions from what you find? Write a brief report.

29. **GLOBALISM** Search the Internet for insurance council websites in other English-speaking countries. You may be surprised how many you will find in other countries. Try to find educational sites similar to the Insurance Information Institute or a state department insurance site. Write a report comparing and contrasting this country's insurance industry with that of the United States.

30. **CRIMINOLOGY** Criminals of all kinds target people who for one reason or another are marginalized by society. For example, illegal immigrants may be chosen as victims because they are afraid of being deported if they go to the police. Research the topic of how criminals choose their victims and write a report or make a presentation.

31. **PUBLIC HEALTH** The U.S. Centers for Disease Control and Prevention (CDC) is an excellent source of medical information. On its website, you will find descriptions and discussions of accepted medical protocol for human diseases. People contesting a denied or partially paid health insurance claim can use printouts from the CDC website to help document their case. Visit the CDC at www.cdc.gov. Think of a disease that recently afflicted someone you know, or search the site to find a disease with which you are not familiar. Print the pertinent page or pages and write a memo to the medical staff at your health insurer explaining why your claim for treatment of this disease should be paid.

A

Accident zone an area of an interstate highway to which automobiles involved in an accident are moved (p. 49)

Actual cash value in homeowner's insurance, current cash value considering depreciation (p. 157)

Adaptive technology in workers' compensation insurance, the means of allowing you to continue to perform your job and meet expectations if an accident prevents you from performing your job in the usual manner (p. 95)

Additional living expenses coverage for loss of use (p. 154)

Aggressive driving unsafe driving actions, such as speeding, tailgating, running red lights, weaving in and out of traffic, or "road rage" (p. 32)

AIME *see* Average Indexed Monthly Earnings

Annuity a retirement plan characterized by a legal contract with an insurance company that provides for either a lump-sum payment or a series of payments (p. 125)

Application the formal document you read and sign for automobile insurance (p. 44)

Assets money or property you own (p. 13)

Average Indexed Monthly Earnings (AIME) a way of calculating Social Security benefits, based on an average of the 35 years you earned the most (p. 130)

B

Base period in unemployment insurance, a time period used to determine eligibility, typically four quarters (one year) (p. 102)

BBB *see* Better Business Bureau

Beneficiary in life insurance, the person or entity who should receive the benefits upon the insured's death (pp. 13, 174)

Better Business Bureau (BBB) alliance of U.S. and Canadian businesses that promotes consumer education and ethical business practices (p. 251)

Binding arbitration an action in which a neutral third party recommends a solution to a problem that both parties must accept (p. 263)

Bodily injury liability automobile insurance that covers physical injury to anyone in other vehicles involved in an accident that is your fault (p. 40)

C

Captive agent an insurance agent who sells only the products of one insurance company and who must comply with company policies (p. 252)

Carpal tunnel syndrome occurs when a nerve running from your forearm to your hand becomes pressed or constricted at the wrist (pp. 88–89)

Cash value the overpayment that accumulates in a life insurance policy (p. 188)

Churning when an insurance agent persuades a customer to replace a perfectly good policy with a new one so the agent can earn a new commission (p. 252)

Claim a written request for reimbursement to cover loss or damage that occurred from a specific event (p. 6)

Claimants unemployed individuals who meet a state's eligibility requirements for benefits (p. 92)

COBRA *see* Consolidated Omnibus Budget Reduction Act

Cognitive impairment a loss of mental capacity that requires you to have substantial supervision to maintain your safety and the safety of others (p. 234)

COLA *see* Cost of living adjustment

Collision coverage automobile insurance that pays for damage to your vehicle in case of collision, no matter who is at fault; includes collisions with other vehicles, animals, or objects (p. 42)

Compound interest interest paid on the ever-increasing total of principal and interest (p. 133)

Comprehensive coverage automobile insurance that compensates you for physical damage to your car, including theft, vandalism, and hailstorms; it covers permanently installed equipment, such as a stereo system, but usually not detachable equipment, such as an antenna (p. 42)

Conditions section the part of an insurance policy that defines the insured's and insurer's duties that, under the terms of the policy, must be fulfilled (p. 46)

Consolidated Omnibus Budget Reduction Act (COBRA) a health plan allowing people to stay insured between jobs, while changing jobs, or in the case of death or divorce; gives employees of companies employing 20 or more people the right to continue their group coverage at their own expense (p. 74)

Contingent (secondary) beneficiary the person or organization who receives the remaining death benefits upon survival of the policyholder and the primary beneficiary (p. 196)

Copayment a small amount of money paid by a health insurance policyholder at the time of medical treatment (p. 65)

Cost of living adjustment (COLA) in disability insurance, a rider that prevents your benefits from losing value due to inflation (p. 216)

Coverage protection for a specific type of loss on an insurance policy, such as flood or fire (p. 6)

Coverages section the part of an insurance policy that details the standard coverages available for the kind of policy purchased, such as liability, medical payments, and property damage (p. 45)

Credit bureaus companies that keep track of your retail credit standing, including mortgages and other loans, payment history, and outstanding balances (pp. 270–271)

Credit score a measure of credit risk calculated by weighting different kinds of information in a credit report using a certain formula (p. 271)

Custodial care assistance with the activities of daily living, such as bathing, eating, and dressing (p. 235)

D

Daily maximums in long-term care insurance, daily fixed amounts of coverage for various kinds of care (p. 236)

Death benefit the sum of money paid to your beneficiary or beneficiaries by the insurance company from which you bought the policy (p. 174); money paid by workers' compensation insurance to compensate survivors if an on-the-job injury results in death (p. 90)

Declarations page the part of an automobile insurance policy that lists important information, such as premiums, coverages, endorsements, and deductibles (p. 45)

Deductible the amount of money you, the insured, agree to pay in the event of a loss, prior to the insurer paying the rest of the claim amount (p. 21)

Definitions section the part of an insurance policy that explains specific terms used throughout the policy, such as "you" or "your," or "family member" (p. 46)

Dependent a child or other person who relies on you for financial support (p. 13)

Depreciation in automobile insurance, the reduction in the value of a car as it gets older (p. 42)

Disability insurance designed to replace all or part of your income if you cannot work or, because of disability, can earn only a reduced income (p. 208)

Diversify to spread risk among many types of investments (p. 122)

Double indemnity a rider that doubles the death benefit if the insured dies in an accident rather than of natural causes (p. 197)

E

Elimination period a clause in a disability insurance policy that specifies how soon after the disability the policy will begin to pay benefits (p. 212)

Employee Retirement Income Security Act (ERISA) sets and enforces minimum standards to ensure employee benefit plans are managed in a fair and financially sound manner for the benefit of participants and their beneficiaries (p. 118)

Endorsements an amendment to your policy that reflects any changes to the standard policy (p. 45)

Entitlement programs health insurance, such as Medicare and Medicaid, provided by the federal and state governments for the citizens deemed most in need of assistance (p. 79)

Ergonomics the design of equipment to increase productivity and reduce worker fatigue and discomfort (p. 100)

ERISA *see* Employee Retirement Income Security Act

Exclusions losses not covered by a policy (p. 46)

F

Fee-for-service (FFS) plan a health insurance plan in which the insured shares the cost of the medical service with the insurer, usually a 20/80 ratio after the insured satisfies the deductible (pp. 65–66)

Fixed whole life premiums premiums that remain constant for the duration of the policy, which is an entire lifetime (p. 190)

Floater a special insurance policy for extremely valuable, unique, or irreplaceable personal property, such as jewelry or art (p. 154)

401(k) plan employer-sponsored defined-contribution plan offered by corporations to their employees, which allows employees to set aside tax-deferred income for retirement purposes (p. 123)

403(b) plan a tax-deferred retirement plan designed for employees of certain nonprofit institutions, such as health care and religious organizations (p. 124)

Fraud deception for the purpose of unlawful gain (p. 105)

G

Graded death benefit policy a policy in which the death benefit is calculated on the amount of time you live (p. 200)

Guaranteed replacement cost in homeowner's insurance, excess replacement cost coverage that may pay as much as 120 or 150 percent of the value of the policy to rebuild your home (p. 153)

H

Health insurance compensation for medical care costs due to disease or injury (p. 14)

Health Insurance Portability and Accountability Act (HIPAA) a health plan allowing people to stay eligible for insurance between jobs, while changing jobs, or in the case of death or divorce; applies to all group health policies no matter what size, employer based or not (p. 75)

Health Maintenance Organization (HMO) the least expensive health care plan that includes a primary care physician who serves as a gatekeeper to other services (p. 66)

HIPAA *see* Health Insurance Portability and Accountability Act

HMO *see* Health Maintenance Organizations

Home health aide in long-term care, the person who helps the recipient bathe and dress, changes the bed, and performs other housekeeping tasks, as well as socializes and supports the individual (p. 224)

Homeowner's insurance a binding legal contract between you, the insured, and the insurer, that protects you, your home, and belongings if they are damaged or destroyed (pp. 144–145)

I

Indemnity policies long-term care policies that specify daily coverage amounts for various kinds of care (p. 236)

Independent agent an agent who sells the products of several insurance companies instead of just one (p. 254)

Individual retirement account (IRA) savings plan designed to help individuals save for retirement; traditional and Roth are the two basic types (p. 127)

Inflation guard clause increases the policy coverage of homeowner's insurance each year based on the changes in building costs in your area (p. 158)

IRA *see* Individual retirement account

Insurability ability of an individual who has applied for insurance to be accepted by the insurer (p. 17)

Insurable interest represents someone or something of value that, if lost, would cause financial harm to the insured; those having an insurable interest include family members and business partners (pp. 174–175)

Insurance protection against risk that financially compensates individuals in case of loss (p. 4)

Insurance fraud deceptive or dishonest insurance practices, ranging from exaggerating a homeowner's claim for a baseball thrown through a window to setting up phony offshore corporations (p. 272)

Insurance policy a written contract between the insurer and the insured, designed to cover specific future losses such as theft, accident, fire, flood, illness, or death (p. 6)

Insurance score a calculation designed to help determine insurance risk based on an individual's credit history and credit rating and to predict the likelihood of a policy applicant causing a loss to the insurer by filing claims (pp. 271–272)

Insured individual who buys insurance (p. 6)

Insurer the insuring company (p. 6)

Integrated policy in long-term care, a policy that specifies a total dollar amount that may be spent on specified types of care, subdivided into a daily, weekly, or monthly dollar limit (p. 236)

Internal limits the maximum amount a health insurer will pay per day for medical treatment (p. 78)

L

Law of large numbers protection against financial loss by insurance companies achieved by spreading the risk of costly medical care among many customers over many years (p. 61)

Liability legal responsibility to provide compensation for certain types of injury or loss (p. 10)

Life insurance a legally binding contract between the insurance company and the insured; in exchange for payment of premiums, the insurer agrees to pay a specified death benefit to the beneficiary/beneficiaries named in the policy (p. 177)

Life pool in life insurance, the insurance pool into which premiums collected from policyholders are placed; death benefits are paid from this pool (p. 177)

Lifetime limit the maximum a health insurer will pay in the insured's lifetime (p. 77)

Lockout when an employer withholds work from employees by closing down during a labor dispute (p. 102)

Long-term care (LTC) insurance designed to cover substantial expenses involved in the extended care of individuals who have difficulty with basic functions such as eating, bathing, or dressing (p. 221)

Loss of use refers to your home or rental property being uninhabitable due to a loss; expenses for loss of use may include the cost of a temporary rental home or hotel room, meals, and parking (p. 154)

Lost wages benefits in workers' compensation insurance, payments equaling about two-thirds of lost income (p. 95)

LTC insurance see Long-term care insurance

M

Managed care a health insurance plan that provides comprehensive medical care to all members, who pay a premium; the principle behind managed care is economy through volume (p. 66)

Medicaid government-provided medical assistance for eligible individuals and families with low incomes and resources (p. 79)

Medical expenses coverage automobile insurance that pays for any physical injuries you or your passengers sustain while in the vehicle or while you are a pedestrian (p. 41)

Medical Information Bureau (MIB) a clearinghouse for medical information about individual policyholders (p. 270)

Medical insurance compensation for medical care costs due to disease or injury (p. 14)

Medicare government-provided health insurance for individuals age 65 or older, under age 65 with certain disabilities, and any age with end-stage renal disease (p. 79)

Medigap (Medical Supplement Insurance) health insurance policies designed to cover expenses not covered by Medicare; they are sold by private insurance companies (p. 80)

MIB see Medical Information Bureau

Misrepresentation when an agent makes claims that are not true about an insurance product (p. 252)

Mortality tables sophisticated statistical averages of how long a person of your age, gender, ethnic background, and so on, can be expected to live (p. 179)

Mortgage decreasing term a particular type of decreasing term insurance tied directly to the policyholder's mortgage interest rate and term and which can be used only to pay off the mortgage (p. 185)

N

Named perils causes of loss specified in an insurance policy (p. 152)

Natural risks occurrences such as earthquakes, storms, and floods that homeowners face in their region of the country (p. 161)

No-fault insurance in auto insurance, coverage that provides compensation in the case of an accident, regardless of who was at fault (pp. 11, 43); in workers' compensation insurance, a plan in which the parties involved in a claim agree not to assign liability (fault), but to resolve the problem in a way both find acceptable (p. 95)

O

Occupational Safety and Health Administration (OSHA) federal agency that sets safety standards for employers (p. 90)

Own-occupation protection extra coverage in a disability policy for those who have a highly specialized and highly paid job, such as a brain surgeon (p. 215)

P

PAP see Personal Auto Policy

Participating policies life insurance policies that may pay dividends calculated on the amount of the policy (p. 189)

PBGC see Pension Benefit Guaranty Corporation

PCP see Primary care physician

Pension Benefit Guaranty Corporation (PBGC) federal corporation that enforces the provisions of the Employee Retirement Income Security Act (p. 118)

Pension plan traditional type of retirement plan that determines ahead of time how much the retiree will be paid (p. 122)

Per claim maximum the maximum amount of money a health insurer will pay for any single claim (p. 77)

Perils sources of danger that result in loss (p. 144)

Permanent insurance life insurance that covers you for your lifetime or until a specified age, such as 100, whichever comes first (p. 188)

Personal Auto Policy (PAP) automobile insurance policy designed for personal use of a private passenger vehicle; the policy covers you and others named in the policy who might drive your car (p. 39)

Personal Injury Protection (PIP) automobile insurance that compensates for lost wages or damages, regardless of who is at fault (p. 41)

Personal liability coverage in homeowner's insurance, protection from claims or judgments made against you, the policyholder, for damages or physical injury caused by you, members of your family, or your pets, or that occurred on your property (pp. 154–155)

Personal property anything not permanently attached, such as cars, RVs, furniture, clothing, and personal items (p. 10)

Physical impairment not being able to perform without assistance two, or sometimes three, of the six basic activities of daily living (p. 233)

PIP *see* Personal Injury Protection

Point of Service (POS) plans health plans that combine the features of an HMO and a PPO; POSs require a primary care physician and referrals (p. 68)

Points penalties accumulated on a person's driving record because of traffic violations and accidents (p. 34)

POS plans *see* Point of Service plans

PPOs *see* Preferred Provider Organizations

Preapproval in health insurance, provides the insurer with the opportunity to determine if a procedure is medically necessary (p. 264)

Predatory pricing the practice of lowering prices of insurance policies temporarily to undercut smaller or less financially healthy competitors; the larger company sustains losses until the smaller or weaker companies are driven out of business, at which time the larger company takes over that share of the market (p. 249)

Pre-existing condition treatment of a medical condition of an applicant for health insurance within six months prior to the application (p. 61)

Preferred Provider Organizations (PPOs) health networks that combine the features of HMOs and fee-for-service (FFS) plans; health plan members can visit any provider in the network by paying a small copayment, and referrals are not necessary (p. 67)

Premiums periodic payments made by the insured to the insuring company; premiums create a pool of money that the insurer invests to earn more money, which is used to compensate the insured for losses (p. 6)

Primary beneficiary in life insurance, the person or organization who receives the death benefits first (p. 196)

Primary care physician (PCP) a physician under the Health Maintenance Organization (HMO) plan who serves as a gatekeeper to other medical services (p. 66)

Primary caregiver in long-term care, the person who attends to all of the recipient's medical needs (p. 224)

Probability the branch of mathematics that measures the likelihood of some event occurring (p. 17)

Product options special features added to a basic insurance policy (p. 20)

Property damage liability automobile insurance that covers damage to other vehicles or other property, such as a fence or garage door, in case of an accident that is your fault (p. 40)

R

Readability when the language in an insurance policy is relatively easy to understand (p. 249)

Real property permanent structures and objects such as buildings, fences, and built-in appliances (p. 10)

Reasonable and customary fee the amount charged by a medical provider approved by an insurance provider (p. 66)

Reasonable cause a basis for firing an employee to which no reasonable person would object, such as gross misconduct or theft (p. 102)

Redline when an insurer refuses coverage to people because they live in certain neighborhoods (p. 162)

Renter's insurance protects individuals who live in a house, mobile home, condominium, or apartment that is owned by another person (p. 146)

Repetitive stress injuries painful and potentially disabling injuries caused by performing the same activity repeatedly for long periods of time (p. 88)

Replacement cost in homeowner's insurance, the current cost of replacing or rebuilding without any deduction for depreciation (p. 153)

Residual benefits disability insurance that protects you when you are able to work part-time but not full-time (p. 215)

Restricted license driver's license, often for teens, that has specific requirements attached, such as the right to drive alone only during daylight hours unless accompanied by an adult age 21 or over (p. 34)

Reverse mortgage an option for paying for long-term care in which a homeowner sells the equity in the home back to the bank, and the bank makes a monthly payment to the homeowner (p. 229)

Rider an amendment or addition to an insurance policy (p. 185)

Risk any situation in which some kind of loss or misfortune is possible (p. 4)

Rollover a transfer of 401(k) funds into a retirement plan offered by a new employer or into an IRA you've opened on your own (p. 124)

S

Schedule to insure particular items, such as jewelry or art, for a specific value of their own (p. 146)

Secondary beneficiary *see* Contingent beneficiary

SEP-IRA *see* Simplified Employee Pension Individual Retirement Account

Settlement recourse the systematic process of disputing a settlement (p. 166)

Severance payment an employer-offered incentive encouraging older, highly paid employees to retire; examples are a lump sum of a designated amount, such as a year's salary, and post-retirement medical coverage (p. 135)

Simplified Employee Pension Individual Retirement Account (SEP-IRA) a retirement plan set up by employers to which only employers or self-employed individuals can contribute funds (pp. 124–125)

Small claims court a special court designed for rapid and simple handling of claims, usually of less than $2,000; small claims courts do not require a lawyer, have a minimal filing fee, and are quick to make a decision (p. 263)

Social Security a federal insurance program providing aid to those who are eligible for benefits, including the retired, the disabled, or the widow/widower or child of someone deceased who is eligible for benefits (p. 130)

Social Security number your primary identification number used by the government (p. 104)

T

Tax-deferred retirement-fund money that is not taxed until it is distributed (p. 115)

Term insurance a life insurance policy limited to a specific length of time, or term; if you die during the term, the death benefits are paid to your beneficiaries—otherwise, the benefits are not paid (p. 184)

Total disability not being able to perform any of the main functions of the job you held when you became disabled or of any similar job appropriate to your education, training, and experience; some insurers require that you not be able to perform *any* job (p. 214)

U

Umbrella policy a special type of liability insurance that sits on top of your auto and homeowner's or renter's insurance to provide extra protection (p. 155)

Underinsured not having enough insurance (p. 7)

Underwriting the process of assessing applicants to determine whether they are good risks for the insurance company (p. 178)

Unemployment insurance temporary benefits to eligible workers who have lost their jobs (p. 91)

Uninsured having no insurance (p. 7)

V

Vested when an employee has worked for an employer for a certain number of years and has thereby become eligible to participate in the employer's pension plan (pp. 118–119)

W

Waiver of premium in disability insurance, a provision saying you don't have to keep paying premiums after you are disabled for a specified period, such as 90 days (p. 217); in long-term care insurance, a provision that enables you to stop paying premiums after you become disabled for a specified period, such as 90 days, without the policy being canceled (p. 237)

Workers' compensation insurance paid by an employer to provide employees with medical care, wage replacement, or death benefits if the employee is injured, disabled, or killed on the job (p. 89)

INDEX

C

Canada
  national health care in, 78
  U.S. auto insurance in, 37
Cancellation, of insurance policy, 46
Captive agent, 252
Carbon monoxide alarm, 149
Carpal tunnel syndrome, 88–89
Cash value, 188–189
Cash value life insurance, 188–189
Casual workers, 96
Caveat emptor, 43
Cell phone laws, 35
Cell phones, driving and use of, 35
Centers for Disease Control and Prevention (CDC), 30
Centers for Medicare and Medicaid Services (CMS), 79
Central America, 7
Certificate in General Insurance (INS), 253
Certification
  of agents, 252
  for medical treatments, 264
Certified Insurance Counselor (CIC), 253
Certified Insurance Service Representative (CISR), 3
Chartered Life Underwriter (CLU), 253
Chartered Property Casualty Underwriter (CPCU), 253
Checkpoint
  Chapter 1, 5, 8, 12, 15, 19, 22
  Chapter 2, 33, 37, 44, 46, 50, 52
  Chapter 3, 61, 63, 68, 72, 76, 78, 80
  Chapter 4, 91, 92, 97, 99, 104, 106
  Chapter 5, 116, 119, 125, 128, 132, 136
  Chapter 6, 147, 150, 156, 159, 163, 166
  Chapter 7, 177, 182, 187, 192, 197, 200
  Chapter 8, 210, 212, 215, 218, 219, 225, 227, 230, 235, 238, 240
  Chapter 9, 251, 254, 259, 265, 272, 274
Chile, 7
China, 7
China Insurance Regulatory Commission (CIRC), 176
Chop shops, 36
Churning, 252
Claim
  for auto accident, 51
  for death benefit from life insurance, 200
  defined, 6
  denial or insufficient payment of, 262–263
  filing guidelines, 260–265
  homeowner's loss, 164–166
  for unemployment insurance, 104–105
Claimants, 92
Claims adjuster, 3
Claims clerk, 207
Claims examiner, 87
Climbing the Ladder (feature), 3, 29, 59, 87, 113, 143, 173, 207, 247
Clutter, danger of fire from, 150
Coalition Against Insurance Fraud, 272
Coal mining, as dangerous occupation, 90
COBRA. See Consolidated Omnibus Budget Reduction Act
Cognitive impairment, 234
Collections, insuring of, 145
Collision coverage, 42
Colombia, 7
Communal home, for the elderly, 226
Communicate (feature), 14, 50, 67, 91, 124, 155, 178, 235, 250
Company ratings, 21–22
Compound interest, 133–134
Comprehensive automobile insurance, 11, 42

Conditional driver's license, 34
Conditional renewability, 217
Conditions section, 46
Condominiums, 145, 158
Consolidated Omnibus Budget Reduction Act (COBRA), 74–75
Consumer advocate representative, 247
Consumers
  insurance fraud and, 272–274
  insurer's responsibilities, 248–254
  rights and responsibilities of, 256–265
  savvy of, 267–274
Contents coverage, 153–154
Contingent beneficiary, 196
Continuing care, 225
Continuous premiums, 191
Contract, insurance policy as, 39, 144, 177, 214, 248–249
Convertibility option, 186
Copayment, in health plan, 65
Corporate ethics and responsibility, 250–251
Cost of living adjustment (COLA), 216
Costs
  from alcohol-related driving accidents, 33
  of automobile insurance, 33–37
  of driving accidents, 30
  increasing, of insurance, 7–8
  of long-term care, 223
  policy pricing, 20–21
  predatory pricing, 249
  reducing your rate, 21
Coverage
  defined, 6
  health plan considerations, 70
  long-term care, 239
  losses exceeding, 52
  workers' compensation insurance, 94–96
Coverages section, 45–46
Crashworthiness of automobiles, insurance costs and, 35–36